A HANDBOOK OF EDUCATIONAL TECHNOLOGY

■ Second Edition ■

■ FRED PERCIVAL & HENRY ELLINGTON ■

**Kogan Page, London/Nichols Publishing
Company, New York**

First published in Great Britain in 1984 by
Kogan Page Limited, 120 Pentonville Road, London N1 9JN
Second edition 1988

British Library Cataloguing in Publication Data

Percival, Fred
    A handbook of educational technology: a
    practical guide for teachers.—2nd ed.
    1. Educational technology
    I. Title   II. Ellington, Henry
    371.3'07'8   LB1028.3

    ISBN 1-85091-547-4
    ISBN 1-85091-449-4 Pbk

First published in the United States of America
in 1984 by Nichols Publishing, PO Box 96,
New York, NY 10024
Second edition 1988

Library of Congress Cataloging in Publication Data

Percival, Fred
    Handbook of educational technology.—2nd ed.
    Bibliography: P.
    Includes Index.
    1. Educational technology — Handbooks, manuals, etc.
    I. Ellington, Henry.   II. Title.
    LB1028.3 1988   371.3'078   87-31381
ISBN 0-89397-297-5
    0-89397-300-9 pbk

Printed and bound in Great Britain by
Richard Clay Ltd, Bungay, Suffolk

Contents

Acknowledgements

We would like to acknowledge the help that we have received from the following people in producing this book:

- [ ] our colleagues Eric Addinall and Barry Murton, for advice and constructive criticism;
- [ ] the two (anonymous) readers to whom the original MS was sent by Kogan Page, whose constructive criticism was of considerable help in producing the final published version of the book;
- [ ] Una Baillie and Margaret Geddes, for typing the MS of this book and for all the other secretarial support they have given us in our work;
- [ ] Bill Black, for taking all the photographs;
- [ ] our Kogan Page editors Jane Wilkinson and Dolores Black.

The male pronoun has been used throughout the book for stylistic reasons only. Readers should interpret this as meaning a person of either sex. We hope that no one will be offended.

Introduction

Since educational technology emerged as a discipline in its own right in the years following the end of the Second World War, whole libraries of books have been written on virtually every aspect of the subject. Despite this wealth of material, however, there has been a noticeable lack of books that can be used as a basic 'primer' in the field, that is, books that give a simple overview of the main aspects of educational technology and explain how adopting an educational technology-based approach can help to improve the efficiency and effectiveness of the average teacher or lecturer.

This book has been written in an attempt to fill this gap, and we see it as having two main roles, namely, as a handbook for practising teachers and lecturers who want to learn something about the principles and practice of educational technology so that they can use it in their day-to-day work, and as a basic text for trainee teachers and students of education who are studying educational technology as part of their courses. The book should also prove useful as an introductory text for students of educational technology.

Since the book is not based on any particular educational system, and deals with the various topics covered in fairly general terms, we also hope that it will prove just as helpful to American, Australian and other English-speaking readers as it does to those in Britain.

The main text of the book consists of 11 chapters, each of which deals with a different aspect of educational technology.

Chapter 1 gives a broad introduction to educational technology, explaining what is meant by the term, introducing the 'systems 'approach' that underlies its thinking, and presenting a brief historical account of the way in which the field has developed since the late 1940s.

Chapter 2 then describes two fundamentally different approaches to education, within the context of which virtually all important developments in educational technology have taken place — the traditional 'teacher/institution-centred' approach and the more recent 'student-centred' approach.

Chapter 3 deals with the subject of educational objectives, the formulation of which should constitute the starting point of any systematic approach to course or curriculum design. It explains the difference between 'aims' and 'objectives', offers guidance on how objectives should be written, and discusses the different types of objectives.

The next three chapters deal with the three main types of teaching methods that can be employed in implementing a course or programme of instruction, Chapter 4 dealing with 'mass instruction' techniques, Chapter 5 with 'individualized learning' techniques and Chapter 6 with 'group learning' techniques. In each case, a general discussion of the various methods that can be used and an analysis of their respective strengths and weaknesses is followed by a review of the different media and techniques that can be used to support them or put them into practice.

Chapters 7 and 8 then deal with the related topics of student assessment and course evaluation, explaining the overall role of each in the instructional process and describing the various techniques that can be used to carry them out.

Chapters 9 and 10 deal with two aspects of educational technology that have become progressively more important during the last 20 years and seem certain to become even more important during the next, looking at the role and organization of resources centres and at the various ways in which computers can be used in education.

Finally, Chapter 11 takes a glimpse into the future, trying to identify the main trends that underlie current educational technology and making informed guesses as to how these will have affected the overall educational scene by the year 2000.

The book also contains four reference sections, which have been included in order to increase its usefulness as a handbook.

The first is a comprehensive glossary of terms used in educational technology, defining over 800 words and phrases that teachers and lecturers are likely to come across in the course of their work; these not only cover the 'hardware' and 'software' aspects of educational technology, but also the highly important intangible aspects of the subject (sometimes described as the 'underware').

The second is a wide-ranging bibliography that lists over 350 books, papers and articles relating to the subjects covered in the individual chapters. This will enable readers to study in greater depth any topic or topics in which they are particularly interested. Full bibliographic details about all books, articles or other publications specifically referred to in the main text are given in the Bibliography under the appropriate chapter heading.

The third is a country-by-country list of some of the main professional bodies, associations and other organizations that are involved in the educational technology field and the various specific aspects thereof.

The fourth and final section is a detailed keyword index to the material covered in the main text.

Introduction to the Second Edition

A Handbook of Educational Technology was first published in 1984 and in light of the many changes that are occurring in the field the authors and publishers felt it was time to bring out a second edition. The authors have taken the opportunity to carry out a comprehensive revision of the book. This revision has taken four main forms.

First, all 11 chapters of the main text have been updated to take account of the various developments that have taken place since the first edition was written. A number of chapters have also had completely new material added to them (Chapters 1, 3, 4, 5, 6 and 7, for example).

Second, the visual impact of the book has been enhanced by introducing a large number of new illustrations, including 20 photographs (which were not used at all in the original version). This, it is hoped, will make the book even more useful to teachers and students.

Third, the glossary of terms used in educational technology that complements the main text has been thoroughly revised and updated. No less than 250 completely new terms have been added, room being made for most of these by removing any terms that had become dated or were judged to be of only peripheral importance.

Fourth, the chapter-by-chapter bibliography that constitutes the second major reference section has also been thoroughly revised and updated, with over 30 new references being added.

Needless to say, the keyword index has also been revised to take account of all the above changes.

CHAPTER 1

The Nature of Educational Technology

Introduction

To most people, the term 'educational technology' is, at best, confusing, and, at worst, downright off-putting. To some, the term is associated solely with the technical equipment and media of education — such as overhead projectors, television, tape-slide programmes, computers, etc. Others take the view that educational technology involves a clinical, systematic analysis of the entire teaching/learning process in an attempt to maximize its effectiveness. Indeed, extreme proponents of the latter view have sometimes been accused of treating learners more like 'impersonalized battery hens' than as 'people with inquiring minds who thrive on intellectual stimulation and human contact' — a view with which we have some sympathy.

Largely because of this confusion over its meaning, there can be little doubt that educational technology has now become a rather unhelpful jargon expression. Indeed, many practitioners working in the field are embarrassed by it, and, in some cases, have even made an attempt to disown it; several former 'educational technology units' in colleges and polytechnics have, for example, been re-named 'educational development units', 'learning units', or something similar. No one has so far managed to come up with an alternative, universally-acceptable name, however, so we appear to be stuck with it for the time being, and, for this reason, we will continue to use the term 'educational technology' throughout this book.

The perceptions of what constitutes 'educational technology' have evolved over a period of about 30 years, and its exact nature is not easily explained. Indeed Kenneth Richmond, in his excellent book *The Concept of Educational Technology* (1970), devotes the first 70 *pages* to a discussion of what educational technology is, and of the different connotations of the word 'technology'.

In this chapter, we will describe some of the general 'aspects' of educational technology, and trace its historical development. We will begin by discussing two quite different perceptions of educational technology, namely the idea of the 'technology *in* education' and the idea of a 'technology *of* education'.

Technology *in* Education

'Technology *in* education' embraces every possible means by which information can be presented. It is concerned with the 'gadgetry' of education and training, such as television, language laboratories and the various projected media, or, as someone once said, 'everything from computers to dinner ticket dispensers'. In other words, technology *in* education is basically the popular impression of what educational technology is all about, namely, *audiovisual aids.*

The general field of audiovisual aids is itself composed of two related but distinguishable areas, namely, *hardware* and *software.* The hardware side is concerned with the actual equipment — overhead projectors, slide projectors, tape recorders, videocassette recorders, television monitors, microcomputers, etc. The software side, on the other hand, is concerned with the various items that are used in conjunction with this equipment — such as overhead transparencies, slides, audiotapes, videorecordings and computer programs.

Technology *in* education is obviously one very important aspect of educational technology. Indeed, historically, many of the college-based 'educational technology units' evolved from units which were previously called 'audiovisual aids units'. By making appropriate use of hardware along with suitable software, it is often possible to improve the efficiency or quality of learning in a given situation, and this was the basis of the first developments in educational technology, as we shall see later.

One of the earliest phases in the evolution of educational technology was the 'hardware phase', in which a great deal of work was done in developing effective instructional equipment which was also reliable, serviceable and within the budgets of schools, colleges and training establishments. However, when such hardware eventually became generally available, it was found that there was a shortage of suitable software to use with it; this triggered off a subsequent 'software phase', in which particular attention was paid to the development of suitable learning materials, often based on the contemporary theories of learning and perception. Thus, even within this early development of educational technology, we can identify changes in the interpretation of the term 'technology'.

Initially, this had distinctly engineering connotations, since the main thrust of educational technology was concerned with the development of items of optical and electronic equipment for educational purposes; subsequently, it became much more associated with psychology and learning theory as the main thrust changed to the development of suitable software for use with this equipment.

However, at this stage in the development of educational technology, many people became aware that there was much in education and training which could be improved by thinking more carefully about *all* aspects of the design of teaching/learning situations. Such considerations led to a new, broader interpretation of 'educational technology' as the entire technology *of* education rather than merely as the use of technology *in* education, with the latter being regarded as merely a part of the former rather than the whole field as had previously been the case. Let us now examine this new interpretation in more detail.

The Technology *of* Education

It could be argued that the principal role of educational technology is to help improve the overall efficiency of the teaching/learning process. In education and training, improved efficiency can manifest itself in many ways, for example:

(a) increasing the quality of learning, or the degree of mastery;
(b) decreasing the time taken for learners to attain desired goals;
(c) increasing the efficiency of teachers in terms of numbers of learners taught, without reducing the quality of learning;
(d) reducing costs, without affecting quality.

It is a value judgement as to which of the above interpretations are more important, and, indeed, such a judgement must be made in terms of the educational, financial and political aspects of individual situations. They are not necessarily mutually exclusive, but (to quote a hypothetical example) it might be found that certain measures that could well improve the quality of learning in a particular situation would also involve an increase in expenditure, so that a decision based on the likely cost-effectiveness of the measures would have to be made.

However, given well-defined criteria by which an improvement in the efficiency of an educational system, situation or process can be gauged, then decisions regarding the exact measures by which this can best be achieved can often be reached by applying a 'technology *of* education' approach. Recommendations for improvement are thus based on a study of the particular system *as a whole*, together with knowledge of appropriate educational research findings and theories of learning. In many cases, ideas and practices drawn from such diverse fields as psychology, sociology, business management and systems analysis are combined with developments in more technical fields such as optics, reprography, acoustics and microelectronics in order to produce the optimum learning or teaching system.

These aspects, which are all part of the technology *of* education, are sometimes called the 'intangible' aspects (or the 'underware', as opposed to the hardware and software already described). In this case, the emphasis is on the *techniques* of teaching and learning rather than on audiovisual aids *per se*. Although the 'intangible' aspects of educational technology are, by definition, less obvious than the 'hardware' and 'software' aspects, they are, nevertheless, just as important (indeed, most educational technologists would say *more* important) when it comes to solving a particular problem.

A 'technology *of* education' approach to educational technology thus involves a systematic, scientific approach to a problem, together with the application of appropriate scientific research, both from 'hard' sciences such as physics and electronics and from social sciences such as psychology and sociology. In applying a technology *of* education approach, changes are not made to a system for their own sake, but only for good educational reasons that are generally based on research findings. Such changes may not always work as intended, but even unexpected outcomes may prove useful to the people involved (and to others) when future developments are being planned.

It is as a technology *of* education that most practitioners view educational technology today. Within this concept, technology *in* education is seen mainly as one of the possible means to an end, with appropriate hardware and software being selected or designed to back up the particular strategy that it is decided to adopt in order to achieve a given set of educational aims or objectives. In some cases, this may involve the use of sophisticated equipment such as video or computers; in others, duplicated worksheets may be all that are required. Here it is important that the educational development or innovation has been *systematically* and *scientifically* planned and executed. It is this 'systems approach' to educational technology which is at the heart of the technology *of* education.

The relationships between the various aspects of educational technology discussed so far are shown in schematic form in Figure 1.1.

The Systems Approach

The systems approach to the design and analysis of teaching/training situations is the basis of the great majority of modern educational technology-related developments. However, the terms 'system' (which we have already used in a number of contexts) and 'systems approach' are jargon terms and can have a variety of interpretations. Let us therefore first take a look at these terms in order to define the way in which we are to use them.

In an educational technology context, a *system* is any collection of interrelated parts that together constitute a larger whole. These component parts, or *elements*, of the system are intimately linked with one another, either directly or indirectly, and any change in one or more elements may affect the overall performance of the system, either beneficially or adversely. A simple system is illustrated schematically in Figure 1.2.

In Figure 1.2 the system consists of four distinct elements A, B, C, D which are related to or dependent upon each other as indicated. Note that some interrelationships may be two-way, while others may be one-way only. These elements may themselves be capable of further

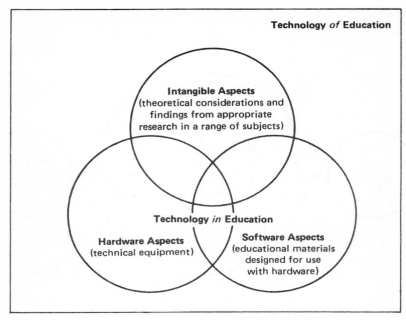

Figure 1.1 **The relationships between
the different aspects of educational technology**

breakdown into other smaller components, and may thus be regarded
as *sub-systems* of the overall system.

The processes of education and learning can be considered to be very
complex systems indeed. The input to a given educational or learning
system consists of people, resources and information, and the output
consists of people whose performance has (it is to be hoped) improved
in some desired way. A schematic representation of systems of this type
is shown in Figure 1.3.

In such a system, the educational or learning process may be so
complex that it can only be considered as a 'black box' whose
mechanisms are not fully understood. However, research into the
nature of the learning process has thrown *some* light on what happens
inside the 'black box'. This has enabled educational technologists
to structure the input to systems of this type in such a way as to try
to improve the output through increasing the efficiency of the learning
process, thus leading to a systems approach to course design based on
existing knowledge of how people learn. Such a systems approach
attempts to mould the input to a course in such a way as to enable the
optimum assimilation of knowledge and skills to take place during the
learning process and hence maximize the quality of the output. It is to
the various elements of such a systems approach to the design of

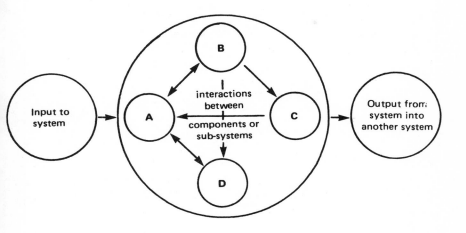

Figure 1.2 **A typical system**

courses, lessons and training programmes that we will be paying particular attention in later chapters of this book.

A simple system for the design of teaching/learning situations is given in Figure 1.4. We have deliberately chosen an extremely basic example of a systems approach to course design. Other writers (for

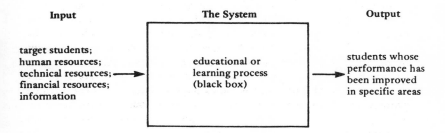

Figure 1.3 **The 'systems' model of the educational or learning process**

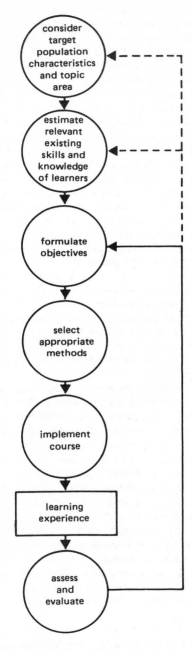

Figure 1.4 **A simplified systems approach to course design**

example, Romiszowski, in his books *The Selection and Use of Instructional Media: a Systems Approach* (1974) and *Designing Instructional Systems* (1981)) have described more sophisticated systems, but we feel that these would be unnecessarily complicated for our present purposes. The components of the system all have sub-elements, which we will discuss in detail in later chapters.

In this simple model, having first taken into account the type of learners and relevant levels of skills and pre-knowledge which the potential learners should possess, we start with the formulation of the objectives, or desired learning outcomes of the course, for a given target population of students. We will look in detail at the nature and role of objectives in Chapter 3. Having specified the objectives (that is, exactly what we are trying to achieve in the course) we are then in a better position to select appropriate teaching/learning methods by which the objectives have a reasonable chance of being achieved. There are far more teaching methods available to choose from than most people realize — indeed a book by Andrej Huczynski lists descriptions of no less than 303 different educational and training methods! The exercise of attempting to match appropriate methods to given objectives is normally done on the basis of a combination of research and experience. The strengths and weaknesses of a range of different teaching methods will be discussed in detail in Chapters 2, 4, 5 and 6.

The next element in the system is the actual implementation of the course. This involves all the logistical arrangements associated with running a course, including structuring and pacing, teaching strategies, selecting appropriate media, and ensuring that all aspects of the course run as smoothly as possible.

The combined result of these first three steps is that a *learning experience* is provided for the target students. How efficient and useful the pre-planning has been can be measured by studying student performance in post-course *assessments*. These assessments should be closely related to the original specified course objectives. Poorly-achieved course objectives should lead the course designers to examine the entire system in order to identify places where improvements can be made. This could involve a change in the original objectives, a revised assessment of students' pre-knowledge, a critical review of the teaching methods used, an examination of the course structure and organization, a consideration of the assessment methods used, or a combination of some or all of these. These deliberations, together with feedback on the course from staff, students, employers, etc can lead to an *evaluation* of the entire concept of the course, which should, in turn, form the basis of an on-going cyclical *course development* process. The topics of assessment and evaluation will be discussed in Chapter 7 and Chapter 8 respectively.

The systems approach to course design is therefore no more mysterious than an attempt to tackle course design through a process of logical development and on-going monitoring and evaluation in order to allow continuous evolution of the course to take place. As indicated earlier, more complicated systems approaches to course design do exist, but these all contain the core elements indicated in Figure 1.4.

Definitions of Educational Technology

We have so far discussed the perception of educational technology from a number of different stances, namely, technology *in* education, technology *of* education, and the systems approach. A number of definitions of educational technology have been produced by different bodies and organizations, and three of these are given below, in order of increasing detail.

Definition 1

'Educational technology is the development, application and evaluation of systems, techniques and aids to improve the process of human learning'.

Council for Educational Technology for the United Kingdom (CET)

Definition 2

'Educational technology is the application of scientific knowledge about learning, and the conditions of learning, to improve the effectiveness and efficiency of teaching and training. In the absence of scientifically established principles, educational technology implements techniques of empirical testing to improve learning situations'.

National Centre for Programmed Learning, UK

Definition 3

'Educational technology is a systematic way of designing, implementing and evaluating the total process of learning and teaching in terms of specific objectives, based on research in human learning and communication and employing a combination of human and non-human resources to bring about more effective instruction'.

Commission on Instructional Technology, USA

All three definitions are similar in that each emphasizes the primary function of educational technology as *improving the efficiency of the process of learning.* As discussed earlier, this is normally done on the basis of what is known as a result of research into the nature of the learning process. Each of the definitions implies a technology *of* education interpretation of the role of educational technology, involving a cyclical, systems approach to the design of teaching/learning situations and the use of whatever methods and techniques are judged to be appropriate in order to achieve one's desired objectives. Note also the strong emphasis on testing and evaluation implicit in each of the definitions.

Educational technology, via the systems approach to course and curriculum design, should therefore be flexible enough to react to new knowledge about the process of human learning, and also to new developments in teaching/learning approaches and methods. Examination of the historical development of the main concerns of educational technology provides an interesting insight into the nature of the subject, so we will now conclude this opening chapter by carrying out such a survey.

Development of the Main Concerns of Educational Technology: The Elton Model

One of the most useful overall pictures of the development of educational technology is that given by Professor Lewis Elton in 1977. He identifies three broad lines along which the field has evolved, namely, *mass instruction, individualized learning*, and *group learning*. Furthermore, he believes that each of these strands has consisted of successive *research, development* and *use* phases, as shown schematically in Figure 1.5.

In essence, Elton believes that educational technology has undergone a progressive change of emphasis since the end of the Second World War, when it first emerged as a discipline in its own right. Initially, there was a concentration on the techniques of *mass instruction*, then a change to *individualized learning*, and finally, during recent years, a move towards *group learning*. In each case, he identifies three broad, overlapping stages in the development, starting with a *research* phase, in which the basic concepts and techniques are developed, then progressing to a *development* phase, in which these basic concepts and techniques are converted into practical teaching and learning techniques together with their associated support materials, and finally leading to a third phase in which the techniques start to achieve widespread *use*. The combined research and development phases have in each case tended to last for roughly 25 years, after which the on-going 'use' phase continues indefinitely. Let us now look in more detail at the way in which each class of techniques has developed, and see where things stand today.

Mass Instruction Techniques

Mass instruction is, of course, as old as education itself, with the 'lecture' and 'expository lesson' being the dominant instructional techniques in virtually all sectors of education and training throughout history. It was, however, only in the period following the Second World War that a systematic effort was made to improve the efficiency

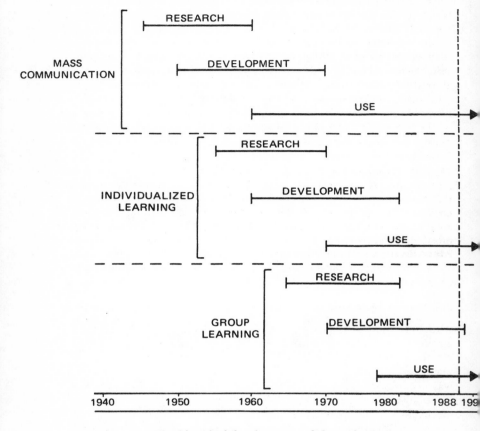

Figure 1.5 **The historical development of the main concerns
of educational technology** (after Elton)

and cost-effectiveness of the method by using the new types of hardware that were starting to become available. By such means, it was
hoped that more people could be educated or trained without necessarily increasing the number of teachers or trainers, and that the overall
effectiveness of the teaching process could be improved. Some important outcomes were the development of basic mass instruction tools
like the overhead projector and 35mm slide projector, and the
increasingly widespread use of 'hardware-based' techniques such as
film, radio and television broadcasting and closed-circuit television.
Indeed, one manifestation of the 'mass instruction' phase of educational
technology was the burgeoning of closed-circuit educational television
systems — like the one that linked virtually all schools in Glasgow.

In retrospect, it can be seen that the 'mass instruction' movement failed to live up to its early promise, largely because it soon became apparent that techniques such as mass teaching by closed-circuit television were strictly limited in the type of educational objectives that they could be used to achieve. They were, for example, totally unsuitable for achieving many higher cognitive objectives, and were also almost completely passive, enabling virtually no student involvement to take place. Partly because of these intrinsic limitations (and partly because of the ever-increasing cost of keeping them in operation) many of the large-scale cable educational television networks that were set up during the 'boom' years of the mass instruction phase have now been closed down or drastically reduced in scale. Nevertheless, other mass instruction techniques such as educational broadcasting have continued to grow in importance, and the various techniques and hardware systems that come under the general heading of 'mass instruction' continue to constitute a very important section of the educational armoury available to the modern teacher or lecturer. Figure 1.6 lists some of the most important of these techniques, and indicates some of their main educational strengths and weaknesses.

Mass instruction techniques are discussed in much greater detail in Chapter 4.

Individualized Learning Techniques

Although individualized learning, in the form of correspondence courses and similar systems, also has a long tradition of use in education, it was only comparatively recently that it became part of main-stream educational technology. The catalyst for this development was *behavioural psychology*, which was pioneered by B F Skinner and his followers during the 1950s. Skinner's work on the *stimulus/response* mechanism, which represented (in many people's view) the first truly 'scientific' theory of learning, first triggered off the bandwaggon *programmed learning* movement that dominated educational thinking during the 1960s. More recently, it led to the development of a wide range of individualized learning techniques (such as tape-slide and the various computer-assisted systems that are now achieving more and more widespread use) as well as to fully integrated individualized instruction systems such as the Keller Plan and Open Learning systems. However, before we trace these developments and uses, let us first look at the basic tenets of behavioural psychology, so that we can better understand the roots of these developments.

Behavioural psychology, like other branches of educational psychology, attempts to discover how learning takes place, and, consequently, how best to promote learning. It is largely predictive in nature, first attempting to discover which conditions are conducive for certain behaviour to occur, and then attempting to reproduce these conditions in order to bring about the desired behaviour.

Technique	Strengths	Weaknesses
Lectures and similar expository techniques	• Can be very cost-effective in terms of student/staff ratio. • Strong in achieving lower cognitive and *some* affective objectives. • Generally popular with both students and staff.	• Strongly dependent on skill of individual lecturer or lecturer. • Weak in achieving most higher cognitive and affective objectives; not suitable for achieving psychomotor objectives or developing communication skills, interpersonal skills, etc. • Student involvement generally low or non-existent. • Pace controlled by teacher; does not allow for different learning rates. • Most lectures are too long for the concentration span of students.
Film and video presentations	• Can be a highly effective substitute for a lecture or part thereof *if* the content and level are suitable. • Can be used to provide realistic illustrative, supportive, background and case-study material. • Tend to be highly stimulating.	• Can be a waste of time unless content and level are appropriate. • Teacher effectively relinquishes control of teaching process to maker of film or video during presentation. • Cannot be used unless suitable hardware is available. • Can be expensive.
Educational broadcasts	• Same basic strengths as film and video presentations, with further advantage that broadcasts are free.	• Same basic disadvantages as film and video presentations (with exception of cost). • Also, timing of broadcasts is generally fixed, making them difficult (or impossible) to fit into a timetable unless they can be recorded — something that can only be done *legally* with certain broadcasts.
Mass practical and studio work	• Can be effective in developing psychomotor and associated skills. • Can help demonstrate relevance of theoretical content of a course. • Students generally enjoy their participative nature.	• Can be a waste of time unless the activities chosen are relevant to the main content of the course. • Generally expensive in terms of time, manpower, equipment and materials. • Often weak in terms of higher cognitive objectives unless very carefully planned.

Figure 1.6 **Characteristics of some of the main mass instruction techniques**

Behavioural psychology theory is based on what is commonly referred to as *stimulus and response*, that is, it assumes that learning has occurred when a specific response is elicited from a learner when he or she is placed in a particular situation and given a particular stimulus. Learning of relatively complex behaviour can (it is claimed) be achieved through an appropriate series of stimulus-response situations. At each stage, the learner must actively participate by performing a set task, after which he or she is then supplied with immediate feedback in the form of the correct answer. This is known as *successive reinforcement*. Skinner also argued that each successive stimulus-response step should be small enough to ensure that the learner is almost always correct in his or her response. Use of these small steps, plus successive reinforcement, led to what behavioural psychologists believed was an efficient way of 'shaping behaviour'.

Skinner's original work was with animals, mostly with pigeons. His later work, which evolved from this, was with humans. Many people have since rejected or at least considerably modified Skinner's model, but it is important to remember that his work led to the beginnings of individualized learning, which now exists in many forms in the education and training fields. We shall look at some of these in more detail in Chapters 2 and 5.

The first application of Skinner's research to the classroom situation came in the form of *linear programmed learning*. In this type of programmed learning, the subject matter is broken down into a sequence of small *steps* (or *frames*) logically following upon one another. Each of the steps represents only a very small part of the concept or skill to be taught. In order to reward the learner and so, in turn, reinforce the learning process, each step contains a certain amount of information and requires the student to respond to a question about the information, while the small size of the step practically guarantees the correctness of the desired response. Immediate feedback on the correctness (or otherwise) of the response is designed to provide suitable reinforcement. Ideally, it should be virtually impossible to take a step without having successfully taken the previous ones. There is thus only one possible path which a student can take through the frames; hence the name *linear* programmed learning (see Figure 1.7).

STARTING   STIMULUS/RESPONSE STEPS
POINT   ➞ ➞ ➞ ➞ ➞ ➞ ➞ ➞ ➞ ➞ GOAL
(PRE-KNOWLEDGE)

Figure 1.7 **The basic structure
of a linear programmed learning sequence**

Skinner's 'essential' ingredients for programmed learning were the use of small steps, the high degree of interaction with the programme, and the 'linear' nature of the sequence. The evidence for the need to use very small steps has subsequently been challenged from a theoretical standpoint, and, in practice, such an approach can very often lead to boredom on the part of the learner. It is now accepted that the optimum step size in any particular learning programme is governed by a large number of considerations, and, as a result, large and/or difficult steps are often incorporated into modern learning programmes, which may also contain a lesser degree of reinforcement than the early programmes developed by Skinner and his followers.

In the 1960s, another form of programmed learning known as *branching programmed learning* was developed. This involved the use of several possible paths through the sequence of steps (frames), with 'remedial loops' being included in order to correct misconceptions identified from student responses to individual steps, which did not necessarily have to be small. Thus, the topic to be studied was taught in a number of alternative ways in such a branching programme, depending on the performance of the learner. Figure 1.8 shows a simple example of a possible structure for a branching programme of this type.

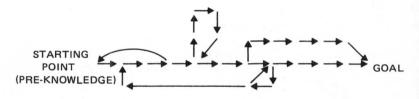

Figure 1.8 **A simple branching programmed learning sequence**

The type of branching structure shown in Figure 1.8, only very much more complex, is the basis of many of the self-instructional programmes that have been designed for use with the computer since the 1970s. Use of the computer in this 'substitute tutor' role allows students to have fast and effective access to what is basically a branching programmed learning sequence. (A review of the present role of computers in education is given in Chapter 10.)

Later developments in individualized learning have involved a much more flexible approach to programme design than that which was used in the relatively strict early programmed learning procedures. As we shall see in later chapters, much of the present use of individualized learning has evolved and been adapted in order to meet the specific requirements of particular educational or training establishments, or in order to satisfy the special needs of particular students (eg students studying on their own at a distance from the parent institution).

Technique	Strengths	Weaknesses
Directed study of material in textbooks	• Can be a highly effective way of teaching basic facts, principles, applications etc, provided that suitable texts are available and the work is carefully structured. • Allows learner to work at his or her own natural pace. • Needs no specialized facilities.	• Requires careful planning and structuring on part of teacher. • Dependent on suitable texts being available in sufficient numbers to cater for the size of class carrying out the work. • Not suitable for achieving many higher cognitive and non-cognitive objectives.
Study of specially prepared notes or programmed texts	• Same basic advantages as directed study of books, and can be even more effective if the material is well prepared. • Can allow learners to interact with the material.	• Preparing suitable material can be very time consuming. • Again, not suitable for achieving many higher cognitive and non-cognitive objectives.
Self-instruction via audio-visual media (audiotapes, video-tapes, tape/slide programmes etc)	• Enables a wide range of educational objectives to be achieved (especially lower cognitive). • Allows learner to work at his or her own pace. • In addition, use of mediated presentation Enables sound, movement, realism, etc to be introduced, thus increasing simulation. • Can save teachers from having to carry out repetitive, time-consuming work (eg teaching certain basic laboratory skills).	• Ideal ready-made courseware seldom available, and preparation of custom-designed material can be both time-consuming and expensive, as well as requiring specialist skills. • Again, not suitable for achieving many higher cognitive and non-cognitive objectives. • Cannot be used unless suitable hardware is available; this can be expensive to provide.
Computer-based learning	• Enables a wide range of educational objectives to be achieved (especially lower cognitive). • Allows learner to work at his or her own pace. • Can allow considerable interaction between learner and instructional programme, and can adapt to the needs of learner; can be highly stimulating. • Can provide (through computer simulations) otherwise inaccessible learning experiences.	• Same basic weaknesses as mediated self-instruction. • In addition, requires computer literacy and (in many cases) a high degree of programming skill on the part of the teacher.
Individual practical studio or project work	• Same basic strengths as mass practical and studio work. • Allows students to work at their own pace.	• Same basic weaknesses as mass practical and studio work.

Figure 1.9 **Characteristics of some of the main individualized learning techniques**

As in the case of the earlier 'mass-instruction' movement, it can, in retrospect, be seen that the individualized learning movement failed to live up fully to its early promise. During the 1960s, programmed learning enthusiasts were predicting the early demise of the traditional classroom teacher or lecturer, claiming that they would be replaced by the new *teaching machines* that they were developing as delivery systems for their programmes. These teaching machines turned out to be the biggest non-event in the history of education, however, partly because of the fact that high-quality software was never produced in the quantities that would have been needed for them to make any real impact, and partly due to the increasing realization that there was much more to education than the teaching of facts and principles. Nevertheless, the individualized learning movement has had a tremendous influence on educational thinking, and the various techniques that it has made available again form a vital section of the modern educational armoury. Some of the more important of these are listed in Figure 1.9, together with some of their main strengths and weaknesses. A more detailed discussion of these various techniques is given in Chapter 5.

Group Learning Techniques

While it can be argued that the 'individualized learning' phase probably had a greater impact on current education and training than the 'mass instruction' phase which preceded it, there are definite limitations to the approach. One of the most obvious stems from the fact that it is, by definition, *individual,* and, as such, cannot enable students to interact with one another and develop group skills such as discussion skills and interpersonal skills. This has led to an increasing realization that the various activities that come under the general heading of *group learning* have a very important part to play in modern education and training.

The theoretical basis for modern developments in group learning is the *humanistic psychology* that was developed by people such as Carl Rogers during the 1960s — a totally different type of psychology from the highly mechanistic behavioural psychology which formed the basis of the programmed learning movement. Humanistic psychology is concerned with how people interact with and learn from one another in small-group situations, and involves the use of the techniques of *group dynamics.*

When used in a learning situation, such techniques generally require no specialized hardware and (in most cases) very little in the way of software other than simple printed sheets and booklets; the emphasis is very much upon the *approach* or *technique* rather than a reliance on specific types of hardware or software.

At the time of writing, group learning is still in the final stages of its 'development phase', although its 'use' phase is now well under way — as evidenced by the widespread use now being made of

Technique	Strengths	Weaknesses
Buzz sessions and similar short small-group exercises	• Constitute an excellent method of introducing variety into a lecture, thus helping to maintain student attention. • Can be used to achieve a wide range of objectives, both cognitive and non-cognitive. • They get students actively involved in a lesson. • They allow feedback to take place.	• They are most useful in a *supportive* role as part of a larger lesson as they are not, by themselves, intended for use as a front-line method of teaching basic facts and principles.
Class discussions, seminars, tutorials, etc	• Same basic advantages as buzz sessions, etc. • In addition, their greater length allows an even wider range of objectives to be achieved, often of a very high level. • Enable relevant topics to be examined in great depth.	• There is a danger that not all the members of a class will take an active part in the exercise unless steps are taken to make sure that they do. • They can cause timetabling problems if a class has to be split up.
Participative exercises of the game/ simulation/ case study type	• They can be used to achieve a wide range of objectives, both cognitive and non-cognitive, often of a very high level. • High student involvement. • Highly stimulating and motivating if properly designed. • Ideal for cross-disciplinary work.	• Most useful in a supportive or illustrative role rather than as a front-line method of teaching basic facts and principles. • Can be difficult to fit into curriculum, especially in case of long exercises. • Must be *relevant* to course to be of real educational value.
Mediated feedback sessions such as microteaching recorded inter-views, or recorded group exercises	• Use of mediated feedback (eg audio or video recording) enables valuable group discussions of student performance to take place. • Can be used to develop a wide range of skills. • High student involvement.	• Some students find method off-putting at first. • Requires suitable hardware and other facilities, often expensive. • Can cause timetabling problems if a class has to be split up.
Group projects	• Suitable for developing a a wide range of objectives, both cognitive and non-cognitive, often at a very high level. • Ideal for developing inter-personal and group skills. • Ideal for cross-disciplinary work.	• There is a danger that not all the members of the group will pull their weight unless steps are taken to make sure that they do. • Assessment of contributions made by individual students can be problematic.
Self-help groups	• Can be of considerable help to isolated groups of learners. • Peer teaching extremely valuable.	• Students require to be motivated to form or join such groups.

Figure 1.10 **Characteristics of some of the main group learning techniques**

participative methods such as games, simulations, interactive case studies, and group projects. Some of the more important types of group learning exercises are listed in Figure 1.10, which again identifies their main educational strengths and weaknesses. A much more detailed discussion of all these various techniques is given in Chapter 6.

Summary of the Main Features of Mass Instruction, Individualized Learning and Group Learning

A summary of the main features of the three aspects of educational technology that are included in the Elton model is given in Figure 1.11. As has already been stated, the results of each of these three phases are still very much with us, and will probably continue to develop and evolve as time goes on. Most of the problems associated with their use are now educational rather than technological. The associated equipment will, in all probability, tend to become as cheap, simple and reliable as possible, while the considerations that determine their use in education and training will depend upon the particular criteria that are considered to be most important in a given situation.

	Mass instruction	Individualized learning	Group learning
Theoretical basis	Industrial technology	Behavioural psychology	Humanistic psychology
Model	Economy of scale	Stimulus-response	Group dynamics
Emphasis of methods	Hardware	Software	Techniques
Results	CCTV; broadcasting	Programmed learning plus derivatives; computer-assisted learning	Interpersonal skill sessions; games and simulations

Figure 1.11 **Summary of main features of the three phases of educational technology**

The evolution of emphasis in educational technology from mass instruction through individualized learning to group learning mirrors the progression from a 'hardware' approach through a 'software' approach to the 'technology *of* education' approach that was discussed earlier in the chapter. One notable example which Professor Elton believes reflects these changes is the development of the Open University in the UK. This institution, originally conceived during the early 1960s as the 'University of the Air', started offering courses in 1971 using the media of television and radio broadcasts, and there was an extensive period of software development (mainly textual) in order to support students studying on an individualized basis. More recently, there has been a much greater concern with providing situations for closer contact with other students and with tutors, and there has generally been a more human, or group, approach to learning, although such developments have been somewhat restricted owing to financial considerations. Although the Open University has always used all three teaching methods (mass communication, individualized learning and group learning) in its courses, there is no doubt that there has been a gradual change of emphasis over the years, and that first individualized learning, and then, more recently, group learning gradually came to play much more important roles than were originally envisaged. In its evolution, the Open University thus represents a microcosm of educational technology itself.

Other Areas in which Educational Technology has Developed

Useful as Elton's model is, there are those who correctly criticize it as being incomplete, and taking insufficient account of the evolving social and technological contexts over the timespan charted. For example, it makes no recognition of the development of other important concerns of educational technology such as the management of innovation and the development of student study skills, both of which will now be examined.

The Management of Innovation

Most of the work of the educational technologist is, almost by definition, innovative. Whether the innovation in question is on a small scale (for example, the development of a tape-slide programme) or much more ambitious (eg the planning of a distance learning course), the success in establishing the innovation as part of the overall educational framework depends on a wide variety of factors (the quality of the innovation, the nature of the potential users, political factors, administrative arrangements etc). Indeed, many highly promising educational innovations have foundered and died because the implementation of the innovation was mismanaged.

As a consequence, the effective management and implementation of innovation has recently been of increasing concern to educational technologists, most of whom have experienced the frustration of seeing many hours of painstaking work failing to realize its potential because of such mismanagement. Indeed, it is not unusual to find educational innovators now spending as much or even more time on fostering an environment in which an innovation can flourish as in developing the actual innovation. This concern is reflected in the literature by a rapidly expanding body of publications on managing educational innovation.

The topic is vast and extremely complex, and, in this book, we do not intend to do more than to underline its undoubted importance in educational technology. For those who want to pursue the subject further, Bolam's article in *Management in Education* (1975) is a useful starting point.

Study Skills Techniques

Another area which has attracted the attention of many educational technologists in recent years is the development of student study skills. Obviously, one way of improving the effectiveness of the teaching/ learning process is to increase the efficiency of learners in assimilating the subject matter covered. For this reason, educational technologists and teachers have used the results of educational and psychological research to devise programmes of activities that are specifically designed to assist students in their study technique. Apart from over 100 'how to study' guides that have been written for students, a number have been written for teachers in order to assist them in devising appropriate activities for students. One of the best of these is by Graham Gibbs, entitled *Teaching Students to Learn: A Student Centred Approach* (1981) and interested readers are referred to this.

The sort of areas covered by study skills include organization of time, effective use of time, reading skills, essay-writing and report-writing skills, note-taking, examination technique, and even job-hunting skills. Also, students in distance learning schemes may have special study difficulties which have to be coped with.

The growing interest in study skills development is further evidence that educational technology is concerned not only with hardware and software, but also with the less tangible aspects of the teaching/learning process.

CHAPTER 2

Basic Educational Strategies

Introduction

In Chapter 1 we discussed, in general terms, the nature of educational technology, and gave a brief historical account of the development of the field to date. In this chapter, we will take a look at two broad, contrasting approaches to education and training, within the context of which virtually all important educational technology-related developments have taken place, namely, the traditional *teacher/institution-centred approach* and the more recent *student-centred approach*. In each case, we will first examine the structure of the system that underlies the approach, then discuss its strengths and weaknesses, and finally identify the main teaching/learning methods that it employs.

The Teacher/Institution-Centred Approach

In the conventional teaching/learning situation, the teacher imparts, to a class of students, subject matter which is laid down in some form of syllabus (or, more often than not, imparts his or her personal interpretation of the syllabus). The classes normally take place at set times and last for a predetermined period, as indicated by a timetable, while the teaching methods are almost invariably of the 'face-to-face' type. The whole system is generally geared towards the smooth operation of the teaching institution, with little or no attempt being made to cater for the different learning styles and particular difficulties of individual students.

The Underlying Structure

A schematic representation of the traditional teacher/institution-centred approach to education and training is given in Figure 2.1.

In such a system, virtually all the decisions as to how a course is to be organized and taught are made either by the institution mounting the course or by the teacher nominated to take the class. The institution decides where and when the class is to meet and how long each session is to last, these arrangements being tailored to fit in with those

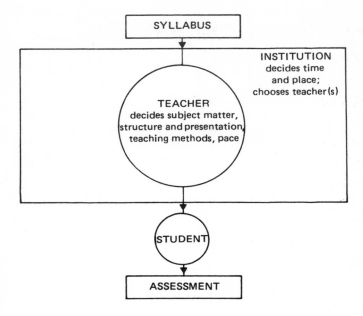

Figure 2.1 **The structure of the system
underlying the teacher/institution-centred approach**

for all the other courses run by the institution. The institution also decides which particular member (or members) of staff will be responsible for actually teaching the class.

The teacher or instructor makes most of the 'tactical' decisions relating to how the syllabus (which is often laid down by an external body of some sort) should be interpreted, in terms of both the specific subject matter to be covered and the level of sophistication at which this is to be treated. Decisions regarding the structuring, sequencing and presentation of the material are also made by the teacher, as are decisions concerning the teaching methods to be used and the pace of the course.

The student normally has little or no say in any of these decisions, and must try to adapt his learning style to the organizational constraints laid down by the institution and to the educational decisions made by the teacher. Finally, the student's ultimate achievement on the course is normally assessed by an examination of some sort, sometimes set externally, with the individual student again having no say regarding how this is done.

Such an approach has its advantages and disadvantages, and these may be viewed from radically different perspectives depending on the level and nature of the course being taught. Let us now examine them in detail.

Advantages

Many of the advantages associated with a teacher/institution-centred strategy stem from the very fact that this represents the traditional approach to teaching and training. Schools, colleges and training establishments are all normally geared to operate via such an approach, and the administrative systems of these institutions are designed to support it. While this administrative convenience is more a reason for the predominance and perpetuation of the teacher/institution-centred approach than an educational advantage *per se*, it is certainly a very important factor. Indeed, any attempt to adopt a radically different approach will almost certainly fail if it is alien to the teaching staff or administratively awkward for the host institution to implement. Most educational and training establishments have decades of experience in operating this traditional system, and students as well as teachers and administrators have become used to it. Also, the 'certification' of learning is strongly geared to existing teacher/institution-centred learning schemes.

Another important advantage of teacher/institution-centred strategies is that they enable institutions to make relatively efficient use of their accommodation and equipment resources and (in terms of timetabling arrangements) fair and effective use of staff time. A set timetable allows a teacher to tackle a course or syllabus in such a way that the teaching programme fits into the time available, thus making sure that all the material is at least 'covered' — a particularly important consideration when students are being prepared for an externally-set examination.

Within this type of strategy, a teacher can attempt to provide a range of different learning situations for the students, all designed to match the type of material being covered and the level and sophistication of the learners. Remedial and/or revision exercises can be provided, and a teacher may well know from experience, and from personal knowledge of the class, what will be the most appropriate teaching method to use in given circumstances. This advantage is particularly relevant when one is dealing with young or inexperienced learners (for example, at primary level) where strong leadership is required in order to provide effective pupil learning opportunities. Many learning activities may certainly involve a considerable proportion of individual or small group work, but the teacher remains firmly at the centre, and his or her experience with such learners is vitally important.

Disadvantages

While sound educational cases can often be made for the use of teacher-centred strategies in particular circumstances, there are many cases, particularly at higher levels of education and training, where strong central control of the teaching/learning situation is hard to defend other than in terms of administrative convenience and teacher/student acceptance. While the traditional system can certainly point to many outstanding successes, cynics and critics of the system might argue that these successes have been achieved *despite* the system and not because of it. A number of strong criticisms have been made of the traditional teacher/institution-centred approach to education and training, particularly in circumstances where it is difficult to argue a strong *educational* (as opposed to an *administrative*) case in favour of it. These include many of the situations encountered in further and higher education, industrial and commercial training, and, to a lesser extent, secondary school education.

One of the most obvious limitations of teacher-centred learning is that it is, by its very nature, extremely dependent upon the skill and ability of the teacher. While this can be a distinct advantage if the teacher is talented and experienced, it can also lead to severe problems for the students if this is not the case. The control exercised by the teacher is that, amongst other things, he interprets the syllabus, structures the content, selects the teaching methods, dictates the pace of coverage, and makes decisions regarding the amount of reinforcement material and remedial work to incorporate. Problems may arise in connection with any or all of these factors, and, in many cases, a teacher has only his or her own experience and intuition for guidance.

Many syllabuses are written in very vague terms, and a teacher must frequently decide upon the level and content of, say, 10 hours of teaching on the basis of a syllabus entry which may consist of only a few words. If the syllabus is written by an external or central organization, some guidance may be obtained from advisers or past exam papers, but the onus and responsibility is still firmly with the teacher. If the syllabus is written in terms of 'behavioural objectives' (see Chapter 3), this particular problem is normally not so serious, since this type of syllabus is generally much more detailed and explicit, requiring less interpretation on the part of the teacher.

Structuring the content is again a task for the teacher, and is usually based on a combination of theory, practical experience, and consultation with colleagues. Even with a small class, the structure adopted is unlikely to be exactly suited to the different levels of pre-knowledge and different learning styles of all the individual students, and the problem obviously becomes even greater with large classes; it is, after all, simply not practicable for a teacher to present the same material in all the different ways that would be needed to match students' individual entry skills and learning styles.

Similar problems are likely to arise with regard to the pace adopted by the teacher, since the students in a class (especially a large one) are likely to differ considerably in the degree to which they have mastered earlier work and in the rate at which they can learn new material. The pace dictated by the teacher will (at best) only be appropriate for part of the class, and, even if the teacher manages to match the pace to the needs of the middle-ability majority, it will almost certainly be too fast for the slow learners (who may, incidentally, have high ability) and will probably be too slow for the high fliers, who are liable to become bored or 'switch off' as a consequence.

Another possible drawback of the teacher-centred approach is that the actual teaching methods that are employed may be inappropriate for teaching towards the desired skills and attitudes. At school level, there is scope for a wide range of teaching methods, but school teachers all too often limit themselves to those methods with which they feel comfortable and to which they are accustomed. Teachers at further and higher education levels are generally even more limited in their approaches, and it is still fair to say that the lecture continues to dominate teaching practice at these levels, often at the expense of alternative methods which may be more appropriate in certain situations.

The amount of reinforcement and revision to be provided is yet another decision that is left to the teacher. It is well established (from psychological research) that the level of skill in executing a given task, or the amount of recall associated with a subject, is very strongly related to the amount of reinforcement or back-up teaching and learning that is carried out. Once again, a good, experienced teacher will almost certainly try to incorporate a reasonable amount of reinforcement into the teaching scheme, but others may either deliberately leave this to the the student to do for himself or may be under such tight time constraints to 'finish' a course that the reinforcement aspect has to be neglected.

Problems can also arise from the very factors that make the teacher-centred approach administratively convenient from an institution's point of view. Classes, for example, are almost invariably timetabled to fit into standard time slots — normally one hour in length in the case of the lectures that form the 'staple diet' of most students undergoing further and higher education. It has, however, been established that the attention levels of both teacher and student fall off rapidly with time, and that the optimum time for a straight lecture is between 20 and 30 minutes — well below the standard length. While it is true that a good teacher or lecturer will probably take steps to counteract this tendency for attention to decrease by (for example) introducing periodic interactive sessions into a lecture or using a variety of methods within a given teaching period, in many cases the problem is either not recognized or simply ignored.

A further weakness of systems that rely on rigid timetables, at all levels of education and training, is that insufficient attention tends to be given to the problems or difficulties that are faced by individual learners. Even when practice sessions or tutorials are arranged, these cannot hope to deal efficiently with all such problems, particularly if they originated in a class talk or lecture given some time previously and are not related to the topic that is scheduled for revision at the time. The scale of this problem is again obviously greater with large classes in further or higher education, but it does also exist at secondary school level and in training courses.

Teacher/institution-centred systems have also been criticized on the grounds that they tend to encourage spoonfeeding of students, and give little scope for individual investigation and choice of appropriate topics of study related to a student's own interests. While the spoonfeeding practice can be defended in the case of many school courses, and also in the case of core courses in colleges, universities and training establishments, it is less easy to defend if one accepts the view that one of the primary functions of education is to foster the development of an inquiring mind and creative thought. It is generally true that teacher-centred staregies at most levels of education encourage neither intellectual curiosity nor an individual student's responsibility for organizing and planning his or her learning.

It must be emphasized that many of the above criticisms of the teacher/institution-centred approach can be of greater or lesser importance depending on the level of education involved, the particular institution, and (most important of all) the individual teacher. However, while it is not suggested that any educational or training system could (or should) be 'teacher proof', it must be pointed out that the success or otherwise of the teacher-centred approach is strongly dependent, in a number of important ways, on the teacher(s) involved. In this lies both its strength and its weakness.

Teaching Methods Used

Within the context of the teacher/institution-centred approach, a wide range of different teaching methods can be used. These range from purely expository methods such as the lecture or talk (see Figure 2.2) to methods which involve a much greater degree of individualized learning or group work. The important point is that all these various activities occur within an educational or training structure which is organized or run by the *teacher*, operating within the fairly rigid constraints of the *institution* in which he or she works.

As mentioned earlier, the almost complete emphasis on the teacher-centred approach at primary school level entails the teacher organizing and controlling virtually all pupil learning opportunities; this may involve, amongst other things, short expositions to the class as a whole, individual work and group work.

At secondary school level, expository methods of one form or another are probably the most widely used teaching technique, with set exercises, group discussions, practical work and a certain amount of individualized learning being used to back these up.

At tertiary level, expositions in the form of lectures, films, broadcasts etc are by far the most common teaching methods, together with private reading and other individual work, tutorials, seminars and practical work. Tutorials are meant to allow students to discuss individual problems arising from lecture work or private reading, but, if not handled properly, they often tend to become 'mini-lectures'.

Figure 2.2 **The 'chalk and talk' lesson — one of the mainstays
of the teacher/institution-centred approach to education**

Seminars that allow discussion of topics within a group and other
group learning methods are becoming progressively more popular
(see Chapter 6). Practical work commonly takes the form of laboratory
and project work in the case of most science and engineering courses,
but may involve anything from television production by students to
first aid, depending on the course.

The Student-Centred Approach

While conventional teaching strategies are strongly dominated by the
teacher and by institutional constraints, student-centred strategies are
designed to provide the student with a highly flexible system of learning
which is geared to individual life and learning styles. In such strategies,
the teacher and the institution play supportive, rather than central roles.

A large number of approaches have been developed and used at
different levels of education. These vary from systems designed to
individualize learning within an existing educational or training environment by extensive use of resource-based learning, to systems where
practically all of the conventional barriers to educational opportunity
have been removed. With the latter, a potential student can be of any
age or background, and can study in places, at times and at a pace
which suits the individual rather than the institution. Such systems are
called *open learning systems*, and are at present engendering a great
deal of interest within the further and higher education and training
sectors in the UK and elsewhere.

The Underlying Structure

The basic structure of the system that underlies the student-centred approach can be represented diagrammatically by Figure 2.3, although not all of the factors shown are applicable in every case. In such a structure, the individual student's requirements are the most important considerations, with all the other components of the system being geared to assist the student to achieve his or her particular learning objectives as effectively as possible.

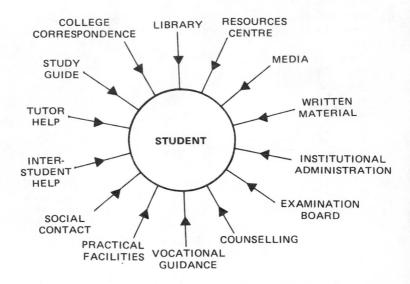

Figure 2.3 **The structure of the system underlying the student-centred approach**

The relationship between the student and his host institution can vary considerably within the context of the student-centred approach, but we can identify at least three basic organizational systems, namely, *institution-based systems*, *'local' systems* and *distance learning systems*. Let us examine these in turn.

1. *Institution-based systems.* Here, the students work at a particular institution, with learning facilities and tutor help being provided by the institution on an 'open-access' basis, and the students attending the institution for study at times and at a pace which suits them. A popular system of this type is the *Keller Plan*, which will be described in more detail towards the end of this chapter.

2. *Local systems.* Here, the host institution sets out to offer the student the facilities normally associated with a correspondence

course and to back this up with on-the-spot institutional support. Such systems are aimed specifically at members of the local population whose personal situations render it difficult or impossible for them to conform to the rigid constraints of the formal education system. The student does not have to attend the college on a regular timetabled basis, and may use a range of individualized learning facilities, both in and out of college. As in institution-based systems, college learning facilities are made available on an open access basis. An example of this type of system is *Flexistudy*, which is becoming increasingly popular in the UK, especially in the field of further education. Figure 2.4 shows part of the 'Learning-by-Appointment' centre in one further education college that offers courses of this type.

3. *Distance learning systems.* Here, most of the learning takes place away from the host institution. Individualized learning materials are provided for the student, and tutorial help may be made available through correspondence or telephone with the institution or via a local tutor (or both). Self-help groups organized by students in a particular geographical area may also occur. Probably the best known example of a distance learning system is the *Open University* in the UK.

In each of the above systems, the student has a high responsibility for many aspects of his or her learning, so motivation must, of necessity, be high. Course material is usually broken up into a number of discrete units, which allow the student to master one section before progressing

Figure 2.4 **A 'Learning-by-Appointment' centre
in a further education college that runs 'Flexistudy' courses**

to the next. As students are permitted to learn at their own rate in such systems, the administrative and tutorial support must be flexible enough to cope with this.

In student-centred courses, the individual course units are often described in detail in the student's study guide. This document may also list the behavioural objectives of each unit, thus enabling the student to have a clear idea of exactly what is expected of him or her (see Chapter 3). Guidance may also be given on how these objectives may be achieved, and this may (ideally) allow the student to select, from a range of alternative methods and routes, those particular ones which best suit his or her personal characteristics.

The learning material that is available in such courses may take several forms. It may be mainly textual, in the form of set books (or sections of books), 'custom-designed' material produced by the host institution, or a combination of the two. Easy access to a library (either an institutional library or, if this is not possible, a good public library) is thus more or less essential for students undertaking a course of this type. Individualized material which has an audiovisual content (for example, tape-slide programmes, videocassettes etc) may also be made available, and so the student must also have access to suitable replay equipment, either at home or through a local college, school or multi-media resources centre. Practical facilities may also be an important component of the course, and these must be made available either in the host institution (or some other local establishment) or in home-based 'kit' form.

An obvious potential problem in any highly individualized study system is that of student isolation, and, in order to prevent this, some mechanism for providing tutorial guidance and remedial help must be built in. In most systems of this type, each student is allocated at least one tutor who can easily be contacted as and when required. Such tutor help may take the form of face-to-face guidance, telephone tutorials or correspondence, depending on the distance between tutor and student and the circumstances of the latter. The role of the tutor is, of course, vital in any student-centred strategy, especially in the early stages, where the student is trying to adapt to a new style of learning. The tutor is in a key position to monitor an individual's progress and to provide strong support in terms of encouragement and counselling. Valuable support for individual students can also be provided through the formation of small local student self-help groups, where common problems can be tackled on a group-discussion basis.

In any student-centred system, the administrative support of the host institution must be geared towards its smooth operation, otherwise the resulting frustration may prove disastrous. This vital area includes making arrangements for recording and monitoring student progress, distributing learning materials, assignments, tutor feedback etc, handling finance, supporting and training teaching staff in materials production, counselling etc, and handling publicity. In addition, the institution's student services staff may provide vocational guidance, as well as ensuring that the examination systems (if applicable) are available and familiar to the student. As with the teacher/institution-centred approach, there are obvious advantages and disadvantages of such strategies. The relative importance of these is again very dependent upon the level of education or training involved, the type of learner, and the specific constraints associated with the institution mounting or hosting the course.

Advantages

In most student-centred learning systems, the material to be learned is much more readily available than in a teacher/institution-centred course. The individual units of study can be learned one at a time, and often in a place which suits the individual's personal circumstances. In addition, students normally have access to well-prepared, well-tested learning materials; hence the quality of the learning material available is less dependent on particular teachers. As the rate of learning is self-paced, the student is not rushed past parts of a course he or she finds difficult, nor is he or she held back on the parts that are easier to master. This aspect makes student-centred learning particularly appropriate for groups that have mixed abilities and/or mixed backgrounds.

Since the course units are normally accompanied by a set of behavioural objectives which spell out precisely what the student will be expected to do at the end of each unit, both student and tutor know exactly what has to be achieved. Such objectives also help the student to focus his or her work towards any subsequent test or examination.

Within most individualized learning units, a variety of different media (such as slides, audiotapes, models, videocassettes, practical exercises, computer-based materials and textual material) can readily be incorporated. The characteristics of different media can thus be exploited to the full, and students tend to find such a multi-media approach both stimulating and motivating. Much of the material produced for individualized use is *interactive* in the sense that it involves the student in active participation and in responding to the learning material rather than simply reading, listening or watching in a purely passive manner. This structured interaction facilitates learning and maintains concentration.

The course units are themselves designed to be student-centred, and, in many cases, there are several ways in which the same course material may be approached. Ideally, students can select, from a range of options, those methods which best suit their individual needs, interests and personal learning styles. Units may be produced in a number of formats, from which the student chooses the most appropriate 'package' in order to achieve the required objectives. Depending on the subject matter, students may be able to select the order in which they study the units of a course, although the sequence will obviously be partly fixed in that some units will depend and build on more basic units. Also, although some 'core' material is generally compulsory, students may usually select from a range of optional, remedial and enrichment units, depending on their individual needs and progress.

With most student-centred learning strategies, tutor help, counselling and guidance are generally more readily available and relevant than in more traditional courses. The role of the tutor is absolutely vital in supporting the individual students as they progress through a course. The advice and academic assistance given can in this case be geared to *individual* worries and problems rather than to more generalized group needs. Also, in such a system, the weaker students have the opportunity of receiving more attention than stronger or more independent students. Indeed, one of the most useful educational outcomes of such courses is that students learn to study effectively on their own, rather than being spoonfed, as is often the case in more traditional systems. It is one of the roles of the tutor/counsellor to help students new to this style of learning to adjust in order to get the most out of the system.

Owing to this close relationship between tutor and student, together with the results of tests on each unit, both tutor and student receive regular feedback on the student's progress. Also, as each unit is successfully completed, both the student and the tutor are assured that something definite has been achieved. This provides regular encouragement and motivation for the student.

On a more general note, student-centred learning systems can provide greater educational and training opportunities for those who cannot attend institutions during 'normal' hours. This applies particularly to those in regular day-time employment and those whose personal situations (for example, dependent relatives, physical disability or problems related to distance) make it difficult or impossible for them to attend regular timetabled classes. Thus, at the levels of further, higher and adult education, a completely new market of potential students has been identified, the exploitation of which may even have implications for the long-term viability of some colleges in these sectors of education. There is vast scope for student-centred open learning courses for training, re-training and career updating. Such courses need be neither long nor certificated, yet can still play a vital role in continuing and community education.

Disadvantages

Since student-centred learning places much more reliance on the active role of the student than does traditional teaching (where the student has a relatively passive role) student commitment and motivation must of necessity be very high. Thus, it may be less appropriate for use with young or inexperienced learners than with older, more mature learners, who have a definite goal to aim for and who enter a student-centred system knowing that they are going to have to work hard and expend effort, not least in organizing their study strategies. Even with a highly motivated group of students, some students may, indeed, never adapt to this style of learning.

There may also be difficulties in setting up a student-centred learning system in terms of the preparation of new materials. Teachers need to learn new skills for the production of good learning materials, and the (often considerable) time required to do this effectively must be found. The difficult and time-consuming nature of this task must not be underestimated. It must never be forgotten that student-centred courses are just as much dependent on good instructional materials as institution-centred courses are on good teachers.

As well as being the producer of learning materials, the teacher has another new role in a student-centred learning system. He is no longer the primary conveyor of information, but adopts a more supportive counselling and tutorial role. This function may be difficult for some teachers to fulfil effectively (or even to accept), and, in many cases, it may be necessary to organize in-service courses and other staff development activities in order to help teachers to carry out their new role effectively.

A further disadvantage of student-centred learning is the rather limited range and type of courses to which the strategy is applicable. Because of the generally prescriptive nature of course units (due to the specification of precise objectives), some may consider that this limits breadth and choice of study. Indeed, most applications of the approach to date have been in courses requiring mastery or updating of basic knowledge, mainly in subjects with a strong factual content and structure such as the sciences, engineering, mathematics and medicine, and also in short training courses. There have, however, also been some developments in arts-based courses. In subjects with a high practical component, it is often extremely difficult to build suitable laboratory work, practical demonstrations and skills-related work into essentially self-paced courses. Also, the student-centred approach is not particularly suitable for any type of learning that makes heavy use of discussion groups.

A student-centred course must obviously have the support of the administrative system of the host institution in terms of funding arrangements and day-to-day operation of the course in matters such as secretarial support, correspondence, telephone calls, access to special facilities (library facilities, computer facilities, laboratories, etc) and providing a suitable examination system.

All of these can cause severe administrative problems, especially if the host institution is not geared up to cope with learners in student-centred schemes. All too often, such learners simply do not fit into the system, and, as a result, are not given the same priority as 'conventional' students when it comes to allocating resources and facilities. A further potential drawback of student-centred learning schemes is that any qualification gained as a result may be regarded as second-rate or inferior to similar qualifications gained by traditional means. While this may have no foundation in reality, potential students may fear that society, employers or the academic community at large may perceive this to be the case, and so they may be deterred from joining such schemes.

Finally, teachers must realize that student-centred learning is not a soft option on their part, and that it requires a tremendous amount of effort in writing and revising suitable units, together with tutorial and counselling duties, marking tests and assignments, and providing student feedback.

Teaching Methods Used

The main teaching methods used in the great majority of student-centred courses are individualized methods of one form or another. Many of the materials associated with individualized learning are highly structured and interactive, although this is not necessarily the case. The materials may or may not have an audiovisual element, depending on the topic being covered and the specific design objectives. A review of individualized learning methods and techniques is given in Chapter 5.

As we have seen, tutorial support is a vital feature of all student-centred learning systems, with the precise nature of this support being strongly dependent upon the situation and location of the individual learner. Some courses may require practical work to be incorporated, but this has to be made as accessible as possible for the student, and may involve the development of individualized kits for use at home, or the provision of more organized facilities within the host institution or some other centre.

Expository methods such as lectures normally have little place in such strategies. However, some student-centred courses have included a certain number of lectures, often on an optional basis, in order to provide an introductory review of a topic or for 'enrichment' purposes.

The Keller Plan Approach

As many readers may have had little or no experience of student-centred strategies, we will now describe the operation of one of the most popular personalized systems of instruction (or PSIs). This system, known as the *Keller Plan*, was developed in the late 1960s by Professor F S Keller of Columbia University in the USA, and is an example of the way in which student-centred learning can be used within a college or similar institution.

In the Keller Plan, the course material is divided into a number of units, each with specified learning objectives, and the students receive a study guide which suggests a number of means of achieving these objectives. Armed with this information, students work largely on their own, using a range of self-instructional materials. The study guide leads students through set text books, and contains supplementary notes, worked exercises, assignments, etc. Some units may also incorporate learning aids such as videos, slides, models and other structured learning materials specially prepared for use in the course. Typically, each unit represents roughly one week's work for an 'average' student, but, as students work at their own pace, this is variable. The student is free to discuss problems associated with the unit with his or her tutor at any time. For this reason, tutors have to be available on a fairly regular basis. Tutors are normally members of the teaching staff, but they may, in certain circumstances, be students who have previously completed the unit successfully. Thus, the possibility of *peer teaching* can be incorporated into a Keller Plan approach.

When a student feels that he has mastered a given unit, that is, he feels that he has achieved all the objectives set, he presents himself for a test (which may be oral or written) and this test must be passed at a predetermined level before going on to the next unit. With the Keller Plan, a high degree of mastery is often required, and pass marks on tests may be of the order of 80 or 90 per cent. There is, however, no penalty for failing, and students may attempt tests on a given unit as many times as is necessary. After each test, the student and tutor discuss any problems which may have arisen during work on the unit, or during the test itself.

In the Keller Plan, lectures, although not a main element of the teaching, are sometimes used to provide an overview of the course material or to illuminate certain aspects of the topics studied. Laboratory work (if required) is normally carried out under the direct supervision of a laboratory assistant.

The basic Keller Plan approach has been modified and adapted to meet a wide variety of needs. Peer teaching is not always used; tests on groups of units (rather than on single units) may be included; a high level of mastery is not always required; and the final grades can be decided using different methods. Whatever the variations, however, the essential elements of the Keller Plan are *individualized learning*, *independent study*, *self-pacing* and *tutor support*. Although the Keller Plan has been used with a wide range of subjects, the most common applications to date have been with medical and science subjects, usually at college or university level.

The distinctive features of other well-known examples of open, student-centred systems of learning (eg 'local' systems such as Flexi-study, and distance learning schemes such as the Open University) are described in Chapter 5.

CHAPTER 3

Educational Objectives

Introduction

In the two preceding chapters, we mentioned the key part played by *objectives* in the systems approach to course and curriculum design. In this chapter, we will try to explain why they are so important.

We will begin by highlighting the key role played by objectives in any systematic approach to the course or curriculum design process and distinguishing them from their 'close relatives' *aims*. We will then give some basic guidelines on how objectives can be written, and outline the different categories of educational objectives that have been identified. Finally, we will review some of the advantages and disadvantages of an objectives-based approach to course design, and suggest how to set about establishing criteria for choosing valid objectives in a given educational or training situation.

An Objectives-Based Approach to Course Design

The formulation of precise educational objectives is usually considered to be one of the first crucial steps in the process of systematic course or curriculum design that was described in Chapter 1 and represented schematically in Figure 1.4. As we showed, this is essentially a cyclical process, and we can see this even more clearly if we rearrange the various elements of the system in the way shown in Figure 3.1.

Within such a system, the original objectives around which a course is developed serve three basic functions. First, they help to define the general direction of the course or curriculum and indicate the sort of material that should be covered. Second, they give some guidance as to what teaching/learning methods should be employed. Third, they are of considerable assistance in planning assessment procedures. The objectives can, of course, subsequently be modified in the light of experience gained during the operation phase; indeed, on-going monitoring, evaluation and tuning of all aspects of a course or curriculum is one of the key features of the system. Objectives should, of course, always be formulated taking due cognisance of the relevant

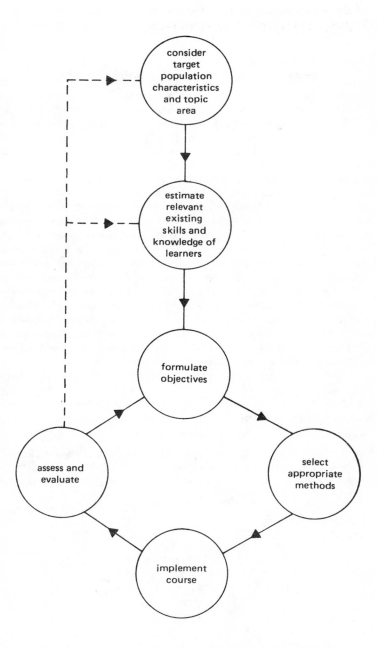

Figure 3.1 **A simplified systems approach to course design**

existing skills and knowledge of the target population, together with their level of maturity and the nature of the topic area in question.

Aims and Objectives

Let us now look at what is meant by the terms 'aim' and 'objective' when used in an educational or training context. In common language, the two terms are almost synonymous, meaning 'that at which we decide to direct our energies'. However, in the jargon-filled world of education and educational technology, they have each been endowed with a special meaning, and, to some, with an accompanying aura of mystique. This is unnecessary — even when they are qualified by the adjective 'educational', or even 'behavioural' — as long as we appreciate the distinctly separate roles and functions.

Educational *aims*, first of all, are normally considered to be broad or general statements of educational intent. They usually indicate the overall purpose or desired goal of a course or part of a course.

Educational *objectives*, on the other hand, are collections of more precise, more detailed statements relating to different aspects of the fulfilment of specific aims. In the generally accepted usage of the word, objectives have taken on the status of definitive descriptions of desirable educational outcomes, often expressed in terms of what students should be able to *do* at the end of their course. (In jargon terms, they express the *terminal behaviour* of the students, and are called *behavioural objectives*.) Thus, objectives should, as a consequence, lend themselves to accurate assessment.

In order to illustrate the difference between aims and objectives, let us look at a specific case, namely, a typical basic chemistry course. One of the general aims of this particular course is given below, together with some of the detailed objectives that have been formulated in order to help ensure that the aim is in fact achieved.

Aim: to develop an understanding of the properties of chemical bonds and of the principles of bonding.
Objectives: At the end of the course, the student should be able to:

1. Define the term *orbital* in terms of the probability of finding an electron in a given region of space;
2. Define the terms *s-*, *p-* and *d- electrons*;
3. Given the atomic number, write the electronic configuration of an atom or ion in terms of s-, p- and d- electrons;
4. Define the terms *ionic*, *covalent* and *co-ordinate bond* and describe these bonds in terms of the electronic interactions involved;
5. From a knowledge of the positions of two elements in the periodic table, describe the likely types of bond formed between these elements;
6. Define the terms *electronegativity* of an element and *polarity* of a bond;

7. List *five* of the important properties of bonds, namely (i) strength, (ii) length, (iii) orientation in space, (iv) polarity, and (v) vibration, and, by suitable choice of examples, describe each of these properties; and so on.

Thus, we see that *objectives* can be considered to be specific sets of well-defined activities that a student must exhibit in order to demonstrate achievement of more loosely-defined *aims.*

Writing Objectives

All too often, teachers, lecturers and trainers state or write objectives for a course or curriculum which are extremely vague, and are, in fact, more like aims than true objectives. Compiling a list of objectives involves carrying out a thorough analysis of the content subsumed under a general aim and listing the chosen objectives in as unambiguous and explicit a manner as possible, so that both student and teacher have a clear idea of what has to be achieved. The precise form of the objectives will, of course, vary considerably, depending on the nature of the people or bodies for whom they are primarily intended (students, staff, potential recruits, internal committees, course validating bodies, etc) but their function should always be that of defining the *behaviour* expected at the end of the course or sequence of instruction.

Because of this, the key part of each objective is the *verb*, which should be carefully chosen so as to describe as unequivocally as possible exactly what the student should be able to do on completing the particular learning activity (or group of activities) that the objective covers.

In order to achieve this clarity of statement, expressions such as 'to know', 'to understand', 'to *really* understand', 'to appreciate', etc should be avoided, since they are far too vague to convey the exact nature of the behaviour being sought. Objectives such as:

'the student should *know* the plays of Shakespeare'
'the student must *develop an appreciation* of thermodynamics' or
'the student should *really understand* Ohm's Law'

tell us little or nothing about what the student will actually be expected to do in order to demonstrate his or her achievement.

Rather, more active, more explicit verbs such as 'state', 'explain', 'define', 'describe', 'predict', 'summarize', 'recognize' and 'criticize' should be used wherever possible, since these can form the basis of much tighter, more clearly-defined objectives. Three examples of objectives that make use of such verbs are given below.

'the student should be able *to name* and *identify* the bones of the human leg'
'the student should be able *to derive* Ohm's Law from first principles'

'the student should be able to *summarize* a 1,000-word article in 50-100 words'

Each of the above examples uses verbs which attempt to define an activity or behaviour in terms of what the student should be able to *do* at the end of the relevant section of the course. As a result, their similarity to examination questions is obvious. Indeed, in courses that are designed using an approach similar to that shown in Figure 3.1, the performance of students in examinations and other forms of assessment provides important information about the suitability of the objectives chosen — information that can be used as a starting point in the next cycle of the course development process. It is no coincidence that, in courses where detailed objectives are *not* clearly stated and made available to the students, the latter place great reliance on past exam papers in order to try to identify the behaviour that is expected of them, that is, in order to determine the 'objectives' of the course.

The Magerian Approach to Writing Objectives

The case for writing very tightly constructed behavioural objectives as an integral part of course, curriculum and lesson design has been strongly influenced by the leading proponent of such objectives — the American psychologist Robert F Mager. His definitive work on the subject, *Preparing Instructional Objectives* (1962), triggered off a 'bandwagon' movement during the late 1960s and early 1970s, a movement that led to the widespread adoption of a rigorous objectives-based approach to the design of courses and teaching materials. Although Mager's stringent 'rules' for formulating objectives are not so strictly adhered to nowadays, his influence still remains strong in many areas of education and training.

According to Mager and his followers, an objective should be written in clear, unambiguous terms that any teacher or student can under-stand without the need for further explanation, and should include the following three basic elements:

1. It should state what the student should be able to *do* at the end of the learning experience (ie should specify the required *terminal behaviour*).
2. It should state the *conditions* or *constraints* under which this behaviour is to be exhibited.
3. It should give a clear indication of the minimum *standard of perform-ance* that is considered acceptable.

Two examples of objectives that have been written in this fashion are given below, and, in each case, we have identified each of the three elements that are required by Mager 'purists'.

(a) 'The student should be able to weigh an object (*element 1*) of less than 100 grams using a single-pan balance (*element 2*) and obtain the correct answer to four decimal places at least nine times out of 10 (*element 3*)'.

(b) 'The recruit must be able to fire five shots from a standard-issue rifle (*element 1*) in 20 seconds at a standard circular target 50 metres away (*element 2*) scoring at least four bullseyes (*element 3*)'.

Formulating objectives in clear, unambiguous behavioural terms can be deceptively difficult, requiring a considerable amount of skill and practice. Clearly, if Mager's criteria were rigidly adhered to, drawing up a full list of objectives for a teaching or training course would be an onerous and time-consuming task, and the resulting list would probably be highly cumbersome and off-putting. Partly for this reason, there has been a move away from the strict Magerian position in recent years, and, although writers of objectives still try to define the required terminal behaviour as explicitly as possible, they often omit the specifications of the conditions under which the behaviour should be achieved and the minimum satisfactory performance.

This relaxation of Mager's criteria has been particularly pronounced in the case of institution-centred courses in the higher education sector. Here, it is often felt that the wide range and complexity of the subject matter make the writing of highly-specific Mager objectives impracticable, quite apart from the fact that they impose (in many people's opinion) unacceptable constraints on academic freedom.

On the other hand, in the case of teaching/learning situations which are more task-oriented or more student-centred in the sense that the student works largely alone, there is no doubt that Mager-type objectives do help to provide the student with a clear idea of *what* has to be achieved, *how* this has to be achieved, and the *level of performance* that is required to demonstrate satisfactory achievement of the objective. As Mager himself put it: 'If you don't know where you're heading, you'll probably end up someplace else, and not even know it'.

Skills Analysis

During the 1950s and 1960s, the 'skills analysis' or 'task analysis' approach, which was originally championed by W D Seymour, became very popular as a means of breaking down a complex task into a sequence of its component parts. Such a breakdown is intended to enable a systematic training system to be devised by re-assembling the various identified sub-skills, and it can also allow for the precise specification of objectives for each stage, as well as for the identification of any necessary pre-knowledge.

Once the separate sub-skills related to a specific overall task have been identified, they can be described, in sequence, on a chart of the type shown in Figure 3.2. This gives a skills analysis for the task of training a person to use a micrometer, a mechanical instrument that is used for measuring the size of small objects with a high degree of

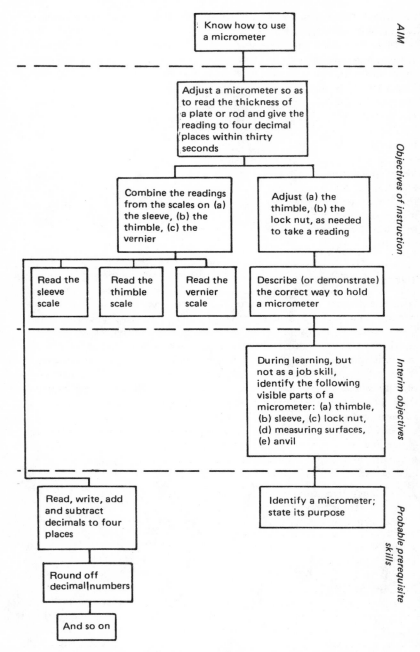

Figure 3.2 **Skills analysis for the operation of a micrometer**

precision. The figure clearly illustrates the hierarchical nature of the various skills identified.

These sub-skills can be translated into objectives for the training system, and careful analysis of such a range of skills can usually be used to identify an optimal sequence for instruction. This approach also identifies skills down to, and below, the prerequisite level, so that appropriate pre-knowledge and existing skills on the part of the learners can be taken into account when designing the training programme.

The skills analysis approach has been particularly widely used in industrial and manipulative skills training contexts, and, indeed, is well suited to many training situations in these areas. However, many other educational and training aims are much less well suited to a skills analysis approach, and instructional designers should be fully aware that there are definite limitations to its use and potential dangers in its mis-use. Indeed, in a wide range of circumstances it is by no means the best, or easiest, or most valid way of determining course design objectives.

Types of Objectives

With the general acceptance of objectives as a key component of the systems approach to course and curriculum design, it has become fashionable to think in terms of broad types of objectives. Here, another American, Benjamin Bloom, has been extremely influential in clarifying and organizing educational thought regarding the classification of objectives. Bloom and his co-workers contend that objectives are attainable in three distinct areas, or domains, to which they have assigned suitably impressive jargon names: the *cognitive domain, affective domain* and *psychomotor domain.* At the risk of over-simplification, these can be thought of as being respectively concerned with *knowledge-related objectives, attitude-related objectives* and *motor skills-related objectives.* Let us now examine them in more detail.

1. *The cognitive domain.* This contains objectives which are related to the acquisition and application of knowledge and understanding, and probably includes the majority of educational and training objectives. As we will show later, Bloom has further categorized this area into six sub-areas, which he claims form an ascending hierarchy, with each sub-area dealing with a progressively higher level of sophistication at which knowledge and understanding can be displayed. An example of a simple cognitive objective might be: 'The student should be able to calculate all the dimensions of a triangle given the lengths of two sides and the size of the angle between them'.

2. *The affective domain.* This contains objectives that are concerned with attitudes and feelings which are brought about as a result of

some educational process. Bloom and his co-workers have again divided this domain into sub-areas, in this case five in number, which they again believe to form an ascending educational hierarchy. In general, affective objectives are much less easy to formulate than cognitive objectives, since the behaviour expected is often difficult to identify and virtually impossible to quantify. Also, although they are often just as important as cognitive objectives (more so, in some cases), they can be extremely difficult to teach towards in a formal educational situation. An example of an affective objective might be: 'The trainee lecturer should learn to exercise empathy when counselling students'.

3. *The psychomotor domain.* This contains objectives that deal with the development of manipulative or physical skills — such as measuring, setting up and using equipment, using tools, drawing graphs, and so on. An example might be: 'The student should be able to assemble and use the distillation apparatus provided'.

Although these three areas might, at first sight, seem to constitute neat and distinct packages, real life does not allow things to be quite so simple, and the domains do, in fact, overlap and interact to a considerable extent. For example, working in a science laboratory or driving a car both involve a broad spectrum of objectives drawn from all three domains, namely, the acquisition and application of knowledge (cognitive domain), the development of appropriate attitudes to safety, together with responsibility and confidence (affective domain), and, of course the development of manipulative ability and motor skills (psychomotor domain). Also, it is normally virtually impossible to bring about desirable attitude changes without an associated increase in knowledge, while, conversely, the development of a positive attitude to work or study will almost invariably exert a favourable influence on the uptake of knowledge. Thus, the cognitive and affective domains are, in fact, intimately linked, and cannot really be considered in isolation. Similarly, the psychomotor domain has links with each of the other domains — albeit not quite so strong.

There is a strong and growing feeling in educational circles that, while cognitive knowledge and psychomotor skills remain important aspects of courses, much more could and should be done to foster and develop broader-based objectives related to the skills required by a student in later life — skills which are much sought after by employers when recruiting new staff. Examples of such 'broader' skills include decision-making, communication, problem-solving, creative-thinking, and interpersonal skills. In a complex and rapidly changing society, students are not likely to succeed for long in the outside world purely on the basis of cognitive attainment. The 'Education for Capability' movement argues along these lines when stressing the importance of *process* rather than *content* in learning. Indeed, if the description of education as 'what is left after the facts have been forgotten' is accepted as having value, then the argument for formulating objectives related to the 'broader skills' area, together with careful consideration of approaches and methods likely to foster their development, becomes very powerful. The classification system proposed by R H Gagné has a category called 'intellectual skills' which includes problem solving as the highest level. It also has a category called 'cognitive strategies' which refers to internally-organized skills that govern the student's behaviour in learning, remembering, and thinking. Being directed toward self-management of learning and thinking, the latter are obviously different from intellectual skills, and are continually being refined with practice as the learner encounters situations that require learning, remembering, and solving or defining problems.

Bloom's Taxonomies of Educational Objectives

Let us now take a closer look at the two highly-influential *Taxonomies of Educational Objectives* that have been published by Bloom and his co-workers. The first, which dealt with the cognitive domain, was published in 1956, while the second, which covered the affective domain, appeared in 1964 (see the Bibliography for further details).

Of the two books, the one dealing with the alleged hierarchical structure of the cognitive domain has been by far the more influential, having had a considerable effect on both curriculum planning and assessment. Bloom's six sub-divisions of the cognitive domain are listed below, in order of increasing sophistication of the mental processes involved.

1. *Knowledge.* The lowest level of cognitive objective. To demonstrate the attainment of objectives at this level, students would be expected to perform such tasks as name the parts of an object, point out a certain object, state a definition, recognize a phenomenon when it is seen, and so on.
2. *Comprehension.* The lowest level of understanding. Activities demonstrating comprehension include selecting an example of a particular phenomenon, giving reasons for a phenomenon, classifying objects into categories, extrapolating trends, translating verbal material into symbolic statements, and so on.
3. *Application.* The application of theoretical statements in real situations. Examples would be for the student to calculate a mathematical result, perform a standard task, use a particular set of rules and procedures, predict the result of a proposed course of action, and so on.
4. *Analysis.* This involves the breakdown of material into its constituent parts, including the ability to analyse elements and relationships of elements, compare and contrast alternatives, justify the adoption of certain procedures, and so on.
5. *Synthesis.* This involves the combination of elements or components

to form new structured wholes. Skills involved include the ability to write an original essay, propose ways of testing hypotheses, derive mathematical generalizations, design systems, and so on.

6. *Evaluation.* According to Bloom, the highest level of cognitive objective, involving making judgements (quantitative and qualitative) about the extent to which material satisfies evidence or criteria. This includes the abilities to indicate logical fallacies in arguments, argue for or against a proposal, compare a work with others of recognized excellence, and so on.

What Bloom is suggesting is the existence of a *continuum* in the development of cognitive attainment from the simple and concrete to the complex and abstract. The six levels should be thought of as milestones on the way to perfect accomplishment rather than watertight categories with specific and exclusive characteristics. By writing objectives at these different levels, a course designer should be able to generate appropriate types of task or assessment questions. The taxonomy does not, incidentally, make any attempt to formulate general rules about how one should teach in order to achieve particular objectives.

Attempts to validate Bloom's taxonomy have, in general, proved inconclusive. However, the results of much of the research which has been done tends to cast doubt on the validity of some of the basic assumptions that were made by Bloom in compiling the taxonomy. A case in point is the assumption that the categories are hierarchically arranged, which is acceptable only if the hierarchy is viewed as progressing *unevenly* from low cognitive levels to higher cognitive levels. For example, the mental processes that are involved in moving from 'comprehension' to 'application' appear to be different in character and more sharply defined than those that are involved in moving from knowledge to comprehension or from 'application' to 'analysis'. Indeed, many educationalists now describe cognitive skills as either *lower cognitive* or *higher cognitive*, rather than referring specifically to one of Bloom's six sub-areas.

Bloom's classification for the affective domain is given below, again in ascending hierarchical order.

1. *Receiving.* Developing an awareness of, and willingness to receive, certain stimuli such as the aesthetic factors of a subject.

2. *Responding.* Showing active attention at a low level, ie taking an interest.

3. *Valuing.* Perceiving phenomena as having worth, and revealing behaviour consistent with this attitude.

4. *Organization.* Conceptualization of values and ordered relationships between values.

5. *Characterization.* Organization of values into a total and consistent philosophy.

To date, very little research designed to test the validity of this proposed hierarchy has been carried out, largely because of the intrinsic difficulties associated with carrying out quantitative measurements of affective changes.

Despite the above reservations regarding their validity, Bloom's taxonomies have been of great value (particularly in the cognitive domain) in that they have provided a useful formalized classification of objectives in an area where formalization is difficult. Their main use has been in analysing objectives and as diagnostic tools rather than as prescriptive tools for setting objectives. Two areas where the taxonomies have had a particularly important impact are *curriculum design* and *assessment*.

In curriculum design, for example, pre-written course objectives often tend to be concentrated in the *higher* cognitive sub-areas of application, analysis, synthesis and evaluation, while the main teaching instruments (lectures and/or individualized study) are perhaps best suited to developing the lower cognitive skills of knowledge and comprehension. Careful analysis of course objectives can point to the need to adopting a much broader range of teaching methods designed to help students achieve objectives that lie in these highly important higher cognitive areas.

In the field of assessment, it is possible, by matching test questions with predetermined objectives at various levels, to devise a test to precise specifications, for example, 40 per cent recall (knowledge), 20 per cent comprehension, 20 per cent application, 10 per cent analysis, 5 per cent synthesis and 5 per cent evaluation. Such a breakdown not only helps teachers and lecturers to clarify their thinking regarding the selection of assessment questions, but also helps them to avoid mistakes like basing a supposedly high-level examination mainly on the simple recall of learned material or attempting to test knowledge of factual material by setting a question based almost entirely on reasoning. A well-stocked bank of suitably graded objective test questions can be extremely useful in pre-specified tests of this sort (see Chapter 7).

Some Advantages of Using Objectives

Detailed, well-written objectives allow both teaching staff *and* students to have a clear picture of the behaviour that is expected of the latter at the end of a course. This can help to provide direction and stability in the course, and can also help to guard against over-reliance on a particular staff member or idiosyncratic interpretation of syllabuses. It is, of course, strongly recommended that the *students* should always be included in this pre-knowledge of objectives. All too often, their only clue to course objectives comes from a study of previous exam papers — a situation that is difficult to defend, since students have quite enough problems to face without being involved in academic 'guessing games'.

Nor is this mutual awareness of objectives limited to the more academic aspects of a course, since it is also possible to employ an objectives-based approach when planning laboratory and other practical work. Here, it should, in principle, be possible to provide the students with a clear indication of the desired outcomes of such work *before* the start of each practical session. The need for such a procedure was emphasized by the results of a recent research project that was carried out in one of the science departments of a large Scottish university. This compared the tutors' intended (but unwritten) objectives with the students' perceptions of the educational objectives of various laboratory experiments, and it was found that any resemblance between the two was purely coincidental!

Another advantage that clear behavioural objectives can provide is in adjusting teaching methods to facilitate the achievement of the stated objectives. If a teacher has made a serious attempt to analyse the objectives of the course he is teaching, and compares his teaching methods with these, some anomalies will probably become apparent. If he is honest, he may well conclude that the methods adopted have only a remote chance of enabling students to attain some of the stated objectives and take appropriate action. However, objectives need not be restrictive, and, within the framework which they provide, there may be many possible routes to the stated goals.

A further benefit which can arise from a clear statement of objectives is that a teacher who is in possession of such objectives should be in a much better position to decide how they may be assessed, since he should know exactly what behaviour he is supposed to be assessing. Different types of behaviour require different forms of assessment, and methods that may be highly appropriate for assessing lower cognitive skills such as knowledge and understanding may well be far less suitable for assessing higher-level skills such as reasoning, creative thinking and logical presentation. This topic will be discussed in detail in Chapter 7.

It is not, of course, being suggested that *all* the objectives of a course can be assessed in a quantitative manner; indeed, in some cases, it is difficult to assess them at all, particularly in the case of those that lie in the affective rather than the cognitive domain and in the broader 'life skill' areas discussed previously. Nevertheless, it is becoming increasingly widely accepted that objectives of this type are an extremely important component of most courses, and may, in some cases, be the longest-lasting and most beneficial outcomes of the course. Thus, it is highly desirable that such objectives be included in the list of course objectives; even though they may be difficult to formally assess they do at least help give direction to the course, as well as focusing attention on the need to use teaching methods that may be capable of achieving them.

Finally, the very act of sitting down to write a list of course objectives can be an extremely useful staff development exercise in its own right. It not only forces a teacher to think deeply about what he is trying to achieve, but, in many cases, also makes him take the first vital step towards a systematic approach to course design and course monitoring.

Some Weaknesses of the Objectives-Based Approach

One danger of adopting an objectives-based approach to course design is that the objectives may be given greater status than they deserve. Despite their name, objectives are anything but 'objective' in the manner in which they are selected and written, since both processes are usually highly *subj*ective in character. Thus, objectives should never be treated as if they are in any way sacrosanct; they are, after all, merely the end result of a value judgement on someone's part.

Another danger inherent in a thorough-going objectives-based approach is that teaching and learning may become so prescribed that spontaneity withers and initiative is stifled. Also, a total concentration on the achievement of clearly-defined objectives may lead to the production of students who are certainly well-trained in specific areas, but who lack the broad spectrum of abilities, skills and desirable attitudinal traits that are normally associated with a balanced, 'rounded' education. When a student is being trained in a skill where straightforward mastery is required (for example, learning the rules for naming chemical compounds or learning how to operate complex machinery) a rigid set of behavioural objectives is usually very much in order. Also, when a piece of individualized instruction involving, say, written or computer-based material is being designed and evaluated, a clear set of objectives is always extremely valuable to both learner and designer. However, when a teacher is concerned with the outcomes of education in its broadest sense, there are many aspects which defy circumscription in the form of set objectives. Indeed, one could argue that it is sheer nonsense to suggest that a teacher should only teach towards that which can be formulated in terms of Mager-type objectives or that which can be rigidly assessed. It is obviously the case that some subjects (eg mathematics and science) lend themselves more readily to a 'straight' objectives approach than others (eg art appreciation and debating); nevertheless, even in subjects of the latter type, it is important that the teaching/learning process should have a *direction*.

A less fundamental, but very practical, weakness of the objectives-based approach is that objectives can be difficult and time-consuming to construct. Many teachers may feel that they simply do not have the time to develop well-written objectives, and, if insufficient time and skill are devoted to the task, the net result may well be anything but beneficial to the course. For example, it is usually the simplest and perhaps the most trivial objectives that are the easiest to write in 'standard format'; this may lead to low-grade objectives of this type dominating a course at the expense of potentially more valuable goals which are not included simply because they are less easy to encapsulate in unambiguous statements.

Choosing Valid Objectives

We have indicated above that the precise choice of objectives for a course is essentially a subjective decision based on a series of value judgements. The factors and requirements involved in the compilation of a set of course objectives generally have their roots in a wide variety of areas, some of the most important of which are listed below.

1. *Vocational needs.* There may be a need for certain specific skills and knowledge, dictated by a student's possible future job, profession or social role.
2. *The cultural view.* The concept of 'the subject for its own sake' which views education as passing on a body of accepted knowledge.
3. *Social factors.* The knowledge, skills and attitudes held to be desirable by the society in which the student lives.
4. *'Student' factors.* The individual student may be interested in attaining certain knowledge or skills.
5. *'Teacher' factors.* The individual teacher may have personal interests and preferences which he or she feels should be built into the course.

Faced with these often conflicting factors, we see how vital it is to carry out a careful and critical analysis of each in order to establish their relative importance — both during the formulation of objectives for a course and throughout the subsequent process of course design and development. The level and function of the course or curriculum itself will also exert a considerable influence on these matters, as will the nature of the institution or environment in which it is to be operated. Finally, we should always remember that course or curriculum development is a *cyclical* process, and that all objectives should themselves be reappraised at regular intervals — not only to determine whether they are being achieved in the course, but also to establish whether they continue to reflect a valid interpretation of the course's direction and emphasis; if they do not, then it is time to change them.

CHAPTER 4

Mass Instruction Techniques

Introduction

Let us suppose that a teacher, lecturer or trainer is involved in the development of a new course or curriculum, and, as a first step, has produced a clear set of objectives. The next step is to choose the most appropriate methods for achieving these objectives, and just how he might go about this task will be the topic of the next three chapters of this book. The particular methods that are eventually chosen will depend on a large number of factors, including the detailed nature of the objectives in question, institutional constraints, student characteristics and his own preferences. They will, however, be of three broad types, namely, those associated with *mass instruction, individualized learning* and *group learning*, so we will look at these three types of instructional methods in turn.

In this chapter, we will examine some of the more common methods that are used in mass instruction, that is, the teaching or training of relatively large groups or classes, usually within the context of a teacher/institution-centred course of some sort. First, we will look at the methods themselves, identifying their main characteristics and discussing their respective strengths and weaknesses. Then, we will turn our attention to the various audiovisual media that can be used to support these different methods, dealing in turn with *non-projected visual aids, projected visual and audiovisual aids* and *audio aids.*

The Main Mass Instruction Methods

In this section, we will discuss four of the most common methods that are used in mass instructional situations, namely *lectures and talks, film and video presentations, educational broadcasts* and *practical activities.* Within each of these categories, there are a wide variety of different approaches and tactics that may be adopted, but, as we will see, a number of generalizations can be made, and it is on these that we will concentrate. It should be emphasized at this point that the techniques of 'mass instruction' may well be received by small numbers of students (or even by individual students) as well as by large audiences. Thus, the term 'mass' is used more in a qualitative than a strictly quantitative sense.

Lectures and Talks

Although the term 'lecture' is normally used in the context of tertiary education and training, we will take it to cover any situation in which a teacher or instructor talks to (or at!) a class of pupils, students or trainees. Despite a plethora of other teaching methods being available, the face-to-face talk or 'lecture' still holds a central position at many levels of education, and will undoubtedly continue to do so for some considerable time to come. It is therefore rather surprising that comparatively little is known about the educational effectiveness of the lecture. Also, what little information *has* been established as a result of controlled, empirical research is not particularly widely known, especially among practising teachers, lecturers and trainers. Thus, the strength with which opinions on the usefulness of lectures are held is frequently greater than the strength of the grounds upon which these opinions are based! In addition, the problem of defining what constitutes a 'good lecture' is exceedingly difficult, since several research studies have indicated that individual students appreciate not only different, but sometimes conflicting things in a lecture.

Some advantages of the lecture method
Undoubtedly, one of the reasons why the lecture has retained its dominant place in the educational and training scene is that the method appears to be highly cost-effective, since it enables high student/staff ratios to be achieved; 100 students can, for example, be taught just as effectively as 10 in a lecture situation (see Figure 4.1).

Another point in the lecture's favour is that it appears to be just as effective as other teaching methods at conveying information *when well done*. The majority of studies which have compared the lecture method with other methods designed for developing lower cognitive skills have not been able to detect any difference that is statistically significant, and those studies which have shown a measurable difference have been approximately equally distributed either way. (It is worth pointing out, however, that *most* teaching methods are not particularly efficient at imparting information; a common figure quoted is approximately 40 per cent recall of information by students immediately after a lecture — and, unless reinforcement takes place, even this ability to recall material falls off rapidly with time.)

Many teachers feel more comfortable using the lecture method than they do using other, perhaps more participative, methods. Also, the lecture method appears to be popular with students, although this may be largely due to familiarity and to a lack of appreciation of the possible advantages of alternative methods of teaching.

Figure 4.1 **A typical lecture in progress**

Some weaknesses of the lecture method
One aspect of the lecture method which causes some concern is that its effectiveness is inevitably very dependent on the skills of the individual lecturer. The ability to organize and explain a topic does not come naturally except to a fortunate few individuals, while fewer still are able to capitalize on their personal charisma in order to 'capture' their audiences. George Brown's book *Lecturing and Explaining* (1978) gives many useful guidelines on the art of structuring and presenting a lecture, and is heartily commended to all who lack these skills, as is the CICED booklet *Some Hints on How to be an Effective Lecturer* (Ellington, 1987).

In addition, the resultant effectiveness of a lecture relies heavily on the ability of the students to learn from it. Here, the range of study skills mentioned in Chapter 1 are extremely important, and it may well be necessary to make a conscious effort to inculcate good study techniques before the full educational potential of the lecture method is realized.

A number of research studies aimed at comparing the lecture with other teaching methods have been carried out. These studies (which are specified and discussed in detail in McLeish's book *The Lecture Method* (1968)) have shown that the lecture is not particularly effective in developing high-level thought amongst students (Bloom's higher cognitive areas), or at teaching towards desirable attitudes (Bloom's affective domain) compared with methods of learning such as group discussions or participative simulations which involve more student activity. Thus, the lecture may not be quite as economical as it is generally believed to be in terms of achieving the entire range of course objectives, especially if a teacher does not appreciate the limitations of lectures and fails to combine their use with other, more active, methods. Many of the disadvantages of the lecture method stem from the fact that students are normally completely passive in lectures, spending most of their time either listening or writing down notes. The method is usually non-interactive, although some teachers attempt to get round this deficiency by building in, for example, 'buzz' sessions (short problem-solving or discussion sessions in which the students work on their own or in small groups and then feed back information based on the task set to the teacher and to the rest of the class.

In a lecture, all students are forced to proceed at one pace, namely, that dictated by the teacher, with usually very little opportunity for feedback from the students. This inevitably produces a wide variation in understanding throughout a lecture class, making the method practically useless for achieving universal mastery of topics. Also, within a lecture structure, individual problems and difficulties cannot normally be dealt with in a satisfactory manner. A related difficulty is that the teacher's perception of a subject is not necessarily the same as that of the students in all cases.

Another problem caused by the passive nature of lectures is that student attention tends to fall off fairly rapidly with time. This fall-off takes the form of an increasing frequency of attention breaks (sometimes called *microsleeps*) in which the student 'switches off' concentration for a short time. The length of time for which a student can maintain full attention to the task of listening and writing is called the *attention span*. In a typical 50-minute 'straight' lecture, student attention span decreases steadily as the lecture progresses. Typically, it falls from about 12 to 15 minutes at the start of the lecture to around 3 to 5 minutes towards the end. Attention breaks usually last for about two minutes, although their pattern of occurrence is affected by a number of factors. It is found, for example, that, if the lecturer includes deliberate breaks in the lecture (practical demonstrations, 'buzz' sessions, visual stimuli and so on), the net effect is that the progressive decline in student attention is temporarily halted. Skilled timing of these variations can improve the attention span pattern considerably, and it is likely that any lecture time that is lost in providing these 'mental breathers' for students is more than recouped in terms of effective student learning.

Thus, for a straightforward, fact-giving lecture, the optimum time for the most effective transfer of knowledge is probably no longer than about 20 minutes, even with comparatively bright students; with young, immature or less able students, it is even shorter. Despite this, virtually all institutions continue to timetable lecture-type classes for much longer periods − anything from 40 minutes to two hours and more.

Thus, if they are to be used to optimum effect, the limitations of lectures *must* be recognized, both by course and curriculum planners and also by the teachers, lecturers and trainers who actually work at the 'chalk face'. The latter, in particular, should realize that lectures are much more effective if they are used in conjunction with a suitable combination of supportive and complementary teaching methods rather than entirely on their own.

Film and Video Presentations

For many years, films have been widely used in education (and, even more commonly, in training situations) as a mass-instructional teaching method in their own right. With the arrival of the videocassette recorder, which makes it even easier to show film-type programmes in the classroom, this practice has become even more prevalent. Thus, an ever-increasing range of films and videocassette programmes are now being made for all sectors of education and training. In addition to being a teaching method in their own right, short films and video clips can be incorporated into lecture-type presentations in order to provide illustrative visual stimulation and variety of approach, to provide enrichment material, and so on.

Some advantages of film and video presentations
Film and video presentations can be used in education and training as an effective lecture-substitute. They are particularly useful if the content has a high visual impact, where a variety of techniques such as animation, time-lapse photography and close-up work can be used to good effect.

Film and video programmes can provide an impression of life outside the classroom which would otherwise be inconvenient or perhaps impossible to achieve. They can, for example, show lifestyles in other countries, scientific processes at the microscopic level, complicated industrial processes, theatrical productions, and so on.

A professionally-scripted and produced film or video programme may well be better structured than its lecture-type equivalent, and is almost certain to be more visually relevant and more stimulating than a lecture, even if the latter is supported by slides and other visual aids. Further advantages are that appropriate films or videos can help to add variety to lecture-dominated courses, and can be used to stimulate discussion and debate.

Some disadvantages of film and video presentations
The most common mis-use of films and videos occurs when the media are used purely for convenience rather than for sound educational reasons. The use of a film or video should not be thought of as an easy option, or 'something to keep a class quiet'. Indeed, it is important that a teacher or instructor should carry out a critical preview of the programme in order to check on its quality and to assess its relevance to

the course. This will enable the teacher or instructor to introduce the programme properly, to explain its context and to prepare for class discussion after it has been shown.

Another possible educational disadvantage of using film and video presentations is that the teacher or trainer effectively relinquishes control over his class for the duration of the presentation, handing over control to the maker of the film or video. This makes it doubly important that such presentations should only be used where they offer some distinct advantage over other, more conventional methods of teaching in achieving a particular set of objectives.

One practical disadvantage of the film and video is that neither can be shown without the appropriate hardware. Also, there is often a financial implication associated with using a programme; indeed, in many cases, hiring or buying a film or video can be quite expensive, particularly if it is to be used in a commercial or industrial training context rather than in an educational situation.

An additional problem associated with the use of videocassette machines to record broadcast television programmes off-air is that there may well be copyright difficulties associated with showing the programmes in an educational or training situation. Although certain programmes are officially classified as 'educational', and can therefore be used with classes, the main television output (parts of which — documentaries, popular science programmes, etc — may in fact have a high degree of educational relevance) cannot legally be recorded on a

Figure 4.2 Use of a video presentation as a lecture substitute

videocassette recorder for subsequent use with a class. Some of these programmes are, however, available for purchase or hire from the appropriate broadcasting authorities.

Educational Broadcasting

Broadcast radio and television have a long history of use in education and training, with programmes designed specifically for class use in schools and colleges being transmitted by a large number of broadcasting organizations in many parts of the world. In most cases, however, the role of such programmes has been limited to that of general interest, 'optional extra' or 'back-up' material, and it is only since the mid-1960s that such broadcasts have been used as front-line teaching tools. As we saw in Chapter 1, this development was pioneered in the UK by the Open University; since then, it has been used as a key part of similar distance learning schemes that have been set up in several other countries, including Israel, Canada and Norway.

Strictly speaking, the use of broadcast radio and television programmes in a distance learning as opposed to a classroom situation should be classed as an 'individualized learning' technique rather than a 'mass instruction' technique in the sense in which we are interpreting the latter term in this chapter. Such programmes are designed to be received by *individuals*, and, in many cases, incorporate features (such as active participation on the part of the learner or viewer) that are more generally associated with individualized learning than with mass instruction. Thus, they are only 'mass instruction' techniques in the sense that they are capable of being received simultaneously by large numbers of people.

Some advantages of educational broadcasts
Educational radio and television broadcasts have the same basic educational advantages as film and video presentations in that they constitute high-quality material that can be used as an effective substitute for, or supplement to, a conventional taught lesson as and when appropriate, thus enabling a teacher, lecturer or trainer to introduce variety into a course. They have a further important advantage in that the material is made available free of charge.

Some disadvantages of educational broadcasts
They also share some of the disadvantages of film and video in that they are always liable to be used in the wrong way (eg for keeping classes quiet or filling slots in timetables) and again entail handing over control of one's class to someone else. A further disadvantage is that the timing of such broadcasts is fixed, so that they may be difficult (or even impossible) to fit into the timetable and cannot usually be previewed before showing to a class. Both of these problems can be overcome by recording the programmes.

Practical Activities

Within most teacher/institution-centred instructional systems, labora-
tory-type classes are a common way of demonstrating the practical
elements of a subject and of 'using the theory'. On the face of it, the
use of practical sessions in this context would appear to be capable
of doing nothing but good; nevertheless, careful analysis of their use
is often necessary if the fullest potential of such exercises is to be
realized.

Some advantages of practical exercises
For subjects in which the development of manipulative (psychomotor)
skills is important, a certain amount of practical experience is obviously
necessary. Indeed, in many cases, there is simply no suitable alternative
to 'hands-on' practice — as in the case of the Pharmacy students shown
in Figure 4.3, for example. However, it should be emphasized that such
manipulative skills must be consciously taught for, and not just allowed
to develop (it is to be hoped) of their own accord.

Another strength of practical sessions is that students generally
enjoy their participative nature, which may also provide a stark contrast
to other, more lecture-oriented classes. Also, such sessions may give
students an idea of some of the real-life applications of topics which

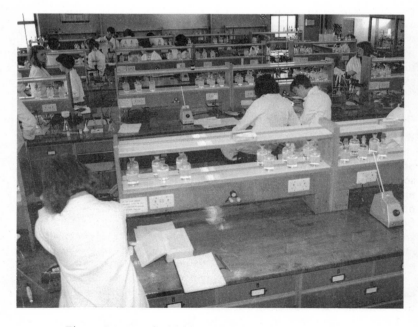

Figure 4.3 **A typical laboratory class in progress in the
School of Pharmacy at Robert Gordon's Institute of Technology**

have only been treated theoretically in lectures, thus helping to demonstrate the relevance of the course as a whole.

Some disadvantages of practical exercises
Practical and laboratory exercises tend to be very expensive in terms of time, manpower, equipment and materials. Hence, the reasons for using practical sessions should be well thought out, and they should not merely be used to fill allocated timetable slots, as is so often the case.

As mentioned in the previous chapter, it is highly desirable that the objectives of each practical session should be stated in advance, so that both staff and students know what should be gained from the work. If this is not done, the results may simply be 'recipe following', with little or no understanding of what is going on, or appreciation of the purpose of the exercise.

The design of practical or laboratory work is all too often completely unrelated to situations and problems which exist in real life. Thus, the perceived relevance of such sessions is often much lower than might be possible with a little more thought and ingenuity on the part of the designers.

Although we have stated that practical sessions have the advantage of illustrating practical applications of more theoretical work, it must be pointed out that student-based laboratory sessions may not be the most economical or efficient means of showing these. In some cases, a simple lecture/demonstration may be much more effective. Thus, while basic psychomotor skills may well be taught extremely effectively in the laboratory, question marks hang over the efficiency of the method in achieving other, higher level objectives that are commonly associated with 'practical work'.

Audiovisual Media used in Mass Instruction

Within the context of the various teaching methods that can be employed as vehicles for mass instruction, it is possible to make use of a wide range of *audiovisual media*, both hardware and software. In some cases, these are used to increase the effectiveness of the teaching method (for example, using visual aids to back up a lecture), while, in others, they constitute a vital part of the method itself (for example, film or video presentations or off-air broadcasts). As the name implies, an audiovisual medium can be thought of as a vehicle through which a message can be conveyed to learners; the medium, in other words, *mediates* between the teacher and the learner, as shown in Figure 4.4.

Thus, it is important that audiovisual media should be carefully chosen for use in particular teaching or training situations because of their suitability and not merely because they 'happen to be available'.

In the remainder of this chapter, we will look at the hardware and software that are associated with mass-instructional teaching methods under three broad headings, namely *non-projected visual aids, projected*

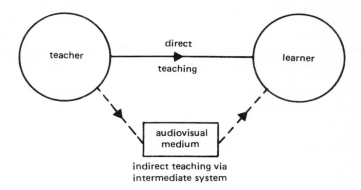

Figure 4.4 **The intermediary role of audiovisual media in teaching**

visual and audiovisual aids, and *audio aids.* In each case, we will discuss the medium in fairly general terms, outlining its main features and identifying its educational strengths and weaknesses rather than giving detailed instructions on its use. Readers requiring the latter type of information are referred to the many books that deal specifically with the use of audiovisual media — Ellington's *Producing Teaching Materials* (1985) and Romiszowski's *The Selection and Use of Instructional Media* (1987), for example. (See the Bibliography for full details of these and other books on audiovisual media.)

Non-Projected Visual Aids

As their name suggests, non-projected visual aids are those that do not involve the use of an optical or electronic projector. They include *chalkboards, markerboards, feltboards, hook-and-loop boards, magnetic boards, charts and wallcharts, posters, flipcharts, mobiles, models, realia* and *handouts,* all of which will now be examined.

Chalkboards
These are still often referred to as *blackboards,* although many are in fact now coloured — usually blue, brown or green. This is because coloured boards produce less glare and reflection, give less 'ghosting' (marks left when the chalk is rubbed out), and generally produce greater legibility then the traditional 'blackboard'.

　　Chalkboards are widely used in all sectors of education and training, and are most suitable for displaying impromptu notes and diagrams during a lesson and for working through calculations or similar exercises in front of a class.

A disadvantage of using chalkboards is that they tend to be difficult to write on and read from; practice in writing and drawing on them is thus often necessary. Chalkboards are also relatively messy to use, and even 'dustless' chalk tends to impregnate one's hair, fingernails and clothes. A further minor disadvantage is that the range of colours of chalk which can be used is often limited.

A major drawback of extensive use of the chalkboard in a classroom is that the teacher has, of necessity, to face away from the class for long periods. This not only means that the teacher is speaking 'into the board' for most of the time, but he also loses the advantage of eye-contact with the class — something that can help to convey meaning and provide useful feedback (by enabling the teacher to spot puzzled looks, loss of interest, etc).

Markerboards

These boards, which are often referred to as *whiteboards*, are used in much the same way as chalkboards, but have a number of advantages over the latter. For example, there is no mess from dust, the range and strength of colours which can be used is much greater, and, in an emergency, the markerboard can double as a projection screen. Against this, care is necessary to ensure that the correct, recommended markers and cleaning materials are used with a given board; use of the wrong markers may result in acute and even permanent 'ghosting' problems.

Feltboards

As its name implies, the *feltboard* is simply a board covered with felt or some similar material. Shapes cut out of felt will adhere to the board if pressed on to its surface, and paper or cardboard cut-outs may also be used by backing them with felt, thus allowing the user to write or draw on the shapes being displayed. To save time, felt-embossed wallpaper is a useful, relatively cheap substitute. Commercially-produced shapes and charts are available for some purposes, although these tend to have limited application.

Feltboards can be used for permanent or semi-permanent displays, but their main application is in situations requiring the movement or rearrangement of pieces, for example, demonstrating table settings, showing traffic movements, carrying out sports coaching, etc. They are also highly portable and comparatively inexpensive.

Hook-and-loop boards

The *hook-and-loop board*, which is also known as a *teazle board* or *teazlegraph*, works on the same basic principle as the feltboard. In this case, however, the display materials are backed with special fabric (such as velcro) which incorporates large numbers of tiny hooks, while the display surface is covered with material incorporating tiny loops with which the hooks can engage. This creates a much stronger bond than that which is formed between two pieces of felt, thus allowing much heavier display materials to be attached to the surface of a hook-and-loop board. Such boards can be used for much the same purposes as feltboards, but only offer a real advantage over the latter in situations where the material being displayed is heavy — demonstrating the components of an actual piece of equipment, for example, or displaying items of realia such as rock samples.

Magnetic boards

Even more useful and versatile than feltboards and hook-and-loop boards are the various forms of *magnetic board*. These come in two main forms — *magnetic markerboards* and *magnetic chalkboards*. The former are sheets of ferromagnetic material with specially-painted light surfaces on which material can be written or drawn using suitable markers or pens, and the latter are sheets of ferromagnetic material covered with a thin layer of dark-coloured vitreous particles, producing a surface on which chalk can be used. Both types of board enable display items made of or backed with magnetic material to be stuck to and moved about on their surfaces, and both enable this moveable display to be supplemented by writing or drawing on the board. Thus, magnetic boards can be used to produce highly-sophisticated displays that enable movement and change in systems to be clearly demonstrated to a class. They are, for example, the ideal medium for demonstrating military tactics or carrying out sports coaching. For coaching a football or basketball team, for example, the field of play can be painted permanently on the board, with the individual players being identified by clearly-marked magnetic discs that can be rearranged and moved about as and when required, and the various movements, run patterns, etc being shown by adding suitable arrows or lines using chalk or marker pens (see Figure 4.5)

Charts and wallcharts

The various forms of *chart* and *wallchart* have always been popular in all sectors of education and training because of their versatility and ease of use, and, even with the spread of more sophisticated visual aids such as slides, films and videos, are still capable of playing an important role in such work. Although the distinction between charts and wallcharts is sometimes a bit blurred, the former term is generally taken to refer to displays on large sheets of paper or cloth that are designed to be shown to a class in the course of a lesson. The latter term is used to describe similar displays that are pinned to a wall or bulletin board and are intended for casual study outwith the context of a formal lesson. Another distinction between the two is that material on charts is usually larger and easier to see or read than that on wallcharts, since the former has to be clearly distinguishable or legible at a distance whereas the latter can be studied at close quarters.

Large numbers of professionally-produced charts and wallcharts, covering a wide range of topics and often incorporating eye-catching

Figure 4.5 **Use of a magnetic board in sports coaching**

features such as photographs, maps, diagrams, graphs and cartoons, are generally available to the educational and training community. In many cases, such charts and wallcharts are available free of charge from commercial organizations as 'goodwill' gestures, while others can be purchased at relatively low cost. Even if such 'ready-made' material is not available for a particular purpose, it is fairly easy to produce one's own, simply by using a little ingenuity and applying basic graphic and design skills.

In an educational or training situation, charts and wallcharts can play a variety of different roles. They can, for example, be used:

☐ to stimulate interest and provide motivation;
☐ to act as a source of ideas or topics for discussion;
☐ to be referred to at random in order to produce gradual familiarization with their content;
☐ to act as an information store and memory substitute.

The prominent display of a chart of the periodic table of the elements in virtually every chemistry classroom and laboratory illustrates most of the above uses.

Posters
These are similar in many ways to charts, but are usually smaller, simpler and bolder in content and style. Their main uses in the classroom are as a means of providing decoration, atmosphere and motivation, although they can also be used to make or remind learners of key

points. As with charts and wallcharts, ready-made posters are available from a large number of sources — very often free of charge.

Flipcharts
These constitute a simple, and, when used in an appropriate context, highly effective method of displaying information to a class or small group. Such charts consist of a number of large sheets of paper, fixed to a support bar, easel or display board by clamping or pinning them along their top edges so that they can be flipped backwards or forwards as required. Such charts can be used in two basic ways. First, they can be used to display a succession of pre-prepared sheets, which can be shown in the required order either by flipping them into view from the back of the suspension system one by one or by revealing each successive sheet by flipping the previous one over the back of the suspension system out of the way. Second, they can be used to provide an instantly-renewable series of blank surfaces on which material can be jotted down on an impromptu basis in the course of a lesson, group discussion or other activity. They can, for example, be used to list replies from class members to questions or ideas generated by buzz groups.

Mobiles
A *mobile* is, in essence, a three-dimensional wallchart in which the individual components can move about. Instead of displaying a related system of pictures, words, etc on the flat surface of a wall, they are drawn on card, cut out and hung independently from the roof or a suitable beam using fine threads. The resulting display, which turns and changes shape as it is affected by random air currents, acquires a vitality which can never be produced in a flat display of the same material. Mobiles can be used in virtually any situation where pupils (particularly younger pupils) have to acquire and consolidate a set of related facts and where a wallchart would normally be used to reinforce this material.

Models
These are often used in cases where movement has to be illustrated (for example, the motion of the planets round the sun, wave motion etc) or when a three-dimensional representation is necessary (eg crystal structures, animal skeletons etc). However, it should always be remembered that, to a large audience in a lecture situation, even the best three-dimensional model invariably appears two-dimensional except to those who are very close. Thus, it is usually worthwhile getting the learners to gather round the model when its salient features are being demonstrated.

Realia
The supreme instructional 'model' is, in some cases, the article itself,

since there are often considerable advantages to be gained from letting learners see or handle the 'real thing' as opposed to a mere representation thereof. In many cases, of course, this will not be practicable on grounds of availability, accessibility, safety, expense, and so on, but there are many other cases where no such objections apply, and, in such cases, serious consideration should be given to the use of realia. When teaching geology, for example, there is simply no satisfactory substitute for getting the class to handle and examine real rock specimens, while the same is true in many aspects of the study of biology, physiology, and similar subjects.

Handouts
Pre-prepared notes, diagrams and tables can be given to students in the form of handouts. This can save the student from tedious and perhaps inefficient note-taking, thus allowing him to concentrate better on what is being said. However, the use of very complete handout notes may encourage laziness or absenteeism, and, for these reasons, some teachers prefer to use partial handouts which list the main points but allow the students to add their own notes in the spaces provided. Thus, the student has some involvement in the process, and interacts better with the handout.

Projected Visual and Audiovisual Aids

These include all visual or audiovisual aids that involve the use of an optical or electronic projector, whether of the front-projection or back-projection variety. For our purpose, we will divide them into six broad groups, namely *filmstrips and filmstrip projectors, slides and slide projectors, overhead projectors, opaque projectors, films and film projectors* and *videocassette and videodisc machines.* Let us now look at these in turn.

Filmstrips and filmstrip projectors
Filmstrips come in two formats — *full frame* (as produced by a standard 35mm camera) and *half frame* (which give smaller pictures, but twice as many of them on the same length of film). It is thus obviously necessary to have appropriate viewing equipment to accommodate the particular type of filmstrip being used. With large classes, a specially-designed filmstrip projector plus a standard projection screen will probably be necessary; most of these projectors can be adjusted to take both formats of filmstrip. With smaller classes or small groups, it may be possible to achieve satisfactory viewing conditions using a *filmstrip viewer* of the type that projects the image being viewed on to the back of a small translucent screen. Most viewers of this type can only be used with half-frame filmstrips, however. Filmstrips covering a wide range of topics are available from a large number of commercial and other organizations, many of these being accompanied by audiocassettes

carrying a synchronized commentary. It is also possible to make one's own filmstrip using a 35mm camera.

The main advantage that filmstrips have over slides is that they are cheaper to mass produce, so that a commercially-available filmstrip tends to be considerably less expensive than a corresponding set of slides. They have, however, a number of disadvantages compared with slides, being less hardwearing, and, because the sequence of frames cannot be altered, less flexible from a user's point of view. A further disadvantage is that a filmstrip can become out of date because of a single frame. For these reasons, filmstrips are sometimes cut up into their individual frames, which are then mounted as slides.

Slides and slide projectors

Ever since the days of the 'magic lantern', *slides* have been one of the simplest and most popular methods of introducing supportive visual material into a lecture or taught lesson. The original 'lantern slides' (which were roughly 3¼" square) are very rarely used nowadays, having been almost entirely superseded by 'compact' 2" x 2" (or 35mm) slides. These consist of single frames of 35mm or similar film mounted in cardboard, metal or plastic binders, often between twin sheets of glass for added protection, and are considerably easier to make, handle, use and store than their more cumbersome predecessors.

Slides are normally shown to a class with the aid of a suitable *slide projector*. Nowadays, these are usually fully automatic, having either linear (straight-through) or circular 'carousel'-type slide magazines. Such projectors can also be linked to a tape-recorder in order to enable synchronized tape-slide presentations to be shown.

If properly designed, slides can be of great assistance to a teacher or lecturer in providing visual reinforcement for what he is saying, and are particularly useful for showing photographs, diagrams, and other graphic material. However, they are also one of the most mis-used of all audiovisual media, largely because of the all-too-common practice of including far too much information on a slide. To be effective, a slide should be clear, simple, and capable of being seen and understood from all parts of the room in which it is being projected. If you are in any doubt about the clarity or legibility of a slide, go to the back of the room in which it is to be shown and see whether you have any difficulty in making it out; if you do, throw it away, for it is almost certainly worse than useless.

Overhead projectors

The *overhead projector* (or *OHP*) is probably the most versatile visual aid that can be used to support mass instruction methods, with the result that its use has become extremely widespread and popular over the last 20 years. Indeed, the OHP has now replaced the traditional chalkboard as the most commonly-used visual aid in many schools, colleges and training establishments.

The OHP has a number of definite advantages over other methods of presenting visual information. A teacher or trainer can, for example, use it in exactly the same way as a chalkboard or whiteboard (for writing up notes, showing diagrams, working through calculations, and so on) but with the great advantage of always facing the class. Another important advantage over the chalkboard or whiteboard is that the OHP can also be used to show pre-prepared material, thus enabling teachers and trainers to build up banks of notes, diagrams, etc that can be used over and over again. Such material can be prepared using a variety of production methods (free-hand writing or drawing, transfer lettering, thermographic or photographic copying, and so on) and can incorporate a wide range of presentation techniques (progressive 'build-up' using overlays, progressive disclosure, animation, movement and re-arrangement of items, etc). Overhead transparencies are also extremely compact, and are therefore easy to store in suitable boxes, large envelopes, folders or files. Compared with other projected aids, the OHP also has the great advantage that it does not require the room to be blacked out, thus allowing students to take notes; indeed it can be used in all but the very brightest light (for example, direct sunlight). The OHP is also clean, quiet and 'user friendly', requiring no technical skill or knowledge on the part of the operator.

Disadvantages of the OHP include the fact that it requires a power supply, and needs a suitable flat (preferably white) surface on which to project its image. Also, unless this surface is inclined forward at the correct angle, the image will probably suffer from 'keystoning' (being wider at the top than the bottom due to the fact that the surface is not at right angles to the axis projection). Unlike chalkboards, OHPs require a certain amount of routine maintenance, and are also liable to break down (generally at extremely inconvenient times), so it is always advisable to have a spare bulb close at hand; some modern machines do in fact have a built-in spare bulb that can be brought into use at the turn of a knob. A further disadvantage is that some users find the glare from the OHP troublesome, although this can generally be overcome by attaching a suitably-positioned shade to the machine.

Apart from these possible 'hardware' difficulties, the main problems associated with the overhead projector stem from the fact that many users do not give sufficient thought to the production of their display material. In many cases, writing is too small or too untidy to be read easily (both, in some cases), quite apart from the fact that it frequently extends beyond the visible area of the transparency (teachers often forget that the illuminated projection area in most overhead projectors is slightly smaller than the standard square acetate sheet, and is sometimes cut away at the corners). As in the case of slides, there is also a tendency to include too much information on a single frame. Finally, teachers tend, if anything, to over-use the overhead projector just because it is so convenient, employing it in situations where other forms of visual aid might, on occasions, be more effective.

Opaque projectors (episcopes)

The *opaque projector*, or *episcope*, can be used to project an image of a small diagram or page of a book directly on to a screen. This has obvious advantages when, for example, the time or technical equipment needed to make an adequate slide is not available, or when the material is only to be used once. The main disadvantages are that complete blackout is usually required, making student note-taking difficult, and that the projection equipment is usually both bulky and noisy. Although modern opaque projectors have been greatly improved in these respects, few schools and colleges have invested in new machines recently. A further disadvantage of projecting pages of books directly is that the material is often difficult to read, and often contains superfluous information; this unnecessary detail may be both confusing and off-putting.

Films and film projectors

Films can be used to fill a number of instructional roles, ranging from front-line teaching to their use for illustrative or motivational purposes. They can, however, be expensive to hire or buy, and, for this reason, custom-built programmes developed 'in house' by schools, colleges or training organizations are now achieving much wider use — usually in video rather than film format.

Most of the standard films that are used for educational or training purposes are 16mm wide, and must be shown using a 16mm projector capable of reproducing the soundtrack, if there is one. Some films are only 8mm wide, however, and this produces further problems since 8mm films come in two formats — *standard 8* and *super 8*. Both formats have the same overall width, but the super 8 film has smaller sprocket holes, allowing a greater area of the film to be used for the pictures. Thus, a compatible projector is necessary for each type of 8mm film, although some 8mm projectors can in fact accommodate both types.

Short, single concept *loop films*, which can be 'slotted' into lectures or practical demonstrations in order to illustrate or demonstrate specific topics, are also produced on 8mm film, the resulting loop being mounted in a special cartridge. Such films can normally only be shown using a specially-designed loop film projector.

Videocassette and videodisc machines

The *videocassette recorder* (*VCR*) is essentially a television receiver minus a display tube, having facilities for recording television and other video inputs and playing back programmes recorded on videocassette. Nowadays, such machines are found in practically all schools and colleges, as well as in many homes. A number of different videocassette formats are now in common use, and since each of these is generally incompatible with all the others, care must be taken to ensure that any tapes purchased or hired will match the available equipment. Many machines have the ability to 'freeze' the picture at a given frame, or to show frames in 'slow motion' — features that have obvious advantages in educational and training situations. However, as mentioned previously, there are stringent copyright restrictions on the types of television programmes that can legally be recorded off-air for use with a class.

Although nothing like as widely used as the videocassette recorder at the moment, the *videodisc player* seems almost certain to play an important part in future education and training. At the time of writing, videodisc players cannot be used to record programmes, but it is expected that the cost of pre-recorded videodisc programmes will, in the long run, become cheaper than the videocassette equivalent. Also, the range of features available on videodisc machines (eg fast search and slow motion reverse) is likely to exceed the capability of even the best videocassette machines. Such machines also seem likely to play an important role in *interactive video* delivery systems, as we will see later (see Chapter 5).

Audio Aids

Apart from off-air radio broadcasts (which have already been discussed), the basic types of audio aid that are most widely used in mass instructional situations are the *tape recorder* and the *record player*. Let us therefore conclude this chapter by taking a brief look at each.

Tape recorders

These can be employed in a variety of roles, the most important being their use to play back pre-recorded audio lectures or talks to a class or to provide illustrative or supportive audio material in the context of a 'live' lecture or lesson. Audio programmes covering a wide range of subjects can be purchased from a variety of commercial and other organizations, and programmes can also be recorded off-air (having regard to copyright restrictions) and prepared 'in-house'. Audiotapes can also be 'pulsed' to allow them to be used in tape-slide presentations.

There are two basic types of tape recorder, namely *reel-to-reel* and *cassette* machines. The former are generally used for making original recordings, and also for editing and mixing work. In most cases, monaural sound is all that is required, but, for certain special purposes (eg music appreciation) stereo obviously has advantages. Recordings made on open-reel machines are generally subsequently 'dubbed' on to compact cassettes, because these are much easier and more convenient to use in a classroom situation. This also has the advantage of keeping the master tape in reserve, so that a new 'using copy' can be run off in the event of damage or loss.

Record players

Although they have now been largely superseded by cassette tape-recorders in many schools, colleges and training establishments, *record players* still provide a convenient method of playing audio material (particularly music and dramatic and literary performances) to a class. Their other main use is as a source of sound effects during the production of audio and video programmes.

The main disadvantage of the record player compared with the tape recorder is the fact that it can only be used to play back material that is commercially available on records. Also, both the machine itself and the records that are played on it are much more liable to damage as a result of careless use or handling. (This is not true of the new *compact discs*, on which the signal is recorded in digital form, but such discs seem unlikely to achieve widespread use in schools and colleges — at least in the foreseeable future — because of the comparatively high cost of the discs themselves and the equipment needed to play them.)

CHAPTER 5

Individualized Learning Techniques

Introduction

In Chapter 1, we looked at the historical development of educational technology, and saw how the subject entered an 'individualized learning' phase during the mid-1950s. We showed how this had its roots in the behavioural psychology-based learning theories of B F Skinner, and how it led to the development of programmed learning and to an associated concern with the design of individualized learning materials.

In Chapter 2, we compared the radically different approaches to the instructional processes that are adopted in teacher/institution-based learning systems and in student-centred learning systems, showing how the latter are designed with the needs of the individual student in mind. In particular, we showed how they are made more flexible and open by reducing institutional constraints and giving the student greater control over how, when, where and at what pace he learns.

In this chapter, we will take a more detailed look at the range of approaches that can be used when developing individualized learning methods and discuss their respective characteristics. (The comparative advantages and disadvantages of the student-centred and teacher/institution-centred approaches have already been discussed in general terms in Chapter 2.) We will then take a brief look at the different types of hardware and software that can be used to support individualized learning methods.

Three Different Approaches to Individualized Learning

In Chapter 2, we identified three basic organizational systems in the context of which some form of individualized student-centred approach can take place, namely *institution-based systems, 'local' systems* and *distance-learning systems.* We will now examine these three systems more thoroughly, and, in particular, will discuss the range of individualized methods that can be adopted within each. However, it should be emphasized at this point that the system of classification that we have adopted below is used purely for convenience. There can, in fact, be a considerable amount of overlap between the approaches and methods that come under the general umbrella of 'individualized learning', so these should be thought of as a continuous spectrum of flexible learning systems, in which the 'sections' that we have identified have no clearly-defined boundaries.

Institution-Based Systems

In most schools, colleges, universities and training establishments, it is generally possible to accommodate some individualization of learning within the context of an overall teacher/institution-centred system. The amount of individualization in the system can vary considerably, from largely traditional courses which provide the option of a limited amount of individualized learning for remedial or back-up work, to highly-flexible personalized systems of instruction, which, although based in an institution, are nevertheless very strongly student-centred. In between, there is a continuous spectrum of emphases, both on the amount and on the type of individualization used.

The simplest, and possibly the most common method, is *unstructured reading* by the student, at home, in the classroom, or in the library. This type of reading may be actively encouraged by the teaching staff, or may be left entirely to the discretion and motivation of the individual student, but, in both cases, the method is self-paced and fairly flexible. Unstructured reading may prove very useful in reading 'around' a subject and in broadening a student's perspectives. However, unless the student has well-defined objectives in mind, the method may be inefficient in terms of time, effort and results.

In this respect, *directed reading* has a distinct advantage, in that the student's attention can be focused more sharply on those aspects of a subject which are deemed to be relevant and important. Directed reading may be used as a front-line teaching method in its own right, or as a back up to traditional expository methods, and may also serve as a foundation for future class discussion or practical work, or for a 'problem-solving' session of some sort.

More formalized attempts can be made to provide individualized learning material for *remedial* or *back-up* purposes, generally through the facilities offered in an institution's library or resources centre (see Chapter 9). For example, students who have been found to have problems in grasping subject matter taught by traditional methods in the classroom can be directed to a range of structured remedial learning packages; these may approach a given topic in a different way from the original teacher, and will probably also allow the student to progress through difficult areas at a more suitable pace. The format of the packages may be textual, audiovisual or even computer-based, but, in this particular context, they are almost always used to complement and support traditional teaching methods, and not to replace them. Other students, apart from those in real difficulties, are generally also free to use the packages on an optional basis. Indeed, research into student use of the remedial/back-up approach to individualized learning has tended to reveal that the middle-ability-to-better students make more use of the available materials than the weaker students for whom the materials were mainly devised. The learning packages used in such systems may either be purchased from a commercial organization or from another institution, or may be custom-made by teachers to support a particular course.

The main advantages of such a system are that students are given access to subject matter that is taught in alternative ways, and that weaker students have a 'safety-net' in the form of well-structured learning materials. In addition, students are introduced to individualized study packages as a legitimate learning method.

On the disadvantage side, it is very rare that there are enough suitable packages available to cover all aspects of a course, so the approach may well be piecemeal. A more serious problem is that those students who would probably benefit most from individualized learning material being available for back-up purposes are the ones who are least likely to use it in practice.

Another approach to individualized learning within an institution is to accommodate it within the four walls of a conventional classroom. Such *individualized classroom work* is most common in primary schools (see Figure 5.1), although a number of secondary school classrooms are now also operated in this mode. In such classrooms, the teacher is basically a manager of resources and learning opportunities for the students, who may be learning at different levels and also at different rates. The learning materials may be of a wide variety of types, but, as a general rule, the more content-based they are, the more highly they are structured. In such a system, the demands placed upon the teacher are much greater than when the teacher is in the traditional 'dispenser of knowledge' role, and it is perhaps only a minority of teachers who would feel comfortable in this alternative role. However, in the case of mixed-ability classes in particular, it is a flexible and appropriate method for allowing each student to work and develop to the limit of his capabilities, without either being left behind by the 'high fliers' or held back by the less able. As the teacher is always present, this system also allows each pupil to be given immediate personal assistance if he encounters a problem, a problem that may be specific to the individual rather than to the class as a whole.

One extremely common student-centred method, employed at all levels of education from the primary school to postgraduate university research, is the *project*. Projects are relatively lengthy activities (ranging in duration from an afternoon to three or four years) in which the student works either independently or within a small group. They involve the investigation of a problem of some sort, the precise area of investigation generally being chosen by the student himself, either on his own or, more usually, in consultation with a teacher or supervisor. Throughout the project, the role of the teaching staff is advisory rather

Figure 5.1 **Individualized work taking place in a typical primary school classroom under the supervision of the class teacher**

than didactic, and it is the student who is largely responsible for making decisions which affect its progress.

Projects constitute an active learning method which allows students an opportunity to exercise initiative, to see practical applications of a subject, to cross subject area barriers, to probe deeply into a particular area of study, and to become responsible for organizing and structuring their activities. One drawback of this method is the difficulty of carrying out a fair and objective assessment of the student's work. This is often done by grading a tangible product of the project (a report, a thesis, a computer program, a model etc), but this may not accurately reflect the total amount of work that has been carried out. It may well be, for many students, that the actual 'planning and doing' aspects are more important educational outcomes than the end product itself.

As mentioned earlier, a number of courses use individualized learning materials mainly for remedial or back-up purposes, in support of more traditional 'front-line' teaching methods. A natural progression is for some courses or parts of courses to use materials as a front-line teaching method in their own right. *Individualized guided study* methods involve the student studying out of class (for example, in the library, in the institution's resources centre, or at home) using a range of carefully-prepared learning materials (textual, audiovisual, or computer-based) to achieve stated objectives. Students are normally provided with a structured *study guide* which can direct them towards appropriate learning materials and provide assignments and other exercises.

The use of individualized guided study for parts of some courses allows teaching staff to use their timetabled student-contact time in a different way. Instead of being almost entirely devoted to information-giving sessions, as is so often the case in traditional courses, class contact time can be used to rectify individuals' difficulties and to provide appropriate remedial work. The time can also be used to investigate the wider implications of the topic under study, and hence, through discussion, attempt to achieve objectives in Bloom's 'higher cognitive' areas, allowing the individualized study methods to cover the more content-related objectives in the 'lower cognitive' areas.

In some institution-based courses, self-instructional learning methods have almost completely replaced more traditional approaches. Learning schemes of this type have been termed *personalized systems of instruction (PSIs)*, the most popular paradigm of the approach being the *Keller Plan* that was discussed in some detail in Chapter 2. Although a number of variations are possible, personalized systems of instruction generally involve individualized learning materials, independent study, self-pacing and tutor support.

Local Systems

Two important areas in which student-centred flexible course developments are currently taking place on an increasingly wider scale are *community adult education* and *further education and training*. In both these sectors, local systems of flexible or open learning are being used to accommodate the special needs and particular situations of potential students who reside in the catchment area of a given college. In many cases, such potential students cannot or will not attend formal, time-tabled institution-based courses, for reasons such as distance, employers' attitudes and policies, age, and family commitments.

Awareness of the need to provide flexible educational, training and re-training opportunities for persons who are constrained in various ways was recently heightened in the United Kingdom by the Manpower Service Commission's 'Open Tech' Programme. This had the following aims:

□ to open up education and training opportunities for adults (most of them already in employment);
□ to secure more and better provision for updating technicians and supervisors;
□ to help employers and employees face up to the challenge of new technology;
□ to help education and training make use of new technology to provide new skills where they are needed.

The three-year Programme, which ended in the Spring of 1987, consisted of a series of sponsored projects, often involving an industrial firm and/or a college (or group of colleges) in developing open learning materials in one particular area. The projects were supervised by a central 'Open Tech Unit', which ensured that there was no unnecessary overlap between them, and that they were properly integrated and evaluated. The Programme was generally considered to have been a great success, and undoubtedly did a great deal to promote open learning in the UK.

Local systems of student-centred learning usually involve a host college or institution in providing (i) a source of learning materials, (ii) a tutorial system, (iii) an administrative system and (iv) a study support system (that is, counselling). The development of suitable learning materials can be one of the most exacting tasks, and is normally achieved via one of three paths: (i) adapting existing material, (ii) providing a study guide to 'conventional' resources, or (iii) developing custom-designed self-contained material. Mechanisms for practical work, student feedback and tutorials have to be carefully thought out; indeed, tutorials are often held over the telephone.

One well-known example of a local student-centred system is *Flexistudy*, which sets out to offer students all the resources of a conventional correspondence course plus local college support. It is targeted specifically at people whose lifestyle renders it impossible for them to conform to the rigid constraints inherent in conventional adult education and training courses. In Flexistudy courses, the student does not have to attend the host institution regularly, does not have to conform to conventional academic terms or years, is able to use a range of individualized learning materials, and has access to tutorial guidance as and when required. In such courses, a whole range of resources of the host institution are made available in order to complement the correspondence and tutor support. These normally include the library, any multi-media, self-instructional resources centre or language laboratory facilities that are available, counselling and career help, and the institution's administrative and examinations machinery. Although the majority of Flexistudy-type developments have, to date, been at the lower end of the adult and further education spectrum, this is not necessarily an intrinsic limiting feature of the system.

In effect, use of Flexistudy allows institutions to offer courses which students (and employers) want, when students want them, by means which suit their circumstances, and from which they can learn effectively. It is one extremely promising method of meeting the demands of recurrent and continuing education and training, and may even have implications for the long-term viability of some colleges. Against this, the development, organization and operation of a Flexistudy-type course is by no means an easy option, requiring tremendous efforts from both teaching and administrative staff, not to mention a considerable amount of self-motivation from the students.

Other examples of flexible local methods include *learning-by-appointment* and *open access* systems. In learning-by-appointment, potential students in the local community can 'sign up' for a given course and make appointments to attend the institution at mutually-suitable times. Normally, a range of individualized learning materials (textual, audiovisual and computer-based) are made available to the student in the institution's library or learning resources centre. In some cases, tutor help can also be 'booked'. Open access methods are less formalized in that the student can have access to the institution at any time. Both methods have proved particularly useful in the field of community education.

Distance Learning Systems

In *distance learning* schemes, all (or nearly all) student learning takes place *away* from the host institution. In some cases, the 'distant student' may be on the other side of the globe from the host institution, and, as a consequence, the student is very dependent on the quality of learning materials available. However, even in such extreme cases, tutor support and feedback on assignments is an integral part of almost every distance learning scheme.

The first distance learning developments came in the form of *correspondence courses*, which still have a place in the distance learning market today. In such courses, the material is almost totally textual, the student being provided with structured course units which direct his learning activities and provide assignments. Students normally receive regular feedback on their performance, and may be required to reach a certain standard before being allowed to progress to the next course unit.

In recent years, distance learning schemes have tended to make use of a much wider range of educational techniques, with *multi-media distance learning schemes* of the type pioneered by the Open University in Britain being developed in many parts of the world. Such schemes can combine a printed student study guide with broadcast material (radio and television), videocassettes, audiovisual learning materials, computer packages, practical 'do-it-yourself' kits, models, books and other textual material. These materials, combined with tutor support (local and distant), student 'self-help' groups and occasional centrally-organized group learning sessions, allow the student to achieve a much wider range of educational objectives than is possible with purely 'correspondence' courses. As well as being educationally desirable, the use of a variety of methods also helps to reduce the strain and boredom of working in isolation.

Media Used in Individualized Learning

In all three of the individualized approaches to learning described above, we have seen that self-instructional teaching materials play a 'front line' role in the learning process, with the actual teacher usually having a managerial and/or counselling role, as shown in Figure 5.2.

As with the exposition-based teaching methods that were discusssed in the previous chapter, a wide range of hardware and software of varying technological complexity is now available to cater for individualized student learning methods.

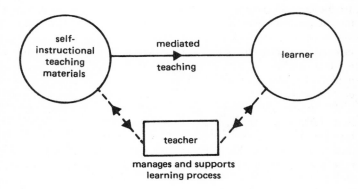

Figure 5.2 **The front-line role of teaching materials in individualized learning**

We will consider the materials used in individualized learning under three broad headings: *textual materials, audiovisual materials,* and *computer-based materials.* Although this distinction has been made for convenience, it is often the case that a combination of media under all of these headings is used to achieve a particular range of objectives in an individualized learning situation. All the media to be described enable students to progress at their own speed and make provision for review and revision; many also provide the student with an on-going check on his progress. Readers who require more detailed information about any of the media described are referred to Ellington's book on *Producing Teaching Materials* (see Bibliography).

Textual Materials

Directed study of materials in text books
Conventional *text books* can often be used in self-instructional situations, although, by themselves, they may not necessarily be suitable for enabling *mastery* of desired material to be achieved. This is because most text books are designed simply to *present* information, not to provide the users with a systematic learning programme. Also, it is very rare to find a single text book that covers all the material in a course or module in the manner that the person responsible for teaching that course or module requires. The effectiveness of text books as vehicles for self-instruction can, however, generally be greatly increased by the use of a suitable *study guide* which structures the

learning process for the students by directing them to suitable chapters (or sections thereof) in appropriate books in a systematic and cumulative way, and provides supplementary notes and assignments, etc.

SOME STRENGTHS OF DIRECTED STUDY OF TEXT BOOK MATERIAL

In the case of certain core subject areas, the course material may well be adequately covered in normal text books, and, if so, such books represent one of the cheapest and most convenient forms of self-instructional materials. Provided that suitable texts are available and the work is carefully structured, directed study of such text books can be a highly effective way of teaching basic facts, principles, applications, etc, i.e. of achieving objectives mainly of the *lower cognitive* type.

Directed study of this type has a further great advantage of allowing each learner to work at his natural pace. Research has shown that learners differ considerably in the rate at which they can assimilate new material effectively, so *any* method that allows self-pacing to take place is almost invariably more effective than a method (like the lecture) in which they all have to work at the pace directed by the instructor.

Another great advantage of the method is that it requires no specialized hardware or other facilities, and no specialized courseware other than standard text books. The latter can either be purchased by the students or made available through a suitable library.

A further advantage of the method is that study can be carried out at any time suitable to the learner, and (provided that the text books involved are not restricted to 'reference only' use within a library) at any convenient place.

SOME WEAKNESSES OF THE METHOD

One possible disadvantage of the method is that it requires extremely careful planning and structuring on the part of the supervising teacher if it is to be fully effective; this, obviously, requires both skill and time.

Also, the method is totally dependent on suitable texts being available. In some cases, it may be possible to insist that all students purchase their own copies of the book or books involved, but, in many cases, this will not be a realistic option. In such cases, it will be necessary to ensure that the books are available in the library in sufficient numbers to enable *all* the students in the class to have suitable access. Ideally, this should be done by purchasing multiple copies and making them available for borrowing, but, if this is not possible, the books should be made available on a 'reference only' basis, for use in the actual library.

A further disadvantage is that the method is not really suitable for achieving many *higher cognitive* and *non-cognitive* objectives. Also, unless a deliberate attempt is made to build in participative student activities through the study guide, study of material in text books can be a very passive form of study, with little or no interaction taking place between the learner and the learning materials; this can lead to boredom and lack of motivation on the part of the students.

Study of specially-prepared handout notes or programmed texts
One of the drawbacks of using text books in self-instructional situations is that they may well be inappropriate either in terms of their level or in terms of their treatment of the subject matter, thus making it unlikely that they will match the objectives of the course and meet the requirements of the students. Use of carefully-prepared and structured *handout notes* produced by the teaching staff offer one means of getting round this difficulty, although the problem of low student interaction with the material may still be present unless deliberate steps are taken to counteract it.

One way of increasing student interaction with textual materials of this type is to produce the notes in the form of a *programmed text.* This involves structuring the material in a series of comparatively small, easily-digestible *steps* (or *frames*) and interspersing those that merely present information (*teaching frames*) with others that require active participation on the part of the learner (e.g. *practice frames,* which provide practice in the material just presented, or *test frames,* which determine whether the learner has mastered the material). Some of the basic structures that can be used with such programmed texts are discussed in Chapter 1, and readers who require more detailed inform-ation are referred to the various texts on programmed learning listed in the Bibliography.

SOME STRENGTHS OF SPECIALLY-PREPARED NOTES AND
PROGRAMMED TEXTS
As a learning method, study of specially-prepared handout notes and programmed texts has all the basic educational advantages of directed study of material in text books, and, if the material is well designed, can be an extremely effective method of achieving a wide range of (mainly) lower-cognitive objectives.

If the material incorporates a high degree of learner participation, this added dimension can make the method even more effective.

SOME WEAKNESSES OF THE METHOD
The main disadvantage of the method is that the task of producing *effective* materials is inevitably extremely time-consuming, and also requires a great deal of skill on the part of the writer. This is doubly true in the case of fields (such as electronics and computer science) that are in a more-or-less continuous state of change, since writers of individualized learning materials in such fields are faced with the on-going problem of keeping their material up to date; indeed they can be faced with a never-ending task rather akin to painting the Forth Bridge! Another major limitation of the method is that, like directed study

of text book material, it is not really suitable for achieving a wide range of higher cognitive and non-cognitive objectives.

A third disadvantage of the method is that it can become extremely boring to students if it is over-used, e.g. if it is the *only* method employed to cover a large section of a syllabus. Because of this, many modern programmed learning sequences that are based primarily on textual materials incorporate some audiovisual or computer-based learning materials as well in order to help maintain student interest and motivation.

Audiovisual Self-Instructional Materials

Audiovisual learning programmes
Although print-based, self-instructional material still has an important place in most individualized learning systems, many self-instructional learning packages now utilize a whole range of audio and visual media to increase their impact and effectiveness. Such packages may include audio and video tapes, filmstrips, loop films, slides, transparencies, models and practical kits as well as conventional printed material, the particular 'media mix' being carefully chosen with the objectives of the topic being covered in mind. For example, in a number of individualized learning packages that have been developed at Glasgow University to teach three-dimensional structures and relationships, printed material, audiotapes and slides have been used in conjunction with custom-built, three-dimensional models and construction kits; using the latter, students can build and examine their own models as directed by the programme (see Figure 5.3). The precise choice of media is therefore very dependent on the objectives that the package is designed to achieve.

A range of hardware of varying degrees of sophistication is available for use with the different types of software mentioned above. A wide variety of expensive automatic playback machines can be purchased for use in institutional libraries and resources centres. However, for students working on their own at home, suitable combinations of relatively inexpensive items of equipment (cassette players, simple slide viewers, etc) are generally just as effective from an educational point of view.

SOME STRENGTHS OF AUDIOVISUAL LEARNING PROGRAMMES

Because of the wide range of media available, audiovisual self-instructional materials can be used to achieve a wide variety of educational objectives, and although these again tend to fall mainly in the lower cognitive range, it is also possible to use them to achieve other types of objectives. By associating manipulative tasks with such materials, for example, they can be used to develop certain types of *psychomotor skills*, and they can also be highly effective in achieving certain types of affective objectives (e.g. in producing desirable attitude

Figure 5.3 **A student of chemistry studying organic chemistry using a self-instructional tape-model programme**

changes). They also have the great advantage of allowing the learner to work at his own pace.

In some cases (e.g. language laboratories, or the tape-model systems developed at Glasgow University), they allow a high element of learner participation to be built into the learning process – another important educational 'plus'. Also, use of appropriate media enables things like sound, movement and realism to be introduced into a presentation, thus again increasing student interest and motivation.

Use of well-designed mediated presentations can save instructors from having to carry out a great deal of time-consuming, repetitive work – e.g. in teaching all the members of a class individually how to use a particular type of machine, instrument or tool or how to carry out a particular process.

SOME WEAKNESSES OF AUDIOVISUAL LEARNING PROGRAMMES
The main weakness of the approach is that suitable ready-made courseware is seldom available, so that the instructor has to produce his own. This is invariably time-consuming, often expensive, and (in many cases) requires specialist skills that the average teacher or lecturer simply does not possess. In some cases, it may be possible to learn the required skills by undergoing suitable staff development (e.g. learning basic video production skills), but in other cases it may be necessary to rely on specialist support staff. Readers interested in developing such skills should find the advice given in Ellington's book on *Producing Teaching Materials* useful (see Bibliography).

Although mediated self-instruction can be used to achieve a somewhat wider range of objectives than self-instruction based purely on the study of textual materials, there are still a wide variety of higher-cognitive and non-cognitive objectives for which the technique is inappropriate.

By its very nature, mediated self-instruction relies totally on the availability of suitable hardware. In many cases, provision of sufficient hardware to enable extensive use of the method to take place may simply not be possible because of its cost, or due to lack of space for the provision of suitable study stations (*carrels*).

Language laboratories

These involve a specialist application of the tape recorder which allows students to interact individually with audio material. Although the original use of such equipment was for language teaching, language laboratories are now also used to present audio programmes in other subjects, and are therefore of more general interest. Basically, a language laboratory allows each student to listen to a master tape and to record and listen to his own responses (see Figure 5.4, which shows students working in this way in a College of Education language laboratory). The teacher can 'listen in' to any one student, and can communicate directly both with individual students and with groups of any size.

Figure 5.4 **Trainee teachers working in a language laboratory**

Language laboratories are an extremely expensive teaching resource, and, for this reason, are largely limited to individualized learning within groups in an institutional setting. The main advantage over the use of individual taperecorders is that, within a group, a teacher may 'listen in' unnoticed, and can therefore monitor each individual's progress and identify those who need remedial work.

Broadcasting media
Through the media of radio and television, broadcast material is readily accessible to individuals in their own homes. The associated hardware can be used to receive programmes transmitted either through an 'open' national or regional network or through a more local network such as a cable distribution or closed-circuit system. Also, by using the appropriate recording equipment, programmes that are broadcast at inconvenient times can be stored on tape and used at the convenience of the learner. Until recently, such off-air recording by individuals was largely restricted to radio broadcasts, but, with the increasingly widespread domestic use of videocassette machines, recording educational television programmes is now just as common.

Through the use of suitably-adapted television sets, recent developments in the field of information technology (such as the British interactive videotex system, PRESTEL) may soon play an important role in individualized learning. In such systems, the viewer can interact with the information shown on the screen via a small keyboard, and the learning sequence can be made appropriate to his individual needs. Developments within this area are progressing rapidly.

Computer-Based Self-Instructional Materials

Computer-assisted learning (CAL)
The computer can play a number of different roles in individualized learning schemes, including front-line teaching, assessment, managing resources and maintaining administrative records. The potential of the computer in each of these areas will be discussed in more detail in Chapter 10.

In an individualized CAL situation, a student may have access to a computer terminal linked to a large 'mainframe' computer, or to a small microcomputer with its own screen or video display unit (VDU). Whatever the hardware used, the computer acts in one of two basic roles in all CAL systems, namely, in a *tutorial* mode or in a *laboratory* mode (although it is sometimes used in a combination of both).

In the tutorial mode, the student interacts directly with the computer, which is programmed to understand and react to student responses. This is basically a sophisticated form of the branching programmed learning that was discussed in Chapter 1.

In the laboratory mode, the computer is essentially a learning resource rather than an instructional device. The computer can be used to simulate a laboratory situation, to model experiments, to provide data-bases, to set problem-solving exercises, and so on. For example, a student can investigate mathematical models of physical systems, and see how specific factors vary under different conditions which he himself can control.

SOME STRENGTHS OF COMPUTER-ASSISTED LEARNING

Whether it is employed in the 'substitute-tutor' mode or in the 'simulated laboratory' mode, use of the computer as a delivery system for self-instructional materials enables an extremely wide range of educational objectives to be achieved, although (as with other types of self-instructional system) these tend to fall mainly in the lower cognitive area. It also enables each learner to work at his own natural pace — a considerable educational advantage, as we have already seen.

Possibly the greatest strength of the computer as a delivery system is that it enables an extremely high degree of learner participation to be built into the instructional process, and also enables the system to adapt to the needs of the individual learner in a way that is simply not possible with other delivery systems.

Use of the computer can also provide (through computer simulations) a wide range of otherwise inaccessible learning experiences. It can, for example, enable learners to carry out simulated experiments in fields like human genetics, macro-economics and sociology where actual experiments are impossible for ethical, economic or practical reasons.

A further advantage of using a computer as a delivery system for self-instructional materials is that it can allow on-going assessment and monitoring to take place automatically if this is thought appropriate. This can be extremely useful, especially if the learner is working in isolation (e.g. on a distance learning course).

SOME WEAKNESSES OF COMPUTER-ASSISTED LEARNING

Computer-based learning has the same basic weaknesses as audiovisual learning in terms of general lack of availability of suitable ready-made courseware, total dependence on the availability of appropriate hardware and the fact that it is not suitable for use in achieving a wide range of higher-cognitive and non-cognitive objectives.

A further weakness specific to computer-based learning is that it requires computer literacy and (in many cases) a degree of programming skill on the part of the person designing the materials. With the development of user-friendly *authoring systems* of ever-increasing sophistication, however, it is now becoming very much easier for non-programmers to write CBL materials than was the case in the past, when ability to write programs in a language such as BASIC or FORTRAN was an absolute necessity for such work.

Other strengths and weaknesses of computer-assisted learning will be discussed in Chapters 10 and 11.

Figure 5.5 **The interactive video work station
used as a delivery system for the BBC's 'Domesday Project'**

Interactive video
Interactive video systems are still very much in their infancy, but
basically they attempt to utilize two relatively well-established teaching
media — *videorecorders* and *computers* — in an integrated teaching
resource. In marrying the two, the aim is to combine a flexible, interactive and accessible teaching programme (through the computer) with
good visual and sound characteristics (through the videorecorder).

A large amount of development work is currently being carried out
on interactive video systems, since their tremendous potential for
providing high-quality learning materials to suit individual needs is
obvious. However, it seems likely that the most important developments will be made by combining microcomputers with videodisc
players rather than with videocassette machines. This is because it is
very much easier to obtain access to specific sequences or frames of a
programme using a videodisc system, since there is no need to wind a
tape forward or backwards in order to do so.

As with interactive videotex, the widespread use of individualized
learning materials that rely on interactive video for their presentation
is still in the future, although perhaps not too far away. Possibly the
advent of the BBC's highly-ambitious *Domesday Project*, which uses
videodisc-based interactive video as a delivery system for a comprehensive data-base on virtually all aspects of Britain (see Figure 5.5),
will provide the necessary stimulus.

CHAPTER 6

Group Learning Techniques

Introduction

As we saw in Chapter 1, educational technology is currently very much concerned with the development of techniques that can be used to promote learning in group situations. Such methods normally involve very little use of technical hardware or sophisticated audiovisual software. Rather, they reflect a 'technology *of* education' approach, their main concern being associated with directing the process of interactive group dynamics towards desirable educational or training goals. As a result, less tangible factors, such as room conditions, seating arrangements, group size and the role of the teacher, may play an important role in determining the success (or otherwise) of such methods. This chapter will begin with a discussion of group learning in fairly general terms, after which a number of specific group learning techniques will be considered.

General Features of Group Learning Methods

The relevance of group learning techniques in an educational or training situation can often be assessed by carrying out a critical analysis of the aims and objectives of the course or programme in question. If the desired outcomes include the development of (for example) oral communication skills, interpersonal skills, problem-solving skills, decision-making skills, critical thinking skills, and certain attitudinal traits deemed to be appropriate, then group learning techniques may be more suitable for teaching towards such outcomes than the various mass instructional and individualized learning methods that have just been described. Indeed, one of the major strengths of a systematic approach to education and training is that when objectives are clearly specified, appropriate teaching methods can be matched with them. The types of outcome which can be achieved through the use of group learning techniques will be discussed in detail later on in this chapter, after we have looked at some basic organizational considerations.

Organizational Considerations

Because of the fact that group learning techniques normally aim to stimulate effective interactive group discussions, it is obviously necessary to use a group of an appropriate size in each particular situation. The optimum group size depends on a variety of factors, including the purpose and nature of the exercise and any constraints that may be laid down by the logistics of the latter; many educational games and simulations, for example, specify the number of participants, particularly if they are highly structured. As a general rule, however, a group should be no larger than about 10 if it is to act as an effective vehicle for promoting group interaction and developing group skills, and, ideally, it should be somewhere between four and six.

In his book *Educational Technology in Curriculum Development* (1982) Derek Rowntree represents the 'group dynamics' that occur in two somewhat different small group situations in the way shown in Figure 6.1.

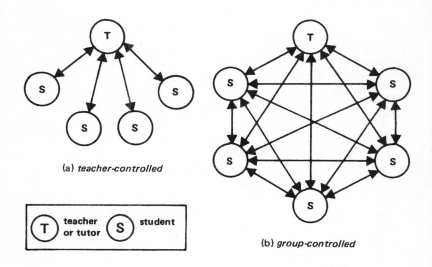

(a) *teacher-controlled*

(b) *group-controlled*

Figure 6.1 **Patterns of communication
in two different group learning situations**

In situation (a), the teacher/tutor controls the discussion, the basic pattern being a succession of dialogues between the teacher and the various individual students. This is the somewhat limited pattern of communication that often takes place within a tutorial-type group environment. In situation (b), we see the multi-way communication pattern that takes place in a group-controlled discussion or seminar, in which the students can interact freely with one another, thus allowing ideas to be built upon from within the student group. Indeed, in such a group environment, it may not even be necessary for the teacher to become actively involved in the discussion provided that it is 'set off' in the right direction.

The role of the teacher in group learning situations is, however, very important, and calls for skills and adaptability which may, for some, be difficult to achieve. First, the teacher must exhibit good organizational skills in planning and structuring the learning experience. Thereafter, his role may be more adaptive and less authoritarian or autocratic than in exposition-based situations. Depending on the form, content and structure of the group technique adopted, and upon its particular educational aims and objectives, the teacher's role may include acting as *group leader* (giving strong direction to the discussion), *group facilitator* (generating self-expression and interaction within the group), *neutral chairman* (controlling the procedure, but not contributing substantially to the discussion), *consultant* (providing assistance and/or information as and when needed) or simply *observer*. In most group exercises, another important aspect of the role of the teacher is in *debriefing* the session. This involves going over with the participants the events that occurred during the group sessions and 'pulling out' any important points that arose, either in connection with the nature and content of the discussions or regarding the processes and interactions within the group itself. Obviously, the points that are highlighted in such a debriefing should be closely related to the main teaching objectives of the exercise.

Group learning activities can range from being highly structured and pre-planned to being essentially free or open discussions. If a structured approach is to be used, the group may be organized in a pre-arranged way, and directed to discuss specific subject matter in a manner that is dictated by the teacher or predetermined by the format of the exercise. On the other hand, if a free or non-directed approach is to be adopted, the group processes are far more 'student-controlled' and flexible, and consequently the learning outcomes are much more difficult to predict. In between these two extremes are a whole range of techniques and approaches which involve the use of groups in a wide variety of different ways.

Some Strengths of Group Learning Techniques

In matching the desired outcomes, or objectives, of a course with the teaching methods likely to achieve them, it soon becomes obvious that no single method is suitable in all circumstances, and that an appropriate 'blend' of teaching methods (exposition-based, individualized and group) may be required. As mentioned above, there are a number of types of objectives for which group learning techniques are particularly useful as a means of teaching. Let us now examine these in turn.

Higher cognitive objectives
Within the general area of knowledge and understanding (Bloom's cognitive domain — see Chapter 3), we have already seen that mass instruction techniques (for example, lectures) and individualized learning methods are well suited for teaching towards the lower cognitive areas of 'knowledge' and 'comprehension'. However, the understanding of factual material and its applications in a number of areas can often be much more effectively investigated in small group situations such as tutorial sessions. Indeed, in most colleges and universities, lectures and tutorials are generally closely linked and complementary.

Cognitive skills that lie further up Bloom's hierarchy (such as those involving the analysis or evaluation of given material) are often most effectively developed by using a group discussion technique of some sort. Here, students can discuss problems and opinions with their peers in a relatively open environment.

Group methods have also proved to be useful in problem-solving sessions, with the students either working individually and interacting with the teacher, or working as a co-operative group in tackling a project of some sort. In such activities, the subject matter is often very specific to the student's course of study. However, exercises that foster the development of decision-making skills through the use of small-group methods need not necessarily be so content-related. Many management-training courses, for example, make use of exercises which enable the participants to improve their decision-making ability through activities in which the processes by which the decisions are reached are much more important than the actual content of the exercise.

Creative thinking skills
In courses that contain objectives which involve the development of creative thinking skills (for example, the ability to perceive new relationships within a topic, or the ability to produce imaginative solutions to given problem situations), group methods have often been found to be extremely useful. In situations where wide-ranging and/or lateral thinking are required, for example, ideas can be 'bounced around' within the group for comment and criticism, with the result that individual group members benefit from the perceptions of others and from the subsequent interactions and discussions.

Communication skills
A number of group learning techniques are ideal vehicles for the development of (or creation of an awareness of the importance of) the various skills that are associated with *oral communication, non-verbal communication*, and *written communication*.

Students are frequently criticized for their inability to express themselves coherently. Group techniques are particularly well suited to helping them to overcome these deficiencies, and, in recent years, a number of exercises have been designed specifically for this purpose. These provide situations in which students can develop oral communication skills (such as presenting and defending arguments and making a meaningful contribution to discussions) and through which they can generally build up their confidence. Ideally, a planned series of such exercises is desirable if significant and long-lasting improvements are to be achieved.

which written work such as essays, laboratory reports, assignments and project reports can be discussed. The purpose of such discussions can be twofold: first, to discuss the content of the written work for the mutual benefit of the group; second, to discuss the form of the written work in terms of, for instance, structure, sequence and clarity of expression. In many cases, open discussion of the latter may well encourage and catalyse improved future efforts.

Finally, group exercises may help the participants to develop an appreciation of the importance of non-verbal communication and to cultivate useful skills in this often-neglected area. This can be achieved through observation of the activities of the group by the teacher, by the actual group members, by independent observers, or via a videotape recording made for later analysis and discussion. Such techniques can be used for a variety of purposes: eg for demonstrating the nature of non-verbal communication to psychology students, or for helping trainee managers to recognize and develop the various non-verbal skills that play such an important part in interviews, meetings etc.

Interpersonal skills
The various skills that are required in order to operate effectively within a group or social situation are often best developed by group learning methods. In many instances, students leaving school or college enter jobs which require them to work in close co-operation with other people. For some, this may involve skills of leadership, administration and delegation, for some, the ability to work as part of a team, while for others it may involve social skills such as those needed in order to deal with the general public. Again, group methods are ideal for putting theory into practice, and a whole range of simulation and role play activities can be used with small groups in order to help develop interpersonal skills of this type.

Desirable attitudinal traits
Research has shown that exposition-based and individualized methods are not particularly effective in the area of attitude (affective) development. It seems that active participation by students and exposure to views different from their own and to criticism by their peers are necessary if attitudes are to be changed, together with a less dominant teacher role than is found in most conventional learning situations. In other words, it appears that *student interaction* is the key to the achievement of such attitude changes.

The vital role that can be played by group methods in this area is self-evident. Such methods can provide an environment in which free discussion can break down prejudices and misconceptions and increase awareness of the range of factors that are involved in any given situation. An example might be the use of group methods to increase empathy towards a minority section of the community, or towards trade unions or representatives of management.

Group activities can also be an extremely powerful means of integrating an individual's cognitive and affective development within the context of a meaningful and relevant learning experience.

Some Disadvantages of Group Learning

Group learning also has a number of disadvantages, some of the more important of which will now be examined.

Organizational difficulties

Running group learning exercises can pose a number of organizational problems, not the least of which is the fact that it is often difficult to fit them into the normal teaching curriculum — particularly if the exercise is a long one or requires a large number of participants, extra teaching staff, special accommodation, etc. This is particularly true of many exercises of the game/simulation/case study type. Also, the fact that such exercises often require the participants to attend briefing or debriefing sessions or to carry out preliminary work can cause complications. Finally, it is often extremely difficult to assess student performance or evaluate the effectiveness of group learning exercises other than on a subjective basis.

Problems of attitude

One potential weakness of all group learning methods is that they require the active co-operation of the participants if they are to succeed. In some cases, however, this co-operation may not be forthcoming. Students may, for example, simply not turn up for the exercise because they feel that it will be a waste of time or are afraid of taking part. In other cases, they may be reluctant to make the very real personal commitment that many group learning exercises require, because they do not feel that they have the necessary skills and do not want to 'show themselves up' in front of their peers.

Nor are these attitude-related problems necessarily limited to students. As we saw earlier, running a group learning exercise can make heavy demands on the staff involved, often requiring them to take on a number of unfamiliar roles which may not fit in with their conception of what their job should entail. This is particularly true of many older, or more traditional, teachers, who, as a result, make little or no use of group learning techniques.

The Main Group Learning Techniques

The type of group technique that is used in a particular teaching or training situation depends on a whole range of factors, including the objectives that it is wished to achieve, the relationship of the exercise with other teaching methods, the maturity of the students, the personality and experience of the teacher, and so on. The techniques described below by no means constitute an exhaustive list of those which can be used in small group situations; they do, however, illustrate a broad cross-section of approaches which vary in their degree of structure, teacher involvement and dependence on subject matter content. Some techniques can in fact be used within other group techniques, while others can be incorporated into exposition-based methods in order to generate student activity, discussion and feedback. More detailed descriptions of these and other group techniques can be found in Abercrombie's book *Aims and Techniques of Group Teaching* (1979).

In order to give this section of the book a workable structure, we will divide group learning techniques into six broad classes, namely, *buzz sessions and similar small-group exercises; class discussions, seminars, tutorials, etc; participative exercises of the game/simulation/ case study type; mediated feedback/discussion sessions; group projects;* and *self-help groups.* Within each of these categories, it is, of course, possible to adopt a wide range of approaches and tactics, but, as we will see, it is also possible to make a number of generalizations, and it is on these that we will concentrate.

Buzz Sessions and Similar Small-Group Exercises

Buzz sessions are short participative sessions that are deliberately built into a lecture or larger group exercise in order to stimulate discussion and provide student feedback. In such sessions, small sub-groups of two to four persons spend a short period (generally no more than five minutes) intensively discussing a topic or topics suggested by the teacher. Each sub-group then reports back on its deliberations to the group as a whole, or sometimes combines with another sub-group in order to share their findings and discuss the implications.

One variation of the buzz group approach is the *one-two-four snowball technique.* Here, the members of a class or large group are first asked to reflect individually on a question, then asked to form pairs in order to look for differences in these responses, then asked to form groups of four in order to arrive at a consensus response. As in the basic buzz group technique, each group of four is then asked to report on its findings to the class or group as a whole.

Some strengths of small-scale group sessions of this type
Buzz groups and similar small-group sessions constitute an excellent method of introducing variety into a lecture or formal presentation,

thus helping to overcome the problems that can arise due to the limitations in the *attention span* of students (see the section on lectures in Chapter 4). Appropriate use of such sessions forces the students to undergo a radical change in their thought processes, thus helping to stop their attention from lapsing.

Such sessions can be used to achieve a wide range of objectives, both cognitive and non-cognitive. They can, for example, be used to develop oral communication and interpersonal skills, as well as being ideal for helping students to develop their powers of decision-making, evaluation and divergent thinking.

Such sessions also serve as an ideal vehicle for getting students actively involved in a lesson, thus increasing the effectiveness of the learning that takes place. They also provide a teacher with a useful mechanism for obtaining feedback from a class.

Some weaknesses of small-scale group sessions
The main limitation of small-scale group sessions of this type is that they are not really suitable for use as a front-line teaching method in their own right, since they cannot, by themselves, be used to teach the basic facts and principles of a subject. Thus, they should only be used in a *supportive* role, in conjunction with other methods such as lectures.

Class discussions, seminars, tutorials, etc

This class of techniques covers a wide range of activities designed to promote discussion between a teacher and a group of students, or within a group of learners.

Class discussions generally take the form of a *controlled discussion* in which the teacher is at all times firmly in control of the situation, either allowing the class to ask questions and controlling the way in which these are discussed, or else guiding the class through a structured discussion of some sort by asking carefully-chosen questions, providing appropriate prompts, and so on. Such discussions can be used in a variety of contexts, e.g. as a follow-up to an expository session such as a lecture or the viewing of a film or video, as a class revision session, as a debriefing session for a game, simulation or participative case study, or as a teaching method in their own right.

Seminars can take a number of forms, and are generally run on somewhat less-restricted lines than class discussions, with the group members themselves having much more control over the course and content of the discussion. One common method of running a seminar is to base it on an essay, paper or prepared talk presented by one of the students in the group, with the group then discussing the presentation in depth. Figure 6.2 shows such a seminar in progress. Another method is to run the seminar as a *free group discussion* of a particular topic, the group either being given broad guidelines on how the discussion should proceed or being left to decide this for themselves.

Figure 6.2 **A typical small-group seminar in progress
in a business school**

Another variation of the seminar approach is the *fishbowl technique.*
Here, half the members of the class involved sit in an inner circle and
conduct a discussion while the remainder sit in an outer circle and act
as non-participating observers; both sections of the group then combine
for a general discussion of what occurred.

Yet another approach to the organization of a seminar is *brainstorming.* This involves group members in spontaneously noting down
or suggesting a range of possible solutions to a problem or question
posed by the teacher, e.g. 'What items would be absolutely essential if
you were marooned on a desert island?' Initially, the suggestions are
compiled without comment, and the group as a whole then evaluates
the various suggestions and modifies or rejects them in the light of the
ensuing discussion. Brainstorming is very useful not only for stimulating
discussion, but also for acting as an *icebreaker* at the start of a seminar
by actively involving every participant right at the beginning. Once the
'ice' has been broken, the group's discussion will probably be a good
deal more free and involve more students than might otherwise be
the case.

Group *tutorials* can also take a variety of forms. One common form
is the *working tutorial*, in which the class (or a section thereof) tackle
course-related tasks set by the teacher or tutor, obtaining help or guidance if they experience difficulties. Another is the *problem-raising
tutorial*, in which the members have the opportunity to ask their tutor
about any matters relating to the course with which they are having
problems.

Some strengths of class discussions, seminars and tutorials
Class discussions, seminars and tutorials can be used to achieve a wide range of educational objectives, both of the cognitive and of the non-cognitive variety. They can, for example, be used to build on *lower-cognitive* objectives (*knowledge* and *comprehension*) that have been developed in lectures or through individualized learning by providing a vehicle for achieving *higher-cognitive* objectives such as *application, analysis, synthesis* and *evaluation* in the areas in question. They can also be used to develop communication and interpersonal skills, and to achieve a wide range of affective objectives such as showing students that there are generally several ways of looking at an issue or making them more tolerant of the views of other people.

They enable relevant topics to be examined in great depth or discussed at considerable length.

Like buzz sessions and similar exercises, they have the great advantage of *getting the learners actively involved in the learning process*, since they are, by definition, participative rather than passive.

Some weaknesses of such methods
With all group learning methods of this type, there is always the danger that some of the members of the class or group will not take an active part in the exercise, leaving all the thinking or speaking to others. Thus, if such an exercise is to be fully effective, it is necessary to take steps to ensure that *everyone* takes part — either by careful structuring or control and/or by limiting the size of the group.

Building group learning sessions such as group tutorials or seminars into a curriculum can cause timetabling and logistical difficulties because of the fact that they generally involve the class being split up, thus making extra demands on staff support and accommodation.

One major drawback of subject-based tutorials and seminars is that there is often a tendency for the teacher to become over-dominant, and, in some cases, to use the session as a 'mini-lecture'. If this happens, the opportunity to achieve the full range of higher-cognitive and other objectives of which such sessions are capable will almost certainly be lost.

Participative Exercises of the Game/Simulation/Case Study Type

During the last decade, the use of *games, simulations* and interactive *case studies* as a group learning technique has increased dramatically. Such exercises were originally largely confined to the military and business management training sectors, but they have now spread to virtually all sectors of education, where they are used in a wide range of subject areas to teach towards a wide variety of educational objectives.

The scope and range of applications of the techniques are much too wide to allow them to be discussed in any great depth here, and interested readers are referred to the various books that have been

Figure 6.3 Chemistry pupils playing a typical educational
game — 'Formulon' (a card game designed to reinforce understanding
of how elements and ions combine to form chemical compounds)

written on the subject. (Ellington, Addinall and Percival, for example,
have written a number of books on the design and educational uses
of games and simulations, and other useful books have been written
by Tansey and Unwin, Boocock and Schild, and Taylor and Walford,
to name but a few — see the Bibliography for details.)

The different types of exercise
In an educational or training context, *games* are exercises which involve
competition and have set rules. The term covers an extremely wide
range of exercises — everything from simple card and board games
to large-scale management games and sophisticated competitions.
When playing a game in a group learning situation, the participants,
acting either individually or in co-operation with others, use their
skills and knowledge to compete with one another in order to 'win'.

Simulations, on the other hand, are exercises that involve an on-going
representation of some aspect(s) of a real situation of some sort. In
many cases, they involve the members of a group in taking part in
role-play, during which each member acts out the part of another
person such as a lawyer, local councillor, trade union representative
or conservationist.

Finally, *case studies* are exercises in which the members of a group
have to carry out an in-depth study of a process, situation, event,
document, etc in order to examine its special characteristics, characteristics that either may be limited to the particular case under examination

or may be general features of the broad set or class to which it belongs. Obvious examples are the group discussions of specific cases that are carried out in the context of medical or legal training, but the case study technique can also be used in a wide range of other areas.

There are also various types of 'hybrid' exercises in the game/simulation/case study field, exercises which have characteristics that are drawn from two or even all three of the basic areas that have just been described.

Simulation games, for example, have a competitive element and also involve a simulation situation, a well-known example being MONOPOLY. Other variations might involve using the actual process of playing a game as a case study in itself (in the study of probability theory, for example) or basing a case study on a simulated rather than a real situation (as in the simulated patient technique developed at McMaster University in Canada for use in the training of medical staff). Such hybrid exercises are described in detail by Ellington, Addinall and Percival in *A Handbook of Game Design* (1982).

Some advantages of games, simulations and case studies

Let us now examine some of the reasons why games, simulations and interactive case studies are useful in a group learning situation.

The techniques constitute a highly versatile and flexible medium whereby a wide variety of educational aims and objectives can be achieved. In a group situation, they can be used to achieve objectives in all parts of Bloom's cognitive and affective domains. Although the methods are no more effective than any other method when used to teach the basic facts of a subject, they have been found to be particularly valuable in teaching towards high-level cognitive objectives relating to such things as analysis, synthesis and evaluation, and also for achieving a variety of affective (attitudinal) objectives. Thus their use is often as a complement to, and a support for, more traditional teaching methods, and they can also be used for reinforcement purposes (see Figure 6.3) or to demonstrate applications or relevance.

The use of a simulated as opposed to a real situation as the basis of a group exercise allows the situation and learning experiences to be tailored to meet the needs of the group, rather than requiring the exercise to be designed within the constraints imposed by the situation. Only very rarely does a real-life situation have all the features that the designer of a case study-type exercise wishes to bring out, whereas a simulated situation can have all such features built in. Also, real-life situations are often much too complicated to be used as the basis of an educational or training group exercise as they stand; the simplification that the use of simulations allows can often overcome this difficulty by reducing the complexity to manageable proportions.

Work by Paul Twelker (see the Bibliography) has indicated that well-designed games, simulations and interactive case studies can achieve *positive transfer of learning*, that is, they can produce in participants the ability to apply skills acquired during the exercise in other situations. It would, in fact, be difficult to justify the use of many exercises of this type if no such transfer of learning occurred.

In many cases, exercises in the game/simulation/case study field constitute a vehicle whereby students can use and develop their initiative and powers of creative thought. This feature may prove increasingly important in the future if the educational system continues to place progressively greater emphasis on the cultivation of divergent thought processes.

Apart from their specifically content-related outcomes, many exercises of the type under discussion help to foster a wide range of useful skills (such as decision-making, communication and interpersonal skills) and desirable attitudinal traits (such as willingness to listen to other people's points of view, or to appreciate that most problems can be viewed in a number of different ways). Indeed, many people believe that it is in these areas that games, simulations and case studies can make their most valuable contribution to education. Exercises which have been designed to involve a high degree of interaction in the group are found to be particularly effective in this regard.

In cases where a competitive element is involved (not necessarily at the expense of co-operation), this can provide strong motivation for the participants to commit themselves wholeheartedly to the work of the exercise. This competitive element may be overt (when sub-groups or individuals are in open competition with one another) or it may be latent (as, for example, when sub-groups or individuals have to perform parallel activities and report their findings to the group as a whole).

Many exercises in this field have a basis in more than one academic discipline, a feature that can help the participants to integrate concepts from otherwise widely-related areas into a cohesive and balanced 'world picture'. Exercises which require the students to formulate value judgements (for example, weighing economic benefits against social costs) or examine problems from a number of different perspectives are particularly valuable in this respect.

Multi-disciplinary exercises have an additional advantage in that they can provide a situation in which participants with expertise in different subject areas have to work together effectively in order to achieve a common end. Interpersonal skills of this type are very import-ant in a student's later life, and constitute an area of education and training in which the multi-disciplinary simulation and simulation game may be the only means of providing practical experience in a school or college environment.

Finally, one universally-observed advantage of game/simulation/case study techniques is that student involvement and motivation are normally very high — features that are particularly beneficial when using these techniques with the less able. In addition, most participants find the approach extremely enjoyable.

Some disadvantages of games and simulations
Apart from the various organizational and attitude-related disadvantages which they share with other group learning techniques (see p 104), there are two main disadvantages that are specifically associated with games and simulations.

First, there is always a danger of using such exercises for the wrong reasons, for example using them as 'diversions' or 'time fillers' rather than for some specific educational purpose. Also, with some 'educational games', it is possible for students to play them purely as games, without deriving any worthwhile educational benefit, because the 'educational' and 'gaming' elements are not fully integrated. (A number of commercially-available card games tend to have this weakness to some extent, as do many board games.)

Second, if a game or simulation is to be of any real use in a given educational situation, it must not only be capable of achieving the desired educational outcomes but must also be properly matched to the target population with which it is to be used; in other words it must be pitched at a suitable level. It is, however, very unusual to find an exercise that is ideally suited to the purpose which the teacher/tutor has in mind, so it may be necessary to carry out a certain amount of adaptation or modification, or even to 'start from scratch' and design a completely new exercise. Obviously, this requires a certain amount of expertise and (preferably) some previous experience.

The role of the teacher
In most exercises of the game/simulation/case study-type, the role of the teacher is mainly organizational, with the actual activities that take place within the exercise being largely under the control of the students. The extent to which an exercise is pre-structured (and hence the extent of student freedom) can, however, vary considerably.

One of the most important roles of the teacher is in *debriefing* the participants after the completion of the exercise, such debriefing being absolutely vital if the full educational value is to be derived from their experience. The form of the debriefing will depend on the nature and function of the exercise concerned, but should generally include the following four elements:

1. review of the actual work of the exercise, and discussion of any important points raised by the students;
2. discussion of the relationship between the exercise and the subject matter on which it is based (for example, discussion of the degree of realism in the case of a simulation);
3. discussion of the group processes which occurred during the exercise;
4. discussion of any broad issues raised.

The debriefing session is particularly important in the case of exercises that involve role play, or which place the intrinsic subject matter in a social, political, economic or environmental context; indeed in such cases, it is often the most important part of the whole experience.

Mediated Feedback/Discussion Sessions

Another important class of group learning techniques includes all those that involve mediated feedback on and discussion of an activity of some sort. One well-known example is *microteaching*, which is widely used in the training of teachers. In microteaching, attention is focused on specific teaching skills, which the trainee teacher practices for short periods (from 5 to 20 minutes) with a small group of pupils (usually 4 to 7). The session is recorded, usually on videotape, and is then played back to the trainee teacher, normally in the presence of other trainees, in order to obtain immediate feedback and catalyse discussion of the performance. The resulting group feedback (together with the supervisor's comments and any observations made by the actual pupils) help the student teacher to analyse his performance, and thus enable him to restructure the lesson in order to teach it to a second group of pupils. Again, this is followed by immediate video replay, so that further analysis and evaluation can take place in order to identify any areas where further improvement could be made. By employing this 'teach-reteach' cycle, it is possible to give the student teacher the opportunity to put into immediate practice what he has learned from the video replay and from the peer group and other feedback on the previous attempt.

There are many variations of microteaching, and indeed, such video-replay methods for analysing performance are now used in many areas of skills training other than teaching practice. Examples include the recording of simulated interviews or other interactive situations for subsequent analysis, criticism and discussion by a class.

Some strengths of mediated feedback/discussion sessions
Use of mediated feedback followed by class or group discussion provides an ideal vehicle for in-depth examination of a whole range of situations and processes (individual presentations, simulated interviews, group dynamics situations, and so on).

Such techniques can be used to develop a wide range of useful skills, including the skills associated with the situation or process being examined and the various skills that are developed by the subsequent critical discussion (communication skills, evaluative skills, and so on).

Again, such techniques have an extremely high 'learner involvement' factor — a great educational advantage, as we have seen earlier.

Some weaknesses of such techniques
One of the main drawbacks of such techniques is that some students may well find them rather off-putting at first; thus, getting the most out of such techniques may require considerable skill and empathy on the part of the organizing teacher.

Another obvious disadvantage is that the technique requires suitable hardware to be available, and may also require back-up by technical staff. Use of techniques of this type may also cause timetabling problems, particularly if a class has to be split up for the work.

Readers who want to learn more about microteaching and similar techniques are referred to the books that have been written on the subject by Brown and by Hargie and Maidment (see the Bibliography).

Group Projects

One group learning technique that has become increasingly popular in recent years is the *group project*. Here, students carry out project work in small co-operative groups (generally containing between 3 and 6 people) rather than as individuals. Such group projects can be carried out as teaching exercises in their own right (e.g. for providing part of the practical or case study work of a course, as in Figure 6.4) or can be built into other, larger exercises (e.g. in the form of *syndicate* work).

Some strengths of group projects
Group projects can be used to achieve the same basic range of objectives as conventional practical and project work (see Chapter 4), and, in addition, help the participants to develop the various interpersonal skills that are so essential for success in later life. Furthermore, the constructive exchange of ideas and division of labour that are generally associated with group projects can make such exercises far more useful

Figure 6.4 **Students at Robert Gordon's Institute of Technology carrying out a mathematical modelling exercise as a group project**

learning experiences than individual projects, with the group being able to produce work of a quality that would probably be completely beyond even the best students if they had to work on their own.

Group projects are also ideal vehicles for cross-disciplinary work, an aspect of education that is assuming more and more importance as traditional subject barriers become less rigid than was the case in the past.

Some weaknesses of group projects
One obvious weakness of such exercises is the problem of making sure that all the members of the group play their full part in the work; in such projects, it is often all too easy for a lazy or incompetent member to 'opt out', leaving his colleagues to do all the hard work. It is therefore important to try to build into such projects measures which help ensure that everyone pulls his weight.

An associated problem is that of *assessing* a group project. While it is obviously fairly easy to assess the work of the group *as a whole*, it is generally much more difficult to assess the work of the individual members unless the group is constantly monitored by supervisory staff (something that can be counter-productive). One solution is to build an element of *peer assessment* into the assessment process, e.g. by asking every member of the group to award every other member a mark reflecting his evaluation of their respective contributions of the work.

Self-Help Groups

These arise when students meet on their own (that is, with no teacher or tutor present) in order to discuss common problems, share ideas and generally help one another by a process of *peer teaching*.

In many cases, such groups form spontaneously; in others, some encouragement from the teacher or institution may provide the necessary catalyst. Students obviously need to be motivated to participate in such groups, but the peer teaching aspect can be extremely valuable in helping them to cope with difficulties. In many distance learning courses, such as those offered by the Open University, the formation of self-help groups is actively encouraged, and, in such circumstances, can often do a great deal to help offset the isolation of independent study.

CHAPTER 7

Student Assessment

Introduction

In Chapter 1, we discussed the main features of a systematic approach to course and curriculum design, and in Chapter 3, we argued a case for the formulation of clear, unambiguous objectives as the first stage of such an approach. One cogent argument for articulating objectives in this way is that it puts a teacher in a much better position to know how to assess the attainment of each objective, since he should (as a result of writing the objective) have a fairly clear idea of the behaviour to be measured. Conversely, the feedback obtained from the results of properly-designed assessment procedures often demonstrates a need for changes in the actual objectives of the course or curriculum, as well as in the methods adopted for trying to achieve these.

In the latter situation, the results of the assessment are being used not only to assess the students, but also to help *evaluate* the teaching system itself. It is important at this stage to draw a clear distinction between the processes of assessment and evaluation, because, although the terms are often considered to be virtually synonymous when used in common parlance, they have radically different connotations when used in an educational or training context.

By *assessment*, we mean those activities that are designed to measure learner achievement brought about as a result of an instructional programme of some sort. *Evaluation*, on the other hand, refers to a series of activities that are designed to measure the effectiveness of an instructional system as a whole. Clearly, the results of student assessments may be just one of the areas of evidence that are taken into account in such a process. The role of evaluation and the different types of evaluation procedures will be discussed in detail in the following chapter, while a much fuller discussion of the relationship between assessment and evaluation can be found in a book by Derek Rowntree — *Assessing Students: How Shall We Know Them?* Rev Ed (1987).

In this chapter we will first discuss the general principles that underlie effective student assessment procedures, and will then describe a number of approaches to student assessment and test construction. We will conclude the chapter by giving a review of the range of common student assessment methods, discussing them in terms of their design characteristics, their functions and their respective strengths and weaknesses.

Desirable Characteristics of Student Assessment Procedures

We will now turn our attention to the basic features that should characterize a 'good' student assessment procedure. Such a procedure should, ideally, be *valid, reliable, practicable*, and *fair and useful* to students. Let us now discuss these in turn.

Validity

A *valid* assessment procedure is one which actually tests what it sets out to test, ie one which accurately measures the behaviour described by the objective(s) under scrutiny. Obviously, no one would *deliberately* construct an assessment item to test trivia or irrelevant material, but it is surprising just how often non-valid test items are in fact used — eg questions that are intended to test recall of factual material but which actually test the candidate's powers of reasoning, or questions which assume a level of pre-knowledge that the candidates do not possess.

As we will see later in the review of assessment methods, validity-related problems are a common weakness of many of the more widely-used methods. For example, a simple science question given to 14-year-old schoolchildren ('Name the products of the combustion of carbon in an adequate supply of oxygen') produced a much higher number of correct answers when the word 'combustion' was replaced by 'burning'. This showed that the original question had problems of validity in that it was, to some extent, testing language and vocabulary skills rather than the basic science involved.

Reliability

The *reliability* of an assessment procedure is a measure of the consistency with which the question, test or examination produces the same results under different but comparable conditions. A reliable assessment item gives reproducible scores with similar populations of students, and is therefore as independent of the characteristics and vagaries of individual markers as possible; this is often difficult to achieve in practice.

It is obviously important to have reasonably reliable assessment procedures when a large number of individual markers assess the same question (eg in national school examinations). A student answer which receives a score of 75 per cent from one marker and 35 per cent from another, for example, reveals a patently unreliable assessment procedure.

To help produce reliability, the questions which comprise a student assessment should (ideally) test only one thing at a time and give the candidates no choice. The assessment should also adequately reflect the objectives of the teaching unit. Note that the reliability and validity factors in an assessment are in no way directly linked — a test or examination, for example, may be totally reliable and yet have very low validity, and vice versa.

Practicability

For most purposes, assessment procedures should be realistically *practical* in terms of their cost, time taken, and ease of application. For example, with a large class of technicians being trained in electrical circuitry, it may be convenient to use only a paper-and-pencil test rather than set up numerous practical testing situations. It should be noted, however, that such compromises can, in some cases, greatly reduce the validity of the assessment.

Fairness and Usefulness

To be fair to all students, an assessment must accurately reflect the range of expected behaviours as described by the course objectives. It is also highly desirable that students should know exactly *how* they are to be assessed. Indeed, it could be argued that students have a *right* to information such as the nature of the materials on which they are to be examined (ie content and objectives), the form and structure of the examination, the length of the examination, and the value (in terms of marks) of each component of the course.

Also, students should (ideally!) find assessments useful. Feedback from assessment can give a student a much better indication of his or her current strengths and weaknesses than he or she might otherwise have. In this respect, the non-return of assessment work to students greatly reduces its utility.

Criterion-Referenced and Norm-Referenced Assessment

Two contrasting general approaches to student assessment are *criterion-referenced* and *norm-referenced assessment.*

Criterion-referenced assessment involves testing students in order to measure their performance in tasks described by a particular objective or set of objectives (the criterion). In any systems approach to education or training (which is invariably geared towards the achievement of clearly-specified objectives), it is normal to use some kind of criterion-referenced test for student assessment. In such a test, the *relative* performances of the various individuals in the class are of little consequence — indeed, in the unlikely event of the whole class demonstrating complete mastery of the objectives, this would simply indicate that a highly-successful teaching/learning system had been developed.

A good example of a criterion-referenced test is the standard driving test, in which the learner driver has to demonstrate a certain level of competence before being allowed to 'pass'. His or her performance relative to other learner drivers should (in principle) be of no consequence. This approach contrasts sharply with *norm-referenced assessment*, which is altogether more competitive. Norm-referenced assessment involves tests of ability or attainment which are intended to probe differences between individual students, and hence to determine the extent to which each individual's performance differs from the performance of others of similar age and background.

In cases where there is a choice of questions in a norm-referenced test, a need is highlighted for *standardization* of scores for comparison purposes. A typical norm-referenced test may have a fixed pass rate (say 55 per cent) which is strictly adhered to, no matter how high or how low is the general level of attainment. This is, on the face of it, a much less fair approach to assessment than criterion-referenced assessment, since only *relative* attainment, not *absolute* attainment, is recognized. However, the approach is widely used – in many national school examinations and professional examinations, for example.

Basically, criterion-referenced assessment and norm-referenced assessment differ in the *purpose* for which the assessment is carried out, the *style* in which the component tests are constructed, and, finally, in the *use* to which the information derived from the results of the assessment is put.

In the remainder of this chapter, we will attempt to demonstrate the role of assessment techniques in a general systems approach to course design. Thus, our main concern will be with criterion-referenced assessment related to the attainment of pre-specified objectives and identifiable behaviours.

Test Construction

As mentioned earlier in this chapter, a student assessment should be directly geared towards the stated course objectives (while remembering that not all objectives are formally assessable, yet may nevertheless be very important). The attainment of assessable objectives may be measured in a relatively sporadic programme of *set examinations*, or, more consistently (and possibly less stressfully for students), by some form of *continuous assessment* procedure. However it is done, it is likely that a *combination* of assessment techniques will be necessary in order to assess the range of objectives under investigation validly and comprehensively.

In order to ensure that particular sets of skills are being assessed, some individuals and organizations have drawn up 'tables of specifications' for tests to ensure that due weight is given to all skills and content areas. For example, Figure 7.1 is a typical specification of the cognitive skills to be assessed in the UK Ordinary National

Subject and topic	Ability				
	Recall	Comprehension	Non-routine application	Analysis/ evaluation	Totals
Inorganic chemistry Revision and					
extension	7	6	4	6	23
Chemical reactions	8	10	2	0	20
Group I and II elements	5	10	2	2	19
Group VII elements	5	10	2	2	19
Group V elements	5	10	2	2	19
Totals	**30**	**46**	**12**	**12**	**100**
Organic chemistry Nomenclature	3	2	0	0	5
Stereochemistry	1	6	2	0	9
Hydrocarbons	5	7	4	2	18
Halogen derivatives	1	6	3	0	10
Hydroxyl compounds	2	8	3	2	15
Carbonyl compounds	3	10	3	3	19
Acids and derivatives	3	6	2	1	12
Bases	2	6	2	2	12
Totals	**20**	**51**	**19**	**10**	**100**
Physical chemistry Gases	4	5	3	1	13
Solutions	8	9	6	3	26
Thermodynamics	3	4	2	1	10
Chemical equilibrium	3	3	2	2	10
Electrochemistry	6	7	4	2	19
Ionic equilibria	6	7	6	3	22
Totals	**30**	**35**	**23**	**12**	**100**

Figure 7.1 **Typical tables of specifications for the UK Ordinary National Certificate (ONC) examinations in chemistry**

Certificate (ONC) in chemistry. The course syllabus is written in the form of behavioural objectives, and the specification is given in terms of Bloom's classification of educational objectives (which was discussed in Chapter 3) and the various areas of course content. Tables of this sort, while perhaps a little rigid, do enable exam setters to design assessments to cover the full range of skills (in this case, cognitive skills) that are under scrutiny, and to promote good syllabus coverage. They also ensure that certain skills (eg factual recall) are not over-emphasized, and that due attention is paid to higher cognitive skills.

The type and range of techniques used within a given assessment strategy will depend upon a number of factors — the most important (at least from an educational point of view) being the student behaviours that are specified in the objectives being tested. The basic characteristics of the range of commonly-used assessment methods will now be discussed, together with their respective advantages and limitations.

A Review of Student Assessment Methods

Student assessment methods can have a wide variety of forms. The most common general approach is via some form of written response, ie the 'paper-and-pencil' approach. This approach encompasses a whole range of 'traditional' assessment methods such as *essay-type questions, short notes questions* and *problem-solving questions*, all of which require an extended written response of some sort.

Another form of 'paper-and-pencil' approach involves the use of *objective tests*, although such tests seldom involve the student in writing very much; in most cases, a mark made beside one of a range of possible options, or a single word answer, is all that is required. Also, the word 'objective', when used in the 'objective test' context, can be somewhat confusing, since it neither means that the questions are necessarily related to the course objectives, nor implies that the questions are objectively chosen. The term simply indicates that the answers to such questions can be marked *totally reliably* by anybody, including non-subject specialists, and, in some cases, even by a computer. The most common type of objective question is the *multiple-choice question* (or, more correctly, *multiple-choice item*), together with its range of variations. Other types of objective questions include *completion items, unique-answer questions*, and *structural communication tests.*

Practical tests are often used to assess psychomotor objectives, and include such techniques as *project assessment, assessment of laboratory work*, and other *skill-tests* designed to assess specific manipulative skills. Also in this category are *situational assessment* techniques, which involve students using non-cognitive skills (such as decision-making skills) in a real, or (more likely) in a simulated environment.

There is a range of *unobtrusive assessment* techniques which can take place without the student necessarily being aware that he is in fact being assessed. Finally, variations of self and peer assessment are currently being researched and used.

Let us now look at each of these techniques in turn, starting with traditional paper-and-pencil tests that involve extended writing of some sort.

Traditional 'Extended Writing' Tests

As we have seen, the most common test techniques that fall into this category are *essay-type questions, short notes questions* and *problem-solving questions.* Let us therefore examine these in turn.

Essay-type questions

Essay-type questions are often considered to be one of the 'bluntest' instruments of assessment, having very low reliability and, in many cases, low validity. Often, in a single question, the setter attempts to test *knowledge, reasoning, written communication skills* (including English language skills, and, perhaps, graphical skills and mathematical skills), *creative thinking abilities*, and *interpretation* (not only of the question itself, but often of the implied objectives of the setter). All these factors and skills are interwoven in an extremely complicated matrix, and much is left to the judgement (or caprice!) of the marker. Even with the best of intentions, it is almost impossible to tease these skills out and mark them independently. Even when an *assessment grid* is used, thus enabling the various components of the essay to be marked independently, research has shown that inter-marker reliability is still very poor, with markers varying widely in their scoring of this kind of question. Despite this, essays do have a number of points in their favour.

(a) They give students an opportunity to organize their ideas and express them in their own words. Also, scope is provided for the demonstration of written communication skills and for the expression of unconventional and creative thinking. (These opportunities are, however, often lost when 'essays' consist simply of regurgitated class notes).

(b) They allow students to display a detailed knowledge of related aspects of the course being assessed, as well as a knowledge of relevant topics outwith the course proper.

(c) The questions are relatively easy to set.

(d) Many teachers and users of the results of assessments (eg employers) hold the opinion that student tests and examinations should contain at least an element of essay writing (except, perhaps, in mathematical subjects).

Balanced against these advantages, however, are many disadvantages, some of the main ones being listed below.

(a) Essay questions are exceedingly difficult to mark reliably, and, with only one marker, the subjective element can be considerable. The correlation between the scores of two markers for the same set of answers on different occasions is seldom sufficiently high to justify confidence. Essays are also very time-consuming to mark, especially if the marker adds comments and criticisms in order to provide feedback for the student.

(b) Only a small number of long essays can be answered in a given time, thus effectively restricting the assessment to a few (often student-selected) areas of the course content. Other equally-important areas may be completely neglected, and the total mark may therefore be an unreliable index of the student's grasp of the course as a whole. Also, in an examination which consists of a limited number of essays, luck in 'spotting' questions beforehand is often a significant factor.

(c) Where there is a choice of questions, this enables different students to answer, in effect, different papers, so the same total mark may not represent comparable performances. This will almost certainly be the case when the questions vary in difficulty, in content, in the types of skills involved, and are scored by different markers. For example, a '5 from 8' paper contains a total of no less than 56 different combinations in which the 5 questions can be selected!

(d) Occasionally, students may not appreciate the true intent of an essay question because of inadequate directions (eg 'Write an essay on proteins'). Markers then have the choice of ignoring the answer, accepting the student's interpretation as an answer to a question which was not intended, or adopting an uneasy compromise. Clearly, this adds neither to the reliability nor to the validity of the assessment.

(e) Irrelevant factors often intrude into the assessment, eg speed of handwriting (especially with restricted time), style and clarity of handwriting, and grammatical errors.

Short Notes Questions
In cases where 'short notes' on a subject or topic are required, rather than an extended essay, many of the problems associated with long-essay questions are reduced, although not necessarily eradicated. 'Short notes' questions should (in principle) be more valid and reliable than essay questions, because the marker is able to concentrate more sharply on particular aspects of the answer. In addition, they allow wider coverage of course content, and are generally more specific.

However, although reliability is increased, some deviation in scores may still occur between markers. Also, course coverage may still not be adequate, and students' individual written and presentational skills may again cloud the validity of the questions.

Problem-solving questions
Problem-solving questions are an excellent method of testing some of the middle-to-higher cognitive skills (such as comprehension, application and analysis), and for demonstrating extended reasoning skills. Mathematical, scientific and engineering subjects, in particular, lend themselves readily to assessments of this sort.

With such questions, validity may well be high, but problems of reliability may arise in respect of the marking of partially-solved problems, or answers in which an error is made.

Objective Tests

Objective tests are assessment procedures which can be marked totally reliably. Although such items are often criticized on account of assessing only at low intellectual levels, this is not necessarily the case. It is possible (although more difficult) to design items to test skills in the higher cognitive areas, and even to test logical thinking and skills related to structuring arguments.

Before looking at the characteristics of specific techniques of objective testing in more detail, we will summarize the main advantages and disadvantages of using objective tests in general.

Some of the main points in favour of objective tests are listed below.

(a) The tests can be marked with complete inter-marker reliability.

(b) Large numbers of questions can be answered, thus ensuring a thorough sampling of course objectives and content.

(c) Objective items can be designed to test specific abilities in a controlled way.

(d) The difficulty of the items is often known from trial-testing. Hence, by selection of appropriate items, the difficulty level of the test can be adjusted to meet particular requirements.

(e) Items can be 'banked' and re-used.

(f) There is no need to provide a choice of questions for the students, and, indeed, this is not desirable, since it tends to reduce validity.

(g) Tests lend themselves to inexpensive and easy marking, and also to thorough statistical analysis. This allows investigation of individual difficulties, and also permits the general problem areas of the student population as a whole to be identified.

Against these advantages, objective items have the following disadvantages:

(a) They are very difficult and initially expensive to construct, and considerable preparation time is necessary. Their *apparent* ease of construction often leads to amateurish attempts, resulting in very poor, invalid items. (This, in turn, has been responsible for some of the criticisms levelled at objective tests.) Expert advice is often required in designing items, and all items should be pre-tested in order to measure their level of difficulty and the extent to which they discriminate between the better and poorer students in a given population.

(b) The teacher or marker cannot see the reasoning behind the choice of a wrong answer.

(c) It is difficult or impossible to construct tests to assess certain high-level abilities such as extended reasoning and written communication ability. Thus objective tests are probably best suited for testing lower cognitive skills, and items at these levels are certainly the easiest to write.

Let us now look at the different types of objective test items that can be used.

Multiple-choice items
Multiple-choice items are probably the most widely used component of

objective tests. Several variations on the multiple-choice theme are possible, such as when several items arise out of one situation, graph or set of figures. A number of references to sources of further information on the construction of multiple-choice items are given in the Bibliography.

The advantages and disadvantages of objective items in general (as listed above) apply in full to multiple-choice items.

An example of a multiple-choice item that is designed to test knowledge is given below:

Which city is the capital of Australia?
  (a) Melbourne
  (b) Brisbane
  (c) Sydney
  (d) Canberra.

Multiple-choice objective testing has its own associated jargon, the most common terms being as follows:

Stem: the introductory part of the question out of which the alternative answers arise. Ideally this should be a self-contained question containing all the basic information which the student needs in order to respond to the item, so that he or she does not need to read through the options to discover what is being asked. The stem should be concise, should use unambiguous language appropriate to the student's ability, and should avoid negatives if at all possible.

Options: the range of possible answers. The options should be parallel in content and structure, ie they should all have the same kind of relationship to the stem, and should all follow grammatically from it. Obviously, the item should not contain clues in the structure of the options (eg mixtures of plurals and singulars).

Key: the correct answer. This must be unarguably correct; hence the option 'all of these' should never be used.

Distractors: the wrong answers. These must be unarguably incorrect answers, yet should appear plausible to weaker students.

Non-functioning distractors: those distractors which attract less than 5 per cent of the responses. When an item is re-written, an attempt should be made to replace such distractors with more plausible ones.

Facility value (FV): the fraction (normally expressed as a decimal) of the candidates choosing the key in any given item. Thus, if half the students answer correctly, the facility value for that item is 0.50. In tests of achievement designed to rank students in order of merit, the facility value should lie between 0.35 and 0.85, since very difficult or very easy items do not normally contribute to the role of such a test.

Discrimination index: a figure which represents the degree to which the item separates the better students from the poorer students, since a 'good' item (particularly in an achievement test) is one which the better students should get right and the poorer students should get wrong. There are several ways in which the discrimination index can be calculated, but one of the simplest is to calculate the difference between the facility values for the top third of the population (on the test as a whole) and for the bottom third for each item under consideration.

The discrimination index can obviously never be greater than +1.0, and should always be greater than +0.2 for a 'good' item. A negative discrimination index is a sign of a very poor item that should be either discarded or revised.

When there is a choice of pre-tested items of known quality, the facility values and discrimination indices chosen will depend on whether the test is meant to be of a simple 'pass/fail' type, is meant to produce a meaningful class ranking, is meant to serve as a diagnostic instrument providing feedback on progress for students, or is designed to help evaluate the efficiency of a teaching/learning system.

Completion items and unique-answer questions

In both these types of assessment question, the student must *supply* the answer rather than select from a set of choices provided. Examples are given below:

Completion item: The United States equivalent to the British House of Commons is known as the . . . . '

Unique-answer question: 'What is the equivalent temperature in degrees Centigrade to 185° Fahrenheit? . . . . '

In both these cases the answer is unique, and so the test can be marked reliably; it has, however, to be marked manually. In such items, skills can be examined one at a time, eg mastery skills (recall, using formulae, simple calculations, etc), organizing skills (categorizing, etc) and interpretation skills (of graphs, tables, etc). Such items can, in fact, be set at surprisingly high cognitive levels. Again, relatively full and representative coverage of course objectives and content is possible, since only very short written answers are required.

Structural communication testing

This is a fairly recent development in objective testing in which an attempt is made to carry out a reliable test of a student's ability to select relevant information from irrelevant information and to present structured arguments logically.

Basically, students are presented with a grid containing statements pertaining to a particular topic, all of which are factually correct. The grid can contain any number of statements, but 16 or 20 are typical. Students are then asked questions on the topic, to which only *some* of the statements are pertinent. The student has to select from the grid the *relevant* pieces of information to answer the question(s), and then has to *arrange them in a logical order*, in order to present the argument. Allowance in the scoring can be made if several logical sequences are permissible. In some cases, structural communication testing can be computer-marked.

Practical Tests

Practical tests are highly appropriate in cases when the development of psychomotor or manipulative skills is an important part of a course. Their main drawbacks are that they may be logistically difficult to arrange and administer, and may have low reliability. However, the face validity of actually performing a set task would seem to be high compared (for example) with giving a simple written description of how the task *should* be performed.

Let us now examine some of the most important types of practical test.

Project assessment

In such assessment, a student may be assessed in terms of his or her cumulative work over a period of time, or perhaps on only the end result of the project, such as a working model, the results of a set of experiments, or a computer program. Such assessment can also be carried out on *groups* of students who have collaborated on a group project of some sort. However, this can give rise to problems in assessing the contributions made by the different members of the group unless some form of *peer assessment* is used.

Assessment of laboratory work

In cases where the development of manipulative laboratory skills are important (eg in science courses), assessment of actual laboratory work may be carried out. This usually takes the form of continuous assessment over a period of time or a one-off practical examination at the end of a course or section thereof. The latter has the disadvantage that it may be unfair to students who have an 'off-day', and also to students who react badly to exam pressure but have otherwise performed well during the course. From the marker's point of view, it can also be exceedingly difficult to monitor the progress of even a small number of students effectively during such an examination.

Skill tests

Tests of the ability to carry out specific manipulative tasks may be important in some courses, eg dismantling and reassembling a car engine, cutting hair in a particular way, or repairing a piece of technical equipment. For each of these, a suitable practical test can generally be devised, depending on the circumstances. Such tests are more common in 'training' courses than in general educational courses, however.

Situational assessment

Procedures of this type stem originally from management education, and involve the appraisal of complex decision-making skills. They may involve the student in performing such activities as dictating letters, dealing with personnel problems, formulating agendas, and dealing with budgets or financial problems. The situations that are used in such assessment are normally simulated, and a whole range of activities and crises can be 'built in' to arise in the same way as they might in the real world. Such an approach is often called an *'in-tray'* exercise.

Again, the validity of such a technique would appear to be high, but care must be taken in marking the performance in order to ensure reasonable reliability. To this end, a checklist containing the objectives under assessment provides a useful guide for the marker.

Unobtrusive Assessment

Unobtrusive techniques involve the students being observed and assessed without their prior knowledge. Such techniques can be important in assessing a student's *commitment* and *attitudes* to work, rather than simply his ability to perform tasks under the controlled conditions of more formal assessment. They can, therefore, be more valid than (for example) written examinations, which invariably contain a large element of artificiality. On some occasions, video techniques are used for recording student performance, and for subsequent analysis and assessment of personal skills and traits. However, there are often considerable logistical problems in operating such an approach, not to mention the obvious doubts over the ethics of unobtrusive assessment.

Self and Peer Assessment

The concept of allowing students to assess their own work and the work of other students is gaining considerable ground in educational and training circles. The arguments in favour of *self assessment* include that we should be encouraging students to become more self-critical and more able to judge the worth of their own work. After all, it is likely they will be expected to do this in later work situations. Experience in the use of self assessment has not resulted in the, perhaps expected, finding that students overmark themselves compared to tutor marking. Indeed the correlation is very good, and, if anything, students tend to mark themselves *downwards* and are often extremely critical of their own work. Obviously, preparation is required before such a scheme can be adopted, involving, among other things, negotiation between tutors and students regarding the criteria for assessment and their relative weighting.

Peer assessment is mainly used in group-based projects or other collaborative exercises, when students may mark each other in respect of their contribution to the combined work. Again, negotiation of criteria is necessary, and there is again the possibility of mutual overmarking, although experience so far indicates this is not an overriding problem, and it is argued that the benefits of increased motivation and self-awareness outweigh such worries.

Summary

If one has an area of course content, a list of objectives and an exam specification of required skills, it should be possible to construct a valid programme of assessment by selecting those objectives which can be tested by objective items, those which require short written notes, those which require to be assessed in a practical setting, and those which lie in the area of attitudes and disposition. The few objectives left over (eg those involving extended reasoning or written communication skills) may then need essay-type questions. If everything else has been dealt with by more appropriate methods, the marker can concentrate comparatively single-mindedly on these few areas in the essays, thus tending to make marking more reliable.

In short, an appropriate *battery* of assessment techniques should be used to match specific objectives, thus producing a *practicable* assessment strategy that not only has a high degree of *validity* and *reliability*, but is also *fair and useful to students*.

CHAPTER 8

Evaluation

Introduction

In the previous chapter, we distinguished between assessment and evaluation by describing the former as those activities that are designed to measure *student learning* achieved as a result of a teaching/learning situation, and the latter as a series of activities that are designed to measure the *effectiveness of a teaching/learning system* as a whole. However, we noted that the results of student assessment may well form part of the wider evaluation process.

Within the systematic approach to instructional design which was described in Chapter 1 and which is argued for throughout this book, the role of on-going monitoring and evaluation of the system is of vital importance to its development and evolution. Because of the cyclical and interactive nature of the systems approach, each cycle can benefit from the experiences and feedback obtained from previous cycles. Evaluative feedback can be gained from a wide range of sources and via a wide range of methods, and, in many cases, a whole battery of evaluation techniques are used in order to gain an overall view of the effectiveness of the instructional system in question. Whether this is a complete course, part of a course, a particular teaching session, a self-contained programme, or a teaching aid such as a film or video, the designer (or team of designers) should never be happy with their first attempt, or even with revised versions. If one takes the view that 'the system can always be improved', on-going evaluation should always be an integral part of the design process.

The scope and depth of the evaluation that is carried out in any particular case will vary according to the nature of the situation, as, indeed, will the evaluation methods used. Whatever the circumstances, however, the importance of using evaluation procedures to monitor the instructional system and provide the basis for improvements cannot be underestimated. Feedback obtained from critical evaluation of an instructional system should shed light on the appropriateness of the *teaching methods* used, the *structure* adopted, the *implementation strategy*, the *student assessment methods*, and even the *aims and objectives* themselves. With each successive cycle of the system, the teaching/learning situation should become progressively more finely 'tuned', and should consequently become *more efficient* and *more effective* through a continuous process of evolution and improvement.

In this chapter, we will first describe more fully the philosophy that underlies the role of evaluation in the evolution of instructional processes. In order to do this, we will adopt the basic 'error elimination' approach advocated by the philosopher Karl Popper and adapt it for use in the on-going development of instructional systems. We will then describe two contrasting paradigms (or models) of evaluation — one of which concentrates mainly on the *outcomes* of an instructional system (the *agricultural/botanical* or *scientific approach*), and one which pays more attention to what happens during the educational process itself (the *social/anthropological* or *illuminative approach*). Finally, we will review the range of diagnostic techniques which are commonly used as part of an evaluation strategy, and discuss the evaluation of cost-effectiveness.

Instructional Development by Error Elimination — A 'Popperian' Approach

The philosopher Karl Popper originally used the concept of 'error elimination' to explain how progress is made in developing scientific theories. The same concept can be applied to the logical development and improvement of instructional systems of all kinds. (See the Bibliography for details of Karl Popper's work.)

Underlying Rationale

The 'error elimination' approach to the development of instructional systems is based on two assumptions: first, that the instructional system is not an independent entity, justifying its existence *a priori*, but is part of a total system — fulfilling a specific function by helping to get from Situation A to Situation B as in the diagram below:

Situation A		*Situation B*
Students thought capable of achieving certain objectives, but lacking some or all of the necessary knowledge, skills and attitudes	▶ Instructional system designed to supply all or part of the necessary education and/or training ▶	Qualified people who have achieved the specified objectives, and can proceed to the next stage of education or training (or take their place in society)

The second assumption is that the development and improvement of the instructional system can most effectively be tackled by adopting the general methodological approach proposed by Karl Popper, an approach that can be summarized by the following schema:

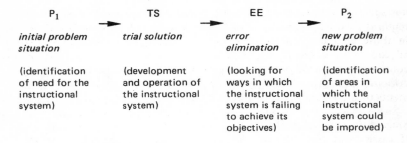

P_1	TS	EE	P_2
initial problem situation	*trial solution*	*error elimination*	*new problem situation*
(identification of need for the instructional system)	(development and operation of the instructional system)	(looking for ways in which the instructional system is failing to achieve its objectives)	(identification of areas in which the instructional system could be improved)

Stages in the Development of an Instructional System

We can see that there are four general stages in the above approach.

Stage 1: the identification of the initial 'problem situation' (P_1)
This itself can be seen as having three sequential stages:

(a) Identification of the desired objectives (knowledge, skills and attitudes) — let us call these X.
(b) Identification of the relevant knowledge, skills and attitudes already possessed by the prospective students — let us call these Y.
(c) Identification of the objectives represented by X-Y, the gap to be bridged by the instructional system.

Stage 2: development and operation of the instructional system (TS)
This falls into two sub-stages:

(a) Designing an instructional system capable of achieving the objectives represented by X-Y (or at least a part of the difference). This involves developing the overall structure, selecting and sequencing the content, choosing appropriate teaching methods, and so on.
(b) Making appropriate administrative arrangements to put the instructional system into operation (ie implementation of the system).

Stage 3: the 'error elimination' process (EE)
This stage involves carrying out a *critical analysis* of stages 1 and 2. It is the key stage in Popper's methodology, according to which a new instructional system can be regarded in the same way as a new scientific theory which has been developed in an attempt to resolve a specific problem situation, but which has not yet been subjected to rigorous experimental testing. According to Popper, such a theory should be tested not by trying to prove it *right* (an impossible task from a logical point of view) but by trying to prove it *wrong*, ie by looking for specific ways in which the theory can be shown to be incompatible with experimental evidence. In the case of a new instructional system, the testing should be carried out not by trying to prove that it is succeeding in achieving its objectives (a very difficult task to do with any degree of rigour) but by looking for ways in which it is manifestly

not succeeding (a much easier task). Needless to say, such an approach requires a healthy attitude towards criticism that is sometimes lacking in those who develop and operate educational and training courses; all too often, these try to defend their course against criticism by contrived arguments and rationalization rather than accepting valid criticism and attempting to rectify the situation through improvements to the instructional system.

Stage 4: identification of the new 'problem situation' (P_2)
If carried out correctly, stage 3 should reveal areas in which the instructional system needs to be improved, and (hopefully) point to how these improvements might be carried out. It therefore leads to a new problem situation, P_2, that can form the starting point of a further development cycle.

$$P_2 \longrightarrow TS \longrightarrow EE \longrightarrow P_3$$

Thus, Popper's methodology is seen to be both open-ended and ongoing, forming a basis for the continuous development of instructional systems of all types.

How the Error Elimination Process may be Carried Out

There are two basic questions that should be asked of an instructional system:

1. Are there any ways in which the instructional system is manifestly failing to achieve its design objectives?
2. Are there any ways in which the organization and logistics of the instructional system are unsatisfactory?

Finding answers to question 1 is essentially a long-term process and can be done:

(a) by surveying students who have undergone the instructional system (ie former students); and
(b) by surveying people who are not directly involved in the instructional system under scrutiny, but who nevertheless may have relevant comments and observations, eg employers who subsequently take on the students, or the teachers and organizers of any subsequent courses or training situations to which the students proceed.

Finding answers to question 2 is usually easier, and can be done:

(a) by surveying the staff who are involved in implementing the instructional system; and
(b) by surveying the students who are involved in the system.

Techniques through which the above information can be obtained are reviewed later in this chapter.

Two Contrasting Paradigms of Evaluation

A major area of debate in educational evaluation is concerned with the relative merits of two distinctly contrasting approaches. On the one hand, there is the so-called *agricultural/botanical approach*, which reflects a 'scientific' approach to evaluation; on the other, there is the *social/anthropological approach*, which is more concerned with the hidden *processes* which occur during an educational experience. The latter approach has become known as *illuminative evaluation*.

The *agricultural/botanical approach* has its origins in scientific experiments set up to assess the effects of specific variables (the nature of the soil, fertilizers, etc) on the growth of crops. Such experiments have tight controls, and the resulting outcomes can be measured relatively easily. When applied to education, this approach has led to the use of systematic, objectives-oriented evaluation procedures. This 'traditional' strategy sets out to measure the extent to which a given instructional system has achieved certain specific goals (its objectives) in relation to the students' pre-knowledge or existing skills. To this extent, the agricultural/botanical evaluation approach measures *output* against *input*, and often treats the differences statistically. Other factors in the system, such as the learning environment, teaching personnel, course content and structure, and teaching methods, normally receive only incidental examination if they are considered at all. This general approach has been used when measuring the relative efficiency of different methods in teaching towards a common end, and also to measure the effectiveness of self-instructional programmes in achieving stated objectives.

By comparison, the *social/anthopological approach* is more concerned with studying the on-going process of education, and, in general, the techniques used are far more subjective and often involve personal value judgements of the results. The arguments in favour of this type of approach are that the variables in educational developments cannot be readily identified or controlled, and that 'inputs' and 'outputs' can be varied, complex, difficult to specify with certainty, and often virtually impossible to measure. In such cases, the evaluator explores the perceptions, opinions and attitudes of staff and students, using a variety of methods, in an attempt to reveal what was otherwise hidden in the educational process. The evaluation process is generally not rigidly structured or constrained, and usually gives the evaluator scope to follow up specific areas of interest as and when they become apparent. Illuminative evaluation of this kind has been referred to as 'attempting to open up the black box of the educational process'. Malcolm Parlett and David Hamilton, amongst others, have been influential in presenting the case for a greater emphasis on illuminative evaluation. (See the bibliography.)

These two basic paradigms of evaluation differ significantly both in their methodologies and in their treatment of results. They also differ in their focus. The agricultural/botanical approach is basically designed to find out if *specified goals* have been achieved. The social/anthrop-oligical approach, on the other hand, is more flexible, and is designed to find out *what* has been achieved and *why*.

Clearly, there must be some middle ground between what, on the one hand, purports to be a purely objective approach, and the largely subjective approach that is embodied in illuminative evaluation. Where the correct balance lies, however, depends to a large extent on what is being evaluated, and for what purpose. A useful review of how appropriate evaluation strategies can be matched with different types of educational development has been given by Tony Becher (1981) — see the Bibliography for details.

A Review of Evaluation Techniques

There is no *single* correct way to conduct an evaluation exercise. One may, for example, be looking for outcomes (whether intended or not) in cognitive, affective and skills areas, and also for an insight into possible problems concerning the implementation and operation of an instructional system. Much depends also on whether one is adopting an 'illuminative' strategy or a more rigid 'objectives-based' approach.

Because of the variety of information that one may be seeking during an evaluation, it is normally advisable to use an appropriate *battery* of evaluation techniques. Some of the possible information sources are listed below:

(a) Results from student assessment.
(b) Student questionnaires and interviews.
(c) Observations of the instructional system in progress.
(d) Feedback from teaching staff directly involved with the instructional system.
(e) Feedback from people having an indirect link with the instructional system.

Each of these approaches generally has an important part to play, regardless of whether the evaluation is of a course or unit of teaching that is still in the process of development (*formative evaluation*) or of a fully-developed instructional system that is already in use (*summative evaluation*).

Let us look at each of these sources in more detail.

Results from Student Assessment

When an instructional system has sharply-defined objectives, a critical study of the results obtained from student assessment (as described in the previous chapter) can be of great assistance in the error elimination process described above. Two basic techniques can be used.

Analysis of student assessments that form a part of the instructional system
When student assessments are an integral part of a course or other

instructional system, the results of and trends indicated by these assessments can usually shed considerable light on the operation of the system as a whole. The evaluator should, as a result, be able to judge which objectives are being well achieved, and, more importantly, which objectives are *not*. When students do not perform as well as expected, there is a traditional tendency to conclude that it is basically the fault of the students. This may occasionally be the case, but, more often than not, there are other factors involved. A systematic approach to instructional design allows *all* aspects of the system to be analysed, and may reveal that there are in fact a number of reasons for unsatisfactory student achievement, for example:

(a)   the teaching methods were not well matched to the course objectives;
(b)   there were problems in the operation of the instructional system;
(c)   the assessment methods used were not suitable
(d)   the objectives themselves were not realistic.

Critical analysis of this sort allows the instructional system to be continuously monitored and progressively 'tuned'.

Analysis of student assessments carried out solely for evaluation purposes
When an instructional package of some sort is being trial tested, or when the relative effectiveness of two methods is being measured, specially designed student assessment techniques can be used to evaluate the effectiveness of the *methods* involved, rather than to assess the *students* themselves. Such approaches are normally essentially 'agricultural/botanical' in nature, and often involve the use of pre- and post-tests, 'control' groups, and statistical analysis of differences. They are one of the standard methods of evaluating new systems, techniques, packages, etc.

Student Questionnaires and Interviews

Obtaining feedback from students regarding their experiences and their opinions of an instructional system is one of the most common approaches to evaluation. The information can be sought through *questionnaires* and/or *interviews*, and can be treated either objectively or in a more illuminative manner. Student feedback can be obtained through a variety of so-called 'self-reporting' techniques. Several of these have been adopted from the field of attitude measurement. Let us now examine some of the more important of these techniques.

Likert scales
Essentially, a Likert rating scale is an attitude measurement instrument consisting of a list of statements, the person responding having to make a judgement on each statement, often selecting one response from a number of degrees of agreement and disagreement. A typical example is shown below:

	Strongly agree	Agree	Disagree	Strongly disagree
1. I find the course easy				
2. The course contains too many lectures				

etc

The number of points on the scale depends on the specific requirements of the setter, although the use of an even number of options has the advantage of making it impossible for students to 'duck the issues' by repeatedly taking refuge in a completely neutral category.

In practice, it is harder to produce 'good' statements than it first appears, and some trial testing of the statements may well be necessary. Indeed, there is a fair amount of skill associated with preparing statements which are *valid* and which, at the same time, provide good discrimination.

Likert scales can be used to monitor students' general opinions of an instructional system. It is also possible to use such statements for comparative purposes, eg by pre- and post-testing the students, or by comparing an 'experimental' group with a matched 'control' group.

Semantic differential scales
This is another type of attitude scale, and it can be used to measure connotations of any given concept for an individual. Here, word pairs of antonyms such as 'valuable/worthless' are joined by a 3, 4, 5, 6 or 7 point scale. The method is based upon the premise that the word pairs are opposites, although this may not always be valid in practice, because particular words sometimes have different meanings for different students. Part of a typical semantic differential scale of the type used in course evaluation is shown below.

I consider the course to be: (mark appropriate box on each row of scale)

easy							difficult
inflexible							flexible
too theoretical							too applied
poorly structured							well structured

Objectives rating scales

Student ratings of the degree of achievement of learning objectives is sometimes used in student feedback questionnaires. Here, the objectives of an instructional system are listed, and the student is asked to indicate whether each objective has been 'well achieved' through to 'not achieved at all'. The rating is generally carried out using a five-point scale, but variations are possible. This type of scale is particularly useful in cases where no other suitable technique exists for measuring the achievement of certain objectives, or as a cross-check on other evaluation techniques.

Free student comments

If students are allowed to respond freely on topics raised in a questionnaire, unexpected outcomes and attitudes may often emerge. Although it may be difficult to categorize free responses, these should normally be sought as a matter of principle, since they can often add a completely new dimension to an evaluation.

Interviews with students

Student interviews are basically a verbal form of student questionnaire. A well-run interview can, however, probe more deeply and sensitively into specific areas of interest than can normally be done in a written questionnaire. One drawback is that individual interviewing is a time-consuming procedure. Thus, the most effective role of sampled interviews may well be to check the validity of a more widely-used formal questionnaire.

Observation of Instructional Systems in Progress

An understanding of the hidden educational processes occurring within an instructional system may be developed by means of careful and sensitive observation of these processes. The observation can be direct and immediate, or may be recorded in some way (eg on videotape) for later analysis. Such techniques are particularly useful when one is evaluating exercises designed to develop communication and inter-personal skills. The ethical problems associated with 'unobtrusive assessment' that were mentioned in the last chapter are not really a problem in this case, as it is the *instructional system* which is under scrutiny, not the students.

Feedback from Teaching Staff Directly Involved with the Instructional System

Through questionnaires, interviews and solicited comments, the opinions of staff directly involved in the implementation and operation of an instructional system can be of great value in course evaluation. Their comments may be influential in evaluating all aspects of the system, including the validity of the objectives, the course structure, the

teaching sequence, the assessment methods, and the day-to-day organization and management.

Feedback from People Having an Indirect Link with the Instructional System

People who do not have a direct link with the actual teaching/learning
system under investigation may still be able to make an important
contribution to its evaluation. Again, questionnaires, interviews and
solicited comments are appropriate means of gathering information.
The advice of *employers*, for example, may be sought if a vocational
course is being evaluated. This may be done at the *formative evaluation*
stage, before a course has been fully developed (in order to assess the
skills and qualities which employers are looking for from students).
It may also be done as part of a *summative evaluation* process (to
gather information on the relevance of the course to the actual work
situation and on the general strengths and weaknesses of former
students).

Similarly, the opinions of *former students* can be important, as they
can comment on the relevance of the course or other instructional
system in retrospect, and perhaps suggest improvements with the
benefit of hindsight and experience.

If a course has *external examiners*, their comments are invariably
extremely influential in course development. This feedback may prove
even more valuable if the external examiners are given some guidance
as to what particular aspects should be commented upon.

Finally, the opinions of *teachers* who subsequently take on a particular group of students for a related course are often highly relevant.
Their comments on the students' strengths and weaknesses may be
important when revising a particular instructional system, or part
thereof.

Evaluation of Cost-Effectiveness

The perceived balance between the cost of an educational programme
or innovation and its educational effectiveness depends upon a
multitude of factors. Deciding whether or not the initial costs and
on-going running costs justify the end results is a value judgement,
involving a wide range of educational, financial, social, and political
considerations. Improvements in the effectiveness of teaching/learning
can also be measured in several 'dimensions', as discussed in Chapter 1.

It is not our intention in this book to deal in any depth with the
complexities of cost-effectiveness. It is, however, important to bear
in mind the overall financial implications and on-going financial commitment associated with *any* educational development, and to weigh these
against the expected educational benefit using whatever criteria are
deemed important.

The financial costing of an educational development is a complex process in itself. Fielden and Pearson, in their book *Costing Educational Practice* (1978), describe a practical approach which they believe could be generally adopted, and give an insight into some of the associated problems, using a number of case studies for illustration. Other interesting case studies of educational costing are provided by Birch and Cuthbert (on open learning methods) and by Fielden and Pearson (on computer-assisted learning). (See the Bibliography for further details.)

Summary

Evaluation is a valuable and, indeed, essential component of the process by which the on-going development of instructional systems occurs. The evaluator has a wide range of techniques at his disposal, and also has several relevant sources of feedback which may assist in compiling a 'total picture' of the system and its effects (both good and bad). No single approach is the best in all circumstances, and, as in the case of assessment, it is generally most profitable to use a battery of appropriate techniques to ensure that the overall evaluation process is as valid and useful as possible.

CHAPTER 9

Resources Centres

Introduction

In Chapter 5, we looked at a range of individualized learning approaches and techniques, all of which give the student greater control over such factors as how, when, where and at what pace the actual learning takes place than is the case in most traditional institution-centred courses, thus making them more flexible from the student's point of view. One of the key components of many individualized learning approaches is a *resources centre* of some sort, in which much of the learning material and many of the aids that are provided to support self-learning may be housed. In this chapter, we will first take a more detailed look at the role of resources centres in education and training, and will then examine some of the practical considerations that relate to their operation.

We will begin by distinguishing between *resources, resources centres* and *resource-based learning*, and indicating how these three concepts are linked. Then we will describe how resources centres are used in different educational systems and at different levels of education. Finally, we will discuss some of the factors that are involved in the planning, organization and operation of a learning resources centre.

Resources, Resources Centres and Resource-Based Learning

In essence, resources, resources centres, and resource-based learning may be thought of as progressively more highly structured systems through which flexible, *student-centred learning* can be achieved. Let us illustrate this thesis by examining each in turn.

Resources

Basically, a *'resource'* in education or training is a system, set of materials or situation that is deliberately created or set up in order to enable an individual student to learn. To qualify as a true learning 'resource', the resource must satisfy all of the following three conditions:

(a) it must be *readily available*;
(b) it must allow student *self-pacing*; and
(c) it must be *individualized*, ie it must cater for the needs of students working on their own.

It therefore follows that a 'resource' must, by definition, be *student-centred*. Thus, in a traditional teacher/institution-centred system involving teaching methods such as lectures or talks, timetabled laboratory classes, and text books, it is only the text books which normally satisfy the criteria for being 'resources', in the sense we have described here. However, in such a course, lectures *could* be made more like true 'resources' by having them 'packaged' in some way, eg by recording them on videocassettes or making them available in some other self-study format such as duplicated notes backed up by audio-tape commentaries. Similarly, a laboratory situation could be made into a 'resource' by allowing more flexible student access to the laboratory facilities than may normally be the case.

Resources can come in many forms. *People* can be 'resources' as, for example, when teaching staff make themselves available on a flexible basis in order to deal with individual student difficulties as and when they arise. Similarly, *places* can be 'resources', as in the case of an open-access laboratory of the type mentioned above. Finally, a whole range of *instructional media* can be 'resources'; examples include books, structured notes, videocassettes, tape-slide programmes, computers, etc. Self-instructional materials in all their various formats are probably the most common type of learning resource, and these are often housed centrally in a *resources centre*.

Resources Centres

A *resources centre* is a place (anything from part of a room, as in Figure 9.1, to an entire complex of buildings) that is set up specifically for the purpose of housing and using a collection of *resources*, usually in the form of self-instructional materials.

Resources centres (which are sometimes given equivalent names such as *learning aids laboratories* or *self-study centres*) may serve the needs of an individual department within a school or college, an entire institution, or even a collection of institutions, as, for example, when several schools are served by a single central resources centre. In many cases, such centres are housed in libraries, which often double up as resources centres by providing for the storage and use of both book and non-book learning materials.

Student use of resources centres may, at one extreme, be very loosely structured, and, in some institutions, may not be an integral component of courses. On the other hand, in strongly student-centred courses, students may spend a large proportion of their time using the facilities offered by such centres.

The different uses that are made of resources centres, and the

Figure 9.1 **A resources centre in a typical primary school classroom**

various factors that are involved in their planning, organization and operation, will be discussed later in this chapter.

Resource-Based Learning

Courses that involve *resource-based learning* generally provide for individual study by including some measure of self-teaching and self-pacing. Such courses invariably make wide use of learning 'resources' in the sense described above, and *may* make use of the facilities of a resources centre. However, true resource-based learning goes far beyond the mere use of a resources centre, involving a highly structured system of individualized, student-centred learning experiences that make full use of both human and non-human resources. The class of resource-based learning systems encompasses all the individualized learning approaches that were discussed in Chapter 5; for example, Keller Plan, Flexistudy and distance learning courses, including all correspondence courses.

Within the broad spectrum of resource-based learning, resources centres *can* be used as a basis for implementing and supporting developments of this type. Such centres are not, however, essential prerequisites for *all* resource-based learning schemes, since it is perfectly possible to operate a resource-based learning system without such a centre.

Several texts which further explain the concepts of 'resources', resources centres and resource-based learning are listed in the Bibliography.

The Role of Resources Centres in Different Educational Systems

Resources centres are exploited in fundamentally different ways in different types of educational institutions, and the way in which they are used also depends to a considerable extent on the nature of the strategic approach to instruction that is adopted.

Within flexible *student-centred* approaches to learning of the type discussed in Chapters 2 and 5, a resources centre may have a key role to play in providing students with a whole range of learning resources, together with any associated hardware that may be required for the use of these resources. Within such flexible learning systems, students are often given free access to a resources centre within a host institution, and are permitted to attend at times which suit *them* rather than the institution. Advice is normally given (via a 'study guide') regarding the range of resources which may be suitable to assist in the achievement of a given set of objectives within a given course unit. Teaching staff may be present in order to assist with any problems or difficulties that may arise, and, as such, constitute another 'resource' within the centre.

In the case of courses which are based on the more conventional, more constrained *teacher/institution-centred approach* (see Chapter 2), the role of resources centres is generally completely different. Here, their role is not so much to serve as a means of providing a front-line teaching facility, but rather to provide remedial or back-up material to support other teaching methods.

In primary and secondary schools, a centralized resources centre may store and supply both book and non-book materials which individual teachers are able to borrow for use with their classes. Similar centralized collections of teaching materials are found in teacher training colleges and teachers' resources centres (see Figure 9.2). In such cases, the resources are most often used as aids within a traditional expository approach rather than for individualized instruction.

Individual use of resources centres by students undertaking traditional teacher/institution-centred courses is often completely voluntary (that is, it is an 'optional extra'), although students may sometimes be directed or recommended to use certain resources by particular teachers or lecturers. All resources are again normally available at most times, but the choice of what particular resource(s) to use is often left to the student. Indeed, students may elect to use the facilities of a resources centre in order to study subjects that are not directly related to the content of their course, for example learning foreign languages for holiday purposes, or studying computer programming out of general interest. However, the main uses of resources centres by such students include remedial study, immediate follow-up of class work, revision before exams, and extra study carried out in order to benefit from an alternative approach to specific subject matter.

Some institution-based resources centres also lay on a programme of displays and exhibitions for general motivation and background interest purposes. This practice is most common in resources centres that are based within a particular department, or which deal only with resources in specific subject areas (eg the biological sciences or health education).

Figure 9.2 **Part of the teaching resources centre in the library of a large teacher training college**

The Planning, Organization and Operation of a Resources Centre

As we have seen, a resources centre can be used in different ways at different levels and in different systems of education. Clearly, the method of use will have a marked effect on how the resources centre is organized and developed. Thus, there are many factors that have to be considered before embarking on the planning and operation of a resources centre, and, in the remainder of this chapter, we will take a detailed look at some of the more important of these.

Constraints

The development of a resources centre is often constrained by a number of factors, including *finance, space, staffing, attitudes,* and *general educational policy.* Let us now look at these in turn.

Finance

Money is obviously required both to set up and to operate a resources centre. An initial outlay is required to buy furniture (for example, study carrels, desks, chairs and storage shelves), to purchase any necessary hardware (for example, microcomputers, tape-slide players, cassette players and videocassette recorders) and to purchase appropriate commercially-available resources (in both print and non-print format). In addition to this 'pump-priming' money (which may be considerable), an annual operating budget is required in order to maintain and enhance the equipment and resources housed within the centre.

Space
Suitable space clearly has to be found in order to site the development. In some cases, it may be possible and desirable to place the resources centre within an existing library; in others, it may be better to use separate accommodation — particularly if the resources centre is to be departmentally rather than centrally based. The amount of space required will obviously be directly related to the amount of use that students are expected to make of the centre. Experience shows that there are liable to be peak times of use (lunch times, free periods, etc), and the size of the development should (ideally) be sufficient to cater for such 'peaks', although in many situations, this is simply not practical.

In addition to providing adequate student spaces, an appropriate amount of storage space is required, both for equipment and for resources; if possible, this should be flexible enough to cater for any planned future expansion of the resources centre.

Staffing
Several staffing problems will almost certainly have to be faced. The cataloguing and administration within the centre should (ideally) be handled by a specialist librarian, but such a person may not be available, so it will often be necessary to find a suitable 'volunteer' to do the job. It may be desirable to use teaching staff within the resources centre as 'human learning resources' to which students can have access, but this may lead to timetabling problems, and also to problems related to staff willingness (or unwillingness!). Finally, some technician back-up is generally necessary in order to check and maintain any audio-visual equipment housed in the resources centre.

Attitudes
Positive attitudes to the resources centre from both staff and students are absolutely vital to the success of the venture. Unless a resources centre is generally considered to be capable of playing an effective and valuable part within the teaching system in which it is to be used, the development is almost certainly doomed to failure. All too often, teaching staff in particular (especially the older members) are highly sceptical regarding the value of a new development such as a resources centre. If this is the case, it may be necessary to take positive steps

to convince them that all the expense and effort are worthwhile, and that a more flexible student-centred approach is capable of producing a significant increase in the overall effectiveness of the learning process.

Politics and policy

Factors ranging from intra- and inter-departmental politics, through general institutional policy to local and central governmental policy, can all affect the development (and effectiveness) of a learning resources centre. For example, if a college of further education is attempting to implement a policy of flexible course provision that includes community education, this will probably stimulate the development of a resources centre in the college; conversely, in the absence of any policy of this type, any attempts to establish such a centre may well be stifled. Similarly, important central government initiatives such as the setting up of the 'Open Tech' programme in the UK (designed to foster the training and re-training of adults at technician level by open learning methods) may give an impetus to the development of resources centres in a wide range of educational institutions and training centres.

Organization and Management

Thought must also be given to a number of other factors, including the centre's *management structure*, the *resources* themselves, the *equipment*, and the *general administration* of the centre. Let us again consider these in turn.

Management structure

Problems related to the *organization, management* and *operation* of a resources centre must be faced on a regular basis, and firm decisions must be made as a result. In some resources centres, these decisions are made by a single person or a small team, whereas in others, a committee of some sort is responsible for deciding policy. Such a committee might involve teaching staff, administrative staff, library staff, educational technologists, students and technicians.

Resources

Basically, the instructional media which comprise the actual learning resources in a resources centre can come from two sources: those that are *'bought in'* from commercial organizations or from other educational institutions, and those that are *'internally produced'* in order to cater for the requirements of a given set of students within a specific subject area.

'Bought-in' resources have the obvious advantage of allowing a usable collection of resources to be assembled relatively quickly. However, some resources, particularly those with an audiovisual component, can be expensive, and, in most cases, their content is not entirely compatible with the objectives of the course in which they are to be used.

Resources which have been *'internally produced'* by a teacher, on the other hand, may be much more relevant to the specific needs of a course, but, at the same time, can be extremely time-consuming to plan, produce and evaluate. In addition, devising effective student-centred learning resources may call for a wide range of new skills on the part of the teaching staff, skills which often have to be nurtured and developed over an extended period.

The various media which might be used in the production of resources have been discussed in detail in Chapter 5, where it was argued that the media should (ideally) be chosen to match the objectives being taught towards. However, the precise choice of media may be influenced by other factors, one of the most important being the range of equipment available in the resources centre. If, for example, basic slide viewing facilities are the only visual equipment available, staff will clearly have to use slides rather than filmstrips or video-tapes. Also, when buying in audiovisual resources, care must be taken to ensure compatibility with any standardized equipment already installed; for example, any pre-recorded videocassettes that are purchased should be of the appropriate format to be played on the videocassette players that are available in the centre.

Finally, the effective production of resources within an institution depends on having adequate production facilities available, including reprographic, photographic, graphics, audiorecording, and possibly also television services, together with adequate secretarial support. In some cases, it may also be necessary to provide facilities for reproducing certain types of resources *within the centre itself*. For example, a student-centred course involving extensive use of a resources centre may have a relatively large number of students progressing through the course at roughly the same pace. If reproduction facilities within the centre allow rapid duplication of resources, such as textual notes and audiotapes, this may reduce the need to store multiple copies of particular resources in order to cope with peak demand, and may well result in greater overall efficiency. Where such immediate duplication facilities are not readily available, consideration should be given to the optimum number of copies which are to be held. With 'bought in' materials, copyright restrictions may preclude direct copying, and, in such cases, any additional copies required would obviously have to be purchased.

Equipment
The range and type of equipment that needs to be installed in a resources centre depends on a number of factors, including the nature of the media to be deployed and the amount of money available. For example, if tape-slide instructional programmes are to form a significant proportion of the resources in the centre, specialist machines, through which the audio commentary is automatically linked to the slides by means of electronic 'pulses' recorded on the tape, can be

provided in order to enable students to study these programmes. If finances do not permit the purchase of this type of (relatively expensive) hardware, however, simple manually-operated slide viewers and basic cassette players can be combined to provide a reasonably inexpensive alternative.

The number of sets of equipment to be installed in the centre has also to be determined, and should (ideally) be sufficient to cope with the expected peak demand. If this proves to be impossible, some form of 'timetabling' or booking of student use of the resources centre may well be necessary, albeit somewhat undesirable.

The actual location of the equipment within the centre may also cause problems. If the equipment is permanently set out in the resources centre ready for use, as in Figure 9.3, there may be problems relating to its security. If the equipment is stored centrally, on the other hand, and has to be collected by students every time they want to use it, this inevitably reduces the 'openness' of the resources centre by erecting a (perhaps unnecessary) administrative barrier, and may well deter some students from making full use of the facilities.

As mentioned previously, regular technical maintenance of all audio-visual equipment is extremely important. If minor faults are not immediately rectified, student interest and motivation may again be lost; it is, after all, extremely frustrating for a student to go to a resources centre, get hold of the material he or she wants, and then find that the hardware needed to study it is not working properly.

Figure 9.3 **Some of the equipment in a typical audiovisual resources centre**

General administration

A whole series of factors have to be considered regarding the running and administration of a resources centre. One of the most important of these is the question of whether the students are to be allowed free access (open access) to the resources, or whether access is to be via staff (closed access). In an *open access* system, the resources are usually housed in the main body of the resources centre, so that the students can select and use resources 'off the shelf'. In a *closed access* system, on the other hand, the resources are usually held in a central store, and students must request resources more formally. This factor is linked both to the staffing levels that are available to run the resources centre, and to the degree of student supervision that is thought necessary for educational, operational and security reasons.

Regardless of whether open or closed access is used, the resources of the centre must be systematically catalogued in some way in order to facilitate efficient retrieval. Where resources are stored on a closed access basis, or are intrinsically 'non-browsable' (eg videocassettes), it may help to annotate the catalogue entry with a fairly detailed description of the contents of the resource. The importance of a good cataloguing system becomes progressively more crucial as the number of resources in the centre increases. Indeed, in the case of a resources centre where a large collection of materials is being built up, there is a strong case for placing the cataloguing of the resources in the hands of a specialist audiovisual librarian.

Other administrative duties which may be important in a resources centre include arranging the booking and borrowing of resources (since it may be desirable for students to be able to use the resources outside the premises of the resources centre itself). Also, someone must be responsible for obtaining for preview and eventually purchasing resources produced elsewhere, on the basis of staff recommendations or other appropriate criteria. A further duty may be the keeping of records of usage of resources, possibly for the purpose of student 'credit' assessment, or, alternatively, for more administrative reasons such as assessing relative demand for different resources or establishing the level of use made of the resources centre.

Finally, the possibility of using 'human resources' in the centre has already been raised. Normally, these will be full-time teachers or lecturers who have a certain amount of 'resources centre duty' built into their timetables, but they can also be part-time members of staff or retired staff who are brought in specially for the purpose. It is also possible to make use of senior students in such a role.

Educational Considerations

Once the idea of setting up a resources centre has been firmly established in a school or college, a number of additional factors regarding the educational (as opposed to the administrative) aspects of its operation and function have to be taken into account. These include *integration with the teaching/learning system, the role of the teacher, student characteristics* and *feedback and evaluation,* all of which will again be examined in turn.

Integration with the teaching/learning system
We have already pointed out that there are many possible ways in which resources centres can be used in educational and training systems. One key decision that has to be made is whether the resources centre is to operate in a 'front line' role or in an optional 'back-up' role.

Within the context of an open, student-centred learning facility such as a resources centre, the amount of guidance given to students in the selection and use of resources must strike an appropriate balance between constructive direction and freedom of choice on the part of the learner. This depends upon just how 'open' and 'flexible' the learning situations can be while still remaining relevant to the course objectives.

When a resources centre is used within a strongly student-centred, self-paced course, there is also the very real problem of coping (on the one hand) with students who complete work quickly, and (on the other hand) with those who fall far behind. Some resources centres do in fact provide 'mind-broadening' or 'enrichment' materials for the 'high-fliers'. Another approach is to use the better students to help their weaker colleagues through a process of *peer teaching.*

In many schools and colleges, there is an increasing awareness of the need to integrate the actual teaching and learning process with the entire range of available support services. This has led some institutions to combine library, computer and media resources under one 'umbrella' service in order to co-ordinate their activities, and thus (it is hoped) to best serve the needs of the institution's courses and students.

The role of the teacher
In a resources centre, the role of the teacher effectively changes from being the sole supplier of information to being a provider of counselling based learning course, the teacher is much more a 'manager of resources' based learning course, the teacher is much more a 'manager of resources than a 'provider of information'. As we saw in Chapter 5, this role is not easy for some teachers to adopt, especially if skills related to the in-house production of resources have also to be learned. These factors indicate a very real need for appropriate staff development programmes on such things as the production of resources, the organization of resources centres, and the use of resource-based learning.

Student characteristics
It is a well-established fact that different students learn in different ways. To cater for individual differences in learning style, it may well be desirable to present similar information in alternative resource

formats. In some instances, there may even be a case for introducing small-group teaching methods for the benefit of those who find studying on their own particularly difficult (eg self-help groups).

When the main role of a resources centre is that of being an 'optional extra', there is often the additional problem of attracting those students who have seldom or never used the facilities on offer. It is a disturbing fact that many institutions which provide resource material of a remedial or 'back-up' nature find that it is the *better* students who use it voluntarily, rather than the weaker students who would, perhaps, have most to gain.

Feedback and evaluation
As with all learning situations, feedback obtained from both students and staff regarding their problems and experiences relating to resources centres can be of considerable value in determining where and how improvements need to be made. We saw in the previous chapter that on-going evolution based on such feedback should be a feature of *all* components of an instructional system, and it is probably true to say that this is particularly important in the case of a resources centre, especially if it plays a key role in the work of the pupils or students who use it.

CHAPTER 10

Computers in Education

Introduction

In Chapter 5, we made brief mention of the role which computers can play in the area of self-instructional teaching and learning. In this chapter, we will take a broader look at the different ways in which computers can be used in education and training. These uses are almost certain to become progressively less expensive — and, at the same time, progressively more sophisticated and versatile — as a result of developments in the field of microelectronics and information technology. The resulting widespread presence of computers in schools, colleges and training establishments, as well as in the home and in many common areas of everyday experience, already means that our society has a young, computer-literate element capable of making maximum educational use of the adaptable learning facilities that can be developed through computers, and that element is becoming progressively larger every year.

For the benefit of readers who are unfamiliar with the computer field, we will begin by defining a few basic terms and explaining the functions of the different components of a computer system. Then, we will examine the different ways in which the computer can be used in education, looking at its use as a 'supercalculator', its role in computer-assisted and computer-managed learning, its use as a data-base, etc. Finally, we will look at some of the factors that affect the educational use of computers — factors that may well be instrumental in determining whether computers are allowed to play the revolutionary role of which they are potentially capable.

Basic Concepts and Terminology

A *computer* can be defined as a device which is able to accept information, apply some processing procedure to it, and supply the resulting new information in a form suitable to the user.

The great majority of modern electronic computers, particularly those that are used for educational purposes, are *digital computers*. By this we mean that the information that they handle is converted into *digital* form (that is, into a code based on the binary number system,

Figure 10.1 **Part of the central processing unit and back-up memory of a typical mainframe computer**

Figure 10.2 **A typical microcomputer work station in use**

which only uses two symbols — 0 and 1) before processing. Computers that are designed to handle data which have not been converted into digital form are known as *analogue computers*, and are mainly used for specialized technical or scientific purposes.

Digital computers are often subdivided into *mainframe computers, minicomputers* and *microcomputers. Mainframe computers* are large, highly-expensive machines (costing at least several hundred thousand pounds) which normally require a custom-built suite of rooms in which to house them and a highly-trained team of staff to operate them — the type of machines that are installed in the central computer units of large organizations such as universities. Part of such a computer is shown in Figure 10.1. *Minicomputers* are basically simpler, cheaper versions of mainframe machines — the type of computers that might well be used by a small business or college or by a major section of a larger organization. *Microcomputers*, on the other hand, are small, 'desktop' machines that can be purchased for as little as a few hundred pounds or less and can be used for a wide range of purposes — everything from straightforward calculations to word processing and interactive video. These are the machines that are now finding their way into our schools and colleges in ever-increasing numbers, a typical example being shown in Figure 10.2.

All computers consist of three basic systems, as shown in schematic form in Figure 10.3.

Figure 10.3 **A simple schematic diagram of a computer system**

Input System

The *input system* is the system whereby information is fed into the computer. This information can be of two types, namely, instructions to the computer (the *computer program*, written in a special code — known as a *programming language* — whose nature depends on the nature of the computer and the specific use to which the program is to be put) and data (the material on which the computer will actually operate). Both types of information can be fed in via a wide range of systems, but the one most likely to be encountered is the *keyboard terminal*, a typewriter-like device whereby instructions or data can be fed directly into the computer to which it is connected. Instructions and data can also be fed into a computer in the form of coded patterns of holes in punched cards or tape, coded patterns of magnetic pulses on magnetic tape or disks, or patterns of bars or symbols that can be 'read' using a variety of optical scanning devices. A user can also feed graphical information into a computer via a variety of *graphics tablets* and *digitizers*, devices that convert such information into digital form capable of being handled by the computer. Other methods of communicating with computers (eg by speech) are currently being developed.

Central Processing Unit

The second major part of a computer system is the *central processing unit (CPU)*, which is the part where the actual processing of the material fed into the computer takes place. This consists of three separate subsystems, namely the *memory* system (where instructions and data are stored in coded form), the *arithmetic and logical unit* (where standard arithmetical and logical operations are applied to the coded signals that represent these instructions and data) and the *control unit* (which co-ordinates all the functions of the CPU by interpreting and executing instructions held in the computer memory).

Output System

The output of a computer can be presented in three different ways. First, it can be produced as *hard copy* — alphanumerical or graphical information that is actually printed on paper using a device such as a line printer or graphical plotter. Second, it can be produced in the form of *soft copy* — similar information that is temporarily displayed on the screen of a *video display unit* (a device similar to a television set). Third, it can be produced in the form of a coded signal of some sort, a signal that can be either used directly for some immediate purpose (for example, control of another machine or system) or passed into a storage system for future reference or use. Storage systems that are used for this purpose include punched cards and tape, magnetic tape and discs, and a variety of 'optical' devices such as videodiscs.

A much fuller, non-technical account of all the above topics can be found in *A Handbook of Computer-Based Training* (1983) by Dean and Whitlock (see the Bibliography).

The Different Roles of the Computer in Education

Over the last decade, the range of uses of the computer in education has expanded rapidly. At first, its role was largely confined to that of a 'supercalculator', but it is now also used in a wide variety of other ways, some of the more important of which are examined below.

Use of the Computer as a Supercalculator

This was the original — and, for some time, the only — role of the computer in education, namely, as a tool for carrying out complicated and/or time-consuming calculations as part of academic research programmes. Digital computers are ideally suited to this form of use, since they enable calculations that would previously have taken hundreds or even thousands of man-hours to be completed in a matter of seconds. As computers became progressively more powerful, their usefulness in this role continued to increase steadily, and they have now become an indispensable research tool in a wide range of subject areas. The use of the computer as a 'supercalculator' is not limited (as was often previously the case) to research scientists and academic staff of universities and polytechnics. In the authors' own colleges, for example, students at all levels — from first-year undergraduates to postgraduate research students — are making increasing use of the computer as a tool in their day-to-day work, and we have no doubt that the same is true in countless other establishments. As a matter of routine, students now use computers to calculate the slopes of graphs, carry out statistical tests on data, and compute the results of experiments — tasks that were, until comparatively recently, all carried out manually using such stone-age aids to calculation as slide rules or (as in the case of one of the authors of this book) logarithmic tables. The availability of computers (and their near-relatives, pocket calculators) to carry out calculations of this type has already had an impact on education, particularly at secondary and tertiary level, that can truly be described as revolutionary.

Use of the Computer to Teach about Computers and Computer Programming

Following on from their original applications in academic research, computers eventually started to be used for teaching *about* computers and computer programming. During the 1970s, this use of the computer became increasingly widespread, until, at the present time, there is hardly a secondary school or tertiary education establishment in the industrialized world that does not include at least *some* computer science or computer programming in its curriculum.

Furthermore, this teaching of basic computer literacy is no longer confined to students of mathematics or computer science or students in traditional computer-using disciplines such as science and engineering, as was (until comparatively recently) largely the case. It is now becoming increasingly widely recognized that almost all tomorrow's citizens will have to acquire computer literacy if they are to be able to cope with the technological complexities of everyday life — or, at the very least, should be given an idea of the vital role of computers in the modern world. Clearly, the use of computers as vehicles for the achievement of these various educational goals is almost certain to continue to increase.

Use of Computers as Direct Aids to the Teaching/Learning Process

A third way in which computers have been able to make a major contribution to education and training is in *computer-assisted learning* (CAL), in which the computer plays a key role in the teaching/learning process. When employed in this role, the computer is normally used in one of two distinct modes (although, in some cases, it is used in a combination of the two). In the first, the computer acts as a *substitute tutor* with which the student can participate in an on-going dialogue via an interactive terminal of some sort. In the second, it acts as a *simulated laboratory*, providing facilities whereby the student can carry out 'experiments' on a model system that has been programmed into the computer. Because of the importance of these two modes of operation, we will now examine them in some detail.

The 'substitute tutor' mode

In the 'substitute tutor' mode, the student interacts directly with the computer, which is programmed to react to student responses to the questions which it sets. The computer may then ask supplementary questions, or provide additional learning information, before requiring the student to respond once more. This adaptive style of learning is directly descended from the programmed learning movement of the 1950s and 1960s (see Chapter 1). It is essentially similar to 'branching' programmed learning, but is capable of being much more sophisticated than the latter because of the greater flexibility and data-handling capacity of computers compared with early 'teaching machines' or programmed texts. For example, in tutor mode CAL, a student may not be directed to a remedial exercise purely on the basis of a single response; his pattern of responding over a period of time, or even over an entire lesson, may be taken into account by the computer. Such a facility is obviously very useful when basic skills such as mathematical or reading skills are being learned.

Normally, tutor-mode CAL may be just one of the several self-instructional techniques that are employed in a given student-centred educational or training situation. Such a combination of approaches obviously leaves room for flexibility, and allows a closer matching of teaching methods with the course objectives to be achieved.

When a computer is used interactively in a self-instructional capacity, the form of student responses is dependent upon the sophistication of (a) the computer, and (b) the computer program. A simple program may require a student to respond to a given question from a multiple-choice set of options by typing in the code for the selected response. More sophisticated packages may allow the student to respond freely in his own words, the computer being programmed to identify key words, phrases, or numbers, and to respond accordingly.

An example of a section of interactive dialogue between a student and a computer is given in Figure 10.4. In this, the computer is assisting the student to plan a chemistry experiment, and the student may in fact investigate various possible experimental methods by interacting several times with the computer. In the dialogue, the student responses are italicized.

You are required to investigate experimentally the chemical equilibrium
of the system: $Fe^{3+} + SCN \rightleftharpoons FeNCS^2$ in order to discover how the
equilibrium constant varies as a function of the ionic strength.
You need a method which is both sensitive and discriminating. Which
method(s) do you suggest?

I'm sorry, but I haven't a clue

You first need to consider the physical properties of the individual species,
or of the system as a whole, which you might use.
What feature do all the species involved have in common?

They are all ionic

Good!
So what method or methods might you choose which makes use of this
property?

Conductivity methods

Yes — a conductance method.
Is a conductance method sensitive? (Very, Fairly, Not Very, Not at All)

Very

No. A conductance method is only fairly sensitive.
Is it a discriminating method?

Yes

Conductance methods are only really discriminating when applied to H^+
ions: for all other ions, the readings are rather similar.
Do you want to consider this method further?

No

What other method(s) might be more discriminating and sensitive?

Possibly a colourimetric method

Good. Are colourimetric methods sensitive?

and so on

Figure 10.4 **Extract from a 'tutor' mode CAL dialogue**

The 'simulated laboratory' mode

In the 'simulated laboratory' mode, the computer is more of a learning
resource than a direct instructional device. In this mode, practical
situations can be modelled on the computer, thus allowing the system
to be studied as changes are made to key variables. The simulated
practical situation can come from a wide variety of subjects, and
developments in computer simulation have taken place in such diverse
areas as medicine, engineering, geography, mathematics, the physical
sciences, economics, business and management training, and military
training.

Examples of situations which might point to the use of computer simulations include the following:

(a) where a conventional practical demonstration is either extremely difficult or impossible (eg in manipulating a country's national economy);
(b) where the apparatus or machinery required is either not readily available or is too complicated or expensive for general classroom use (eg in training off-shore oil drilling personnel);
(c) where a conventional, real situation would take an unacceptably long time to investigate (eg experiments in population dynamics or genetics).

Figure 10.5 gives an example of a 'laboratory mode' CAL application. In this case, a complex, highly-expensive industrial process (the production of ammonia) has been modelled on the computer. This process is impractical to carry out in the science laboratory owing to the high pressures involved, but, with the aid of the computer, students are able to discover the effects of altering various conditions (temperature, pressure, and concentration ratio) on the efficiency of the process. When interacting with the computer, the students enter simple replies to the computer's requests for information. The figure shows a sample print out, with the user's inputs again italicized.

For a more general discussion of the role of simulation exercises in education and training, see Chapter 6.

Use of Computers in an Administrative or Managerial Role

Yet another area in which computers have been used in education is in an administrative or managerial role, helping with, for example, the overall administration of the system, timetable planning, budgetary control and the management of the teaching/learning process.

In this last role, which is known as *computer-managed learning* (CML), the computer does not make a direct contribution to the teaching/learning process, as is the case in CAL. Rather, it acts in a supportive and/or supervisory role, relieving the teacher or trainer of various tedious or time-consuming managerial tasks and thus allowing him to devote more time to teaching and to meeting the specific needs of individual students. Thus, in a smoothly running CML environment, there is a balanced partnership between the teacher, the students and the computer.

In CML, the role of the computer is largely clerical, although it can be argued that it is more efficient and cost-effective than human clerical assistance could ever be. There are four roles normally associated with the computer in a CML system. First, it can generate, mark and analyse tests for diagnostic or assessment purposes. Second, based on what is previously known about each student and about the structure of the course, it can provide individual guidance to each student,

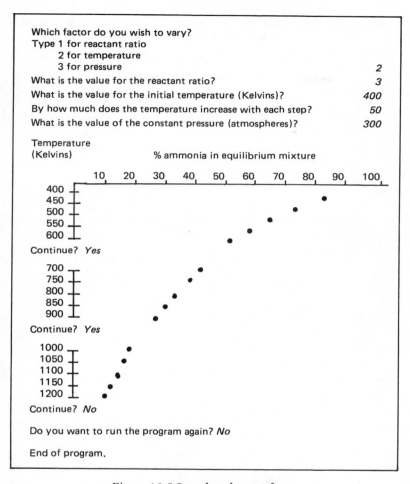

Figure 10.5 **Sample print out from
a 'laboratory simulation' mode CAL exercise**

directing or advising him on the best choice of route through a structured set of course materials or modules. This is normally based on the assumption that the majority of students should follow one of a limited number of well-defined routes. Third, the computer can be used to store and update records of test performances and progress through the course. Finally, from its accumulated records, it can report on the progress of the student body as a whole, and on the operation of the course in general, to individual students, the course tutors, and the course planners. The emphasis on each of these four factors will obviously vary according to the particular requirements of a given CML approach, although the administration and operation of assessment is at the heart of most CML applications. With properly constructed computer-marked tests, the marking is (by definition) totally reliable. However, this normally restricts the type of questions to the different forms of objective items such as multiple-choice questions and structural communication tests (see Chapter 7 for a full discussion of student assessment techniques). The tutoring time saved by utilizing computer-based assessment can be considerable, and can allow the teacher to allocate a greater proportion of his time to direct student contact.

Use of the Computer as a Data-Base

Although most people tend to think of the computer mainly as a machine for carrying out complicated calculations with great speed and accuracy, its ability to store and facilitate the subsequent retrieval of information is equally important. Indeed, it is this latter feature that has led to one of the most important uses of the computer in modern society, namely, as a *data-base.*

One of the first manifestations of the 'new information technology' explosion that is currently changing the nature of industrial society was the establishment of vast computerized repositories of information such as the US-based ERIC system and the British PRESTEL interactive videotex system. These differ from conventional reference libraries and data-banks in that the information they contain is stored electronically, and is accessible from virtually any distance using a remote computer terminal connected to the central computer by telephone link. The development of such computerized data-bases has not only revolutionized the world's library systems, but is also having a tremendous impact on education — particularly at tertiary level. Students who wish to carry out a literature search in a given field, for example, no longer have to do so manually, but, by linking up with the appropriate bibliographic data-base (which is often located on the other side of the world) can obtain abstracts of virtually every paper, article or book that has ever been written on the subject. Some of the long-term implications of developments of this type will be discussed in greater detail in the next chapter.

It is, of course, also possible to make use of the information-storing capabilities of the computer at a more 'local' level — by, for example, creating custom-built data-bases for specific educational purposes like the two described below.

Example 1

Much of the work that is requested of students is often boring and repetitive. If, for example, it is necessary to take 20 readings during the course of a lengthy scientific experiment, it may not be educationally necessary, or desirable, for the students to repeat the actual practical activity more than a couple of times. By feeding a student's first few results into a computer in which a suitable data-base has been established, the computer may then generate the required number of additional readings, which the student can then examine and interpret just as if he had obtained them by experiment. In a similar way, use of a suitable computer data-base can save students from having to carry out repetitivecalculations.

When using the computer in this manner, it is necessary for the teacher to distinguish between appropriate tasks and inappropriate (often time-consuming) tasks associated with the achievement of given goals. Very often, a balance can be struck in which the computer can be used to eliminate the main burden of the latter while still retaining those tasks that are essential to the student's development.

Example 2
As we saw in Chapter 7, writing and validating objective test questions is a difficult and time-consuming task. Thus, once a suitable question of this type has been produced, it seems sensible that it should not simply be used on a 'once off' basis, but should be stored for future use. The computer represents an ideal vehicle for this type of storage, and can be used to build up an extensive bank of objective questions over the years. Specific questions can then be culled from such a bank for particular purposes − by, for example, calling up all questions containing certain keywords and then selecting the most suitable by inspection.

Factors Affecting the Educational Use of Computers

There is no doubt that computers and new information technology are potentially capable of causing profound and far-reaching changes in our educational system − changes that are at least comparable to those that were eventually brought about by the mass use of the old information technology of the printing press. We will look at some of these in the final chapter of this book, but first let us discuss some of the factors that are likely to determine to what extent, and at what rate, the computer revolution will be realized.

Technical Factors

Although enormous progress has been made during the last 10 years, there are still a number of technical factors that militate against the use of computers in our schools and colleges becoming even more widespread and far-reaching.

Probably the most important is the fact that it is still generally necessary to learn what are basically new languages (the various programming languages) in order to be able to communicate effec-tively with computers − something that undoubtedly prevents large numbers of people from even trying to use computers in their work or studies. It is true that 'user friendly' software packages and authoring systems, which do not require users to be familiar with the programming language in which the program is written, are becoming increasingly available, but there is still a long way to go before the communication barrier is completely broken down. Indeed, some commentators believe that computers will only achieve universal accepance when users can actually *talk* to them using ordinary language — as in science fiction situations such as 'Star Trek'. Given the phenomenal rate of progress in computer development, that day may not be all that far off.

Other technical problems relate to the use of the large time-sharing mainframe computers that have now been set up in most of our large colleges and universities. Here, students gain access to the machine via remote terminals, and (unless they are lucky enough to be carrying out their studies in an institution that has enough terminals to meet the peak demand) often experience difficulties in gaining access to a terminal when they want it. Even when they do succeed in gaining such access, they often find that the machine is so overloaded with work from other people that they experience long and frustrating delays in having their own material processed. Over a period of time, an equilibrium is generally established, but not necessarily one that meets the needs of the students, who often have their motivation to use the computer reduced as a result. Nor is the problem necessarily removed by increasing the capacity of the machine, since each successive enhancement merely leads to an increase in usage which very quickly causes the system to become saturated once again. Thus, most central computer service units in colleges and universities find themselves trapped in a perpetual 'Catch 22' situation! No doubt these problems will eventually disappear as time-sharing machines become progressively capable of handling more and more users without undue delays, but, for the foreseeable future at any rate, they will probably remain with us.

Technical problems are not limited to the 'hardware' side of computer operations, since serious difficulties can often arise regarding the compatibility of software, that is, the use of software that has been designed for use with one type of machine on other machines. Such problems even arise with software 'packages' that are designed for use with a variety of machines, since technical standards regarding programs and supportive documentation are seldom rigidly adhered to. Compatibility problems have become even greater in recent years with the proliferation of different types of microcomputers, but, as in the case of the other technical problems that are associated with the educational use of computers, these are probably merely teething troubles that will be overcome in the not-too-distant future, and there appears to be no intrinsic reason why this should not prove to be the case.

Factors Relating to the Availability of Software

With the advent of inexpensive, portable microcomputers, it seems likely that virtually every educational and training establishment in the developed world will soon have access to *some* form of computer hardware. However, while hardware costs are steadily decreasing and computer capacity and sophistication are steadily increasing, appropriate educationally-useful software packages still need to be developed, and this is proving both difficult and time-consuming. Thus, many institutions are finding themselves in a position where they have access to highly-sophisticated computer hardware, but are not in a position to make proper use of it due to lack of suitable software. It was in fact just such a lack of software that prevented teaching machines from making any lasting impact on our educational system.

Given that it can take up to several hundred skilled man-hours to produce, document and validate a *single hour* of high-quality computer-assisted learning material, it is clearly not realistic to expect the average classroom teacher or college lecturer to produce all his own software. Even if he had all the appropriate skills (the necessary programming ability, a feel for educational design, ability to write supportive documentation, and so on) the time element would effectively preclude the production of anything more than a tiny fraction of the material that would be needed to support even a comparatively short course.

Provided that high-quality material was available from other sources, this would give no real cause for concern (after all, no one expects teachers and lecturers to write their own textbooks). However, with a few honourable exceptions (for example, the packages produced by centres of excellence such as Chelsea College, London and the State University of New York), much of the commercially-available CAL software produced until recently has been (to quote Megarry, 1983) 'of dismal quality, poorly documented, gimmicky and unimaginative, some of it actually dangerous in the sense that prolonged inexperienced use could lead to the perpetuation of maladaptive strategies and the learning of errors'. The situation is now starting to improve, but, unless there is a really massive commitment to the production of high-quality software that is capable of making a significant contribution to the main-line teaching work of our schools and colleges, it is doubtful whether computer-assisted learning will ever make the impact of which it is potentially capable.

Attitudinal Factors

Another factor that will almost certainly have a considerable influence on the extent to which computers are used in our educational system is the attitude of teachers and lecturers. Here, as in the case of other fields in which an attempt is being made to introduce revolutionary new technology, there is a very real danger that the people who will actually have to use it will see it as a threat to their jobs, authority or traditional role, and, as a result, will fail to provide the co-operation that is necessary for the success of the innovation.

Gray (1983) cites two examples that clearly illustrate these potential problems. The first was an attempt by one of the largest school districts in the American State of Utah to introduce a comprehensive computer-managed learning system covering virtually the entire curriculum. Based on the concepts of skill mastery learning, the system established specified goals, and provided schools with criterion-based pre- and post-tests together with the appropriate learning strategies and resource materials. The entire system was monitored and administered via the district's central computer, which marked the tests, indicated remedial strategies where appropriate and decided when students should progress to new work.

This highly sophisticated and innovative scheme was developed by dedicated teams of teachers and curriculum specialists, all of whom subsequently spoke with considerable enthusiasm about the resulting educational benefits. However, in the case of the great majority of teachers, who had not been directly involved in the development process, the attitude to the scheme was radically different. Many of these felt that their traditional role had been usurped by the computer, and also resented the fact that their efficiency as teachers was effectively being measured by the on-going programme of diagnostic tests. Thus, although there had hitherto been no history of teacher union militancy in Utah, the teachers demanded — and eventually achieved — the partial dismantling of the control mechanisms and the adoption of a more voluntarist strategy on the part of the district administration.

The second example cited by Gray involved an attempt by an (unnamed!) English polytechnic to introduce a comprehensive personnel management system, based on the use of a central computer to store detailed information about the expertise, timetables and availability of individual members of staff. It was intended that this information would be used to monitor the accuracy of timetabled information, and to provide more precise data concerning the distribution of teaching activities, student group attendance, teachers' work loads, etc. In the event, requests for the relevant information were simply ignored by the majority of staff involved, thus rendering the system ineffective.

In both these examples, the availability of new computer-based technology encouraged educational administration to attempt to introduce systems which they confidently expected would improve the efficiency of their organizations. In both cases, however, the innovations met with strong resistance from the teaching staff involved, who felt that their traditional working practices and professional autonomy were under threat. Clearly, any attempts to introduce innovations of this type are foredoomed to failure unless the co-operation of the teachers involved can be obtained, and it is obviously necessary to proceed with great caution and sensitivity.

Other Educational Factors

Other factors that are likely to affect the extent to which computers are eventually used in our educational system are of a philosophical rather than a practical nature. There is, for example, a very real fear among some educationalists that the ever-increasing use of computers and other aspects of new information technology will lead to an over-dependence on *mediated learning*, as opposed to learning through direct experience (what Bruner and his co-workers called *enactive learning*). Such educationalists argue that there is a need to preserve a balance between the two types of learning, since it will never be possible to provide children with a properly-rounded education by mediated learning alone — a view with which we wholeheartedly agree.

Another argument that is sometimes put forward against the increased use of computer-based technology in our schools is that there is a danger that it will lead to a new form of educational elitism. Some children (it is argued), but not the majority, will gain 'computer literacy' and take advantage of whatever becomes available through the technology that this literacy opens up to them. The very real danger of the emergence of such a new elitism is recognized by several commentators, including computer enthusiasts such as Evans (1981) who concedes that some children will take to computers more readily than others, whether or not the same facilities are made available to all children.

Finally, there is concern in some quarters that the increasing reliance on computer-based learning and new information technology will weaken our traditional public educational systems, thus causing lasting and possibly irreparable damage to the fabric of society. Two arguments are put forward in support of this view. The first maintains that new information technology is likely to prove too expensive to be adopted on a really large scale by the State educational sector, and that its undoubted benefits will therefore be limited to the private sector, which will progressively 'cream off' substantial numbers of able students whose parents can afford to pay for their education. This, it is argued, could lead to the eventual demise of the State system as an effective educational force — with all the potential social damage that this would produce. The second argument maintains that new information technology will eventually become so cheap and efficient that existing educational systems will be rendered obsolete, being replaced by individualized learning carried out at home or at work. Thus, face-to-face instruction will become a rarity, with a resulting imbalance between mediated and enactive learning that will be extremely undesirable from an educational point of view.

All the above issues are discussed in detail in an excellent and thought-provoking book by Hawkridge (1982), and interested readers are referred to this.

Conclusion

If computers are to be used *effectively* in education and training, then they must be used *appropriately*, and their use will certainly not flourish if they are seen merely as an expensive alternative to the classroom teacher. Care must be taken to identify and develop, through the computer, learning opportunities which cannot easily be provided in any other way. In other words, the undoubted strengths of computers must be made the most of; it is in no one's interest simply to use them because of their availability, or to employ them as 'gimmicks', as is all too often the case at the moment. Computers have, in principle, the potential to revolutionize our educational system; let us hope that the opportunity is not lost due to lack of action or mis-use, and that they do not suffer the same fate as the teaching machines which showed such early promise during the 1960s.

CHAPTER 11

A Glimpse into the Future

Introduction

In Chapter 1, we looked at the past history of educational technology, showing how it has developed and (it is to be hoped) matured since the end of the Second World War. In this, the final chapter of our book, we will attempt to look into the future, trying to identify current trends in educational technology and making informed guesses as to how these will affect the educational scene of tomorrow. We hope that this final chapter will help to pull together the various topics that have been examined in earlier chapters, and will thus help readers to put educational technology in its proper perspective.

Current Trends in Educational Technology

We believe that we can identify at least three important underlying trends in current educational technology. The first is a gradual shift towards a more student-centred approach to learning, a shift that is manifesting itself in a steady increase in the use of individualized learning in all its various forms. The second is an ever-widening realization that there is more to education than teaching basic facts and principles, and that a serious attempt should also be made to cultivate the various non-cognitive skills and attitudes that are so important for success in later life; this is leading to a much greater use of group learning methods, which, as we have seen, are ideally suited to this type of role. The third, and probably the most important in the long term, is an almost explosive increase in the use of new information technology in practically all aspects of education and training. Let us now examine these three trends in more detail.

The Shift Towards a More Student-Centred Approach

Traditionally, our educational system has been almost entirely based on the teacher/institution-centred approach described in Chapter 2, a system in which the individual student has little or no say regarding what he learns and how he learns it. Since the end of the Second World War, however, there has been a gradual but definite shift away from this traditional paradigm towards a more student-centred approach, a shift that has, in our opinion, shown definite signs of accelerating during recent years.

First, let us consider our 'formal' educational system — the network of schools, colleges and universities in which most of our education still takes place. Here, the traditional teacher/institution-centred approach still dominates, and we have no reason to suppose that it will not continue to dominate for many years to come. However, it is probably also fair to claim that there has been a slow but steady increase in the use that is made of student-centred learning *within* the traditional system, as evidenced by the much wider use that is now being made of resources centres and of mediated and individualized learning in all their various forms. Thanks, we believe, to the influence of educational technology, more and more teachers and curriculum developers are beginning to appreciate that such techniques are capable of making a valuable contribution to the educational process, and, as a result, are building them into increasing numbers of courses. We confidently expect this trend to continue at all levels of education — from primary schools right through to polytechnics and universities — and are also fairly certain that it will receive a considerable boost by the current information technology 'explosion', which, as we will see below, is making student-centred learning progressively more practicable by making available new and more effective vehicles for mediated learning.

It is, however, outside the traditional educational system that we see the main developments in student-centred learning taking place. Here, the fundamental and (we believe) irreversible changes that are currently taking place in the fabric of Western industrial society seem certain to bring about a massive increase in the demand for education, a large proportion of which seems likely to be supplied in student-centred form. More and more people, for example, are finding that they *have* to continue to study after they finish their full-time schooling in order to gain the extra qualifications and expertise that they need to survive in what is becoming an increasingly technical and computer-based society. Since the traditional educational system is not, in its existing form, ideally suited to meet this need, a number of completely new educational and training systems are currently being set up — many, like the projects in the British 'Open Tech' scheme, being largely student-centred in approach. With the increasing need to retrain people for completely new jobs at regular intervals throughout their working lives, the importance of this type of system seems almost certain to increase.

Equally important, more and more people are now continuing to study because they *want* to, and are enrolling in ever-increasing numbers with institutions such as the Open University which provide flexible, student-centred courses of the type that they can fit into their normal lives without undue disruption. As the working week becomes progressively shorter, and more and more people find themselves at a loose end because of long-term unemployment or early retirement, the demand for this type of course seems almost certain to increase, and we expect that the provision of student-centred 'continuing education' courses will become one of the growth industries of the late 1980s and the 1990s.

The Spread of Group Learning

We saw in Chapter 1 that, according to Professor Lewis Elton, educational technology has gone through three overlapping phases since the end of the Second World War, concentrating on the development first of mass communication, then of individualized learning, and, finally, of group learning (see Figure 1.5). We also saw that the various techniques that are associated with group learning (games and simulations, interactive case studies, structured communication exercises, etc) are now starting to achieve increasingly widespread use in our educational system. We believe that this trend will continue throughout the 1980s, since such techniques are ideally suited for use in teaching towards the various higher-cognitive and non-cognitive skills (for example, decision-making, communication and interpersonal skills) and desirable attitudinal traits that are now regarded as being such an important part of a properly-rounded education.

Since the early 1970s, we ourselves have both been heavily involved in the 'group learning' movement through our work on the development of science- and technology-based games, simulations and case studies. During this time, we have seen such exercises change from being optional extras, employed by a few isolated enthusiasts, to becoming an integral part of an increasing number of courses and curricula, at both local and national level.

In our own colleges, for example, games, simulations and interactive case studies have now been built into the curricula of a number of science and engineering courses, where they are used in two basic roles. First, they are used as vehicles for teaching towards the various higher-cognitive and non-cognitive skills mentioned above, and, in particular, for the teaching of communication studies; indeed, the staff responsible for this rapidly-expanding area of the curriculum have adopted such exercises as one of their main teaching methods. Second, they are used as vehicles for helping students to appreciate the applications and social relevance of the subjects they are studying. This is another area to which progressively greater emphasis has been given in recent years. Feedback from colleagues in other colleges indicates that similar developments appear to be taking place in many other tertiary educational establishments, and we confidently expect this trend to continue.

Similarly, the use of group learning methods appears to be increasing at school level, since such techniques are now starting to be built into a number of national curricula. Two such developments of which we have first-hand knowledge are the use of games and simulations in the AO-level 'Science in Society' course that was developed by the (UK) Association for Science Education (ASE) during the late 1970s, and the use of similar exercises in the Foundation-Level Science course recently developed for use in Scottish secondary schools. In the case of the ASE course, which is now being taught in secondary schools throughout the United Kingdom, the various games and simulations that were custom-built for use in the course have, in the words of Project Director John Lewis, 'proved a great success with all who have tried them,' and are 'clearly a powerful teaching technique'. Figure 11.1 shows pupils at Hazlehead Academy in Aberdeen taking part in one of the ASE simulations − the *Power Station Project*. Feedback received from teachers who have used the exercises developed for use in the Foundation Science course, which is designed for 13 to 15 year olds in the bottom 20 per cent of the ability range, indicates that group learning techniques seem likely to prove equally successful with lower ability pupils − an extremely encouraging result which supports our view that such techniques are capable of making a valuable contribution to education at all levels, and that their use will continue to spread.

The Increasing Use of New Information Technology

One matter on which virtually all educationalists and educational technologists are in agreement is that new information technology seems certain to play an increasingly important role − many would say a dominant role − in future education. It would therefore probably be helpful to start this section by explaining exactly what we mean by the term.

Like 'educational technology', 'new information technology' is not a particularly easy term to define, largely because it denotes a wide-ranging field of activities rather than a single concept or process. Indeed, Hawkridge, in his book on *New Information Technology in Education* (1982) devotes the whole of the first chapter to attempting to answer the question: 'What is New Information Technology?' In essence, however, new information technology can be thought of as the application of new electronic and other technology (computers, communications satellites, fibre optics, videorecording, etc) to the creation, storage, selection, transformation and distribution of information of all kinds. This may not be a completely satisfactory definition, but we hope that it is slightly more helpful to readers than the 'official' definition of new information technology that was recently adopted by UNESCO, namely: 'the scientific, technological and engineering disciplines and the management techniques used in information handling and processing; their applications; computers and their interaction with men and machines; and associated social

Figure 11.1 **Pupils at Hazlehead Academy in Aberdeen
working on the design of a coal-fired power station
as part of the ASE's 'Power Station Project'**

Figure 11.2 **Pupils in the top form of a Scottish primary school
using a microcomputer to develop problem-solving skills**

economical and cultural matters'. (The camel has been described as 'a horse designed by a committee' and the above definition could well be described in similar fashion!)

It is self-evident that new information technology in all its various forms and manifestations is making an increasing impact on education as the years go by, and that this trend currently gives every appearance of accelerating rapidly. In formal education, for example, computers and the various mediated learning systems that make use of them are becoming increasingly widely used at all levels. Initially, these were largely confined to the tertiary sector, but, with the recent appearance of the cheap desk-top microcomputer, the use of computers has now spread throughout our secondary schools and is even starting to make an impact at primary level (see Figure 11.2). If microcomputers continue to become progressively cheaper in real terms, and the various technical and other problems that were outlined in the last chapter can be satis-factorily overcome, their use may indeed eventually become universal, as many commentators currently predict. This would clearly have consequences of the most far-reaching nature, consequences that can indeed probably be compared with those that have resulted from the universal use of the old information technology of the printing press.

New information technology also seems likely to have a comparable impact on informal education — the education that both we and our children constantly receive from the activities of everyday life (watching television, reading books and newspapers, etc) rather than in the context of formal school or college courses. Whatever the criticisms that are levelled at the modern child in respect of traditional academic standards, surely no one would seriously deny that he is considerably better informed than the generations that preceded him, largely as a direct consequence of exposure to television from an early age. With the increasing availability in the average home of products of new information technology such as videorecorders, computer-based data retrieval systems, electronic games, mediated instruction systems, etc, an increasingly large proportion of the education of the child of the future seems likely to take place *outside* school, a development that is again likely to have far-reaching implications both for society and for our educational system.

Education in the Year 2000

Let us now conclude this look at the future by extrapolating the above trends to the end of the century, and trying to predict what changes they are likely to bring to education by then. We appreciate that new technological developments, political and social changes, and other events that are impossible to anticipate at the time of writing, will almost certainly invalidate these predictions in a number of important respects, but we hope that they will prove of interest to readers who would like to know what the future may hold. Readers who regard such speculations as pointless can always close the book now!

Pre-School Education

There seems little doubt that, by the end of the century, most children will have received a significant part of their education before they ever start formal schooling at the age of five or six. Some progress has already been made in this direction, largely due to the presence of a television set in virtually every home, but the possibilities that will be opened up through the mediated learning resources that new information technology seems likely to make available are almost limitless.

By the year 2000, we expect that most homes will contain a basic information/entertainment system, comprising integrated television, sound reproduction, communication, information retrieval and computing facilities. Using this system, members of the household will be able to gain access to multi-channel television networks, probably via optical cable links and/or direct broadcast communications satellites, which will provide programmes of every possible type — including basic educational programmes for pre-school children. These will almost certainly be so interesting, and so attractively presented, that the great majority of children will need no persuasion to make extensive use of them. Similarly, children will very quickly learn to make use of the wide range of packaged material that will be available on videodisc, videocassette and similar media, including electronic games (many of which will have a built-in educational content) and interactive video presentations. Using these mediated resources, many children will probably learn the basics of the 'three Rs' long before they start school, and, once they do, they will be able to make use of an even wider range of computer-mediated resources, including interactive videotex systems and data-bases, which will both no doubt contain large amounts of material specially designed for the entertainment and education of the pre-school child.

Thus, by the time they start school, children will not only be thoroughly familiar with new information technology, but will, through the medium of such technology, have already mastered a significant proportion of the material that they would previously have learned during the first few years of formal schooling.

Primary Education

Despite some dire predictions of the virtual total disappearance of schools, we do not expect the educational system to have changed greatly in terms of its overall structure by the year 2000. Children will still, for example, start full-time schooling at the age of roughly five or six, and will then spend six or seven years in a primary school that is similar in many ways to those we have today. Indeed, most of them will probably still occupy the same buildings, because of the ever-increasing cost (in real terms) of constructing new ones.

We also expect that primary schools will continue to be organized along much the same lines as today, with most children being taught in single-age groups of between 20 and 30 and being under the direction of a single teacher for most of the time. (This is a system that has proved extremely flexible in incorporating all the various educational innovations that have appeared during the last 30 years, so we see no reason why it should not prove to be equally flexible in respect of the challenges posed by the advent of new information technology.)

With regard to the activities that will take place in the average primary school, we again expect that these will be similar in many ways to those that take place in the more progressive primary schools of the present day. Already, most of the work in these schools is organized on pupil-centred lines, with the teacher acting as a manager and supervisor of learning activities rather than a 'fount of knowledge' of the traditional type. The main changes will be in respect of the range of resource materials to which pupils will have access, which will, in addition to the textbooks, work cards and resource sheets of the present classroom, include interactive video and multi-channel cable and satellite television systems, computer-mediated systems such as interactive videotex, word processors and data-bases, and a wide range of mediated learning packages. Mediated individualized learning, based on the use of these systems, will be complemented by a variety of group activities designed to cultivate social, interpersonal, communication and other skills, and also by a certain amount of 'plenary' face-to-face teaching, which will still have an important part to play in primary education.

By the time they reach the end of their primary schooling, children will probably vary greatly in the academic level that they have reached — almost certainly much more so than today because of the greatly increased learning opportunities that new information technology will make available to the 'high fliers'. Nevertheless, we expect the overall standard to be significantly higher than today, with virtually all children being brought to a level where they can benefit from the more advanced education that they will receive in secondary schools.

Secondary Education

As in the case of primary education, we do not expect that secondary education will be all that different in terms of its overall organization from that which we see today. Children will still start their secondary education at the age of about 12, and will still spend a minimum of four or five years in the system, with most of them probably spending even longer at school because of the poor job prospects for unqualified school leavers (which will almost certainly be even worse than they are today). Similarly, most secondary schools will probably occupy the same buildings that they do today.

With regard to their internal organization, we again do not expect any major changes to take place between now and the end of the century. The specialized nature of secondary teaching will still make it necessary for most of the work to be carried out on a single-subject or related-subject basis, although we expect that there will be a significantly greater emphasis on cross-disciplinary studies than is the case at the moment, probably under the direction of teams of teachers with different subject backgrounds. Such studies will probably make extensive use of group learning techniques, such as games and simulations, which, as we have seen, are ideally suited for use as vehicles for cross-disciplinary work.

Although the activities that take place in the actual classroom will obviously vary considerably from subject to subject, there will probably be much less emphasis on conventional face-to-face teaching than is the case at the moment. Pupils will spend a large proportion of their time carrying out individualized study of one form or another, much of it based on mediated resource material (although we expect that textbooks and other printed materials will still have an important role to play). This will be complemented by other, more traditional activities such as practical work, as well as by a wide variety of group learning techniques, with the curriculum in each subject, and the overall curriculum, being designed in such a way as to provide each child with a balanced, rounded education tailored to his particular needs.

Needless to say, tomorrow's secondary schools will make extensive use of the products and techniques of new information technology. In many schools, for example, practically all mathematics and computer studies teaching will actually be carried out via computers, probably using rows of microcomputers or time-sharing terminals laid out in a similar fashion to a present-day language laboratory. Science classrooms will also make heavy use of computers, both for basic teaching and calculation purposes and also to provide computer simulations of laboratory situations (see Figure 11.3). Even non-mathematical subjects such as English and history will almost certainly make considerable use of the new technology. Most English classrooms, for example, will probably contain banks of word-processors (for creative writing) and video terminals (for studying literature contained in data-banks, consulting computerized dictionaries, etc) while history classrooms will probably contain libraries of audio- and videorecordings of archive material, together with the hardware needed to study them on an individual or group basis.

Tertiary and Continuing Education

The area of education that will probably have undergone the greatest change by the end of the century is the tertiary sector — the sector that includes all today's further and higher education colleges, universities, polytechnics, teacher training colleges, and so on. Such establishments will no doubt still exist in the year 2000, but we expect

Figure 11.3 **The classroom of the future?**
The computer room in the physics department of a sixth-form college

that their function will have undergone a significant change. At the moment, the primary role of most tertiary education establishments is to provide long 'one-off' courses that are designed to equip students to hold down a job for the rest of their working lives. No doubt this will continue to be an extremely important part of the work of such establishments, but we expect that they will also become much more heavily involved in providing other types of courses – short updating, extension and re-training courses that people will undertake at regular intervals throughout their working lives, for example, and also courses designed specifically for the unemployed, the retired, non-working mothers, and so on. Indeed, by the year 2000, we feel that continuing education of this type – backed up with almost unlimited opportunities for informal education via the various mediated techniques that information technology will make available – could well have become one of the mainstays of post-industrial society.

The organization of most tertiary-level courses will probably also have undergone a number of significant changes by the year 2000. We expect that they will be much more strongly student-centred than is the case today, with much less emphasis on formal 'face-to-face' teaching and more emphasis on individualized and resource-based learning and on group learning. As in the case of primary and secondary education, much of the former will be based on new information technology, with which the students of the year 2000 will be just as familiar as they are with textbooks today. They will, for example, make extensive use of computer terminals, both to gain access to mediated learning programmes and data-banks and to carry out calculations, simulated laboratory work, exercises and creative work. Essays and assignments, for example, will probably be carried out using word-processors, which teaching staff will probably also use to scrutinize, mark and annotate students' work.

As a result of the above changes, teaching staff will spend much less of their time in timetabled contact with their students and much more creating, modifying and updating teaching packages and resource materials of one form or another. Much of their work will probably be done via computers, with each member of staff having his own personal terminal via which he can gain access to data-banks, create new material, carry out research, and so on.

Final Word

Needless to say, one extremely important aspect of tomorrow's educational system will be the training and staff development of teaching staff, something that will probably take place on a regular on-going basis rather than on a once-off pre-service basis as is usually the case at the moment. Such training will be designed to ensure that teachers and lecturers are not only thoroughly familiar with and proficient in the use of the new techniques that information technology has made available, but are also able to organize the learning activities of their pupils or students in a systematic and effective way, making appropriate use of group learning and individualized learning as well as conventional expository teaching. They will, in other words, be expected to have a thorough understanding of the principles and practice of educational technology. We hope that this book will go some little way towards helping the teachers and lecturers of today to gain such an understanding, and realize that educational technology can be of considerable assistance and benefit to them in their everyday work.

Glossary of Terms used in Educational Technology

A

Ability profile a chart or diagram which provides a graphical representation of an individual's scores in respect of a number of separately-assessed aptitudes and abilities, and which thus gives a balanced picture of his overall ability.

Accessory materials a US term for any teaching materials that are used to supplement basic textbooks, eg audiotapes, tape-slide programmes, video materials, etc.

Achievement test a test designed to measure a person's knowledge, skills, understanding, etc, in a given area at a particular time, as opposed to his potential for learning.

Acoustic coupler a device that enables a remote terminal to be connected to a computer via an ordinary telephone link by using a *modem* to convert the digital signal into an analogue signal and then converting it back into digital form after transmission.

Active, activity learning learning which involves active participation on the part of the learner.

Adjunctive programme a type of instructional programme which incorporates a set of questions which are presented to the learner at the end of a text (or section of a text) in order to determine what has been learned.

Advance cue, signal synonyms for *synchronizing signal.*

Advance, advanced organizer an overview of new material which is presented before teaching (or exposing a learner to) the material in order to prepare the learner's cognitive structure.

Affective (adjective) relating to attitudes, feelings or values; see also *affective domain.*

Affective domain one of the three broad sets into which Bloom and his colleagues classify learning objectives, containing all those connected with attitudes, feelings and values (see Chapter 3).

Agricultural/botanical approach (to evaluation) a scientific approach to evaluation that involves measuring the extent to which specific objectives are achieved by an instructional system under controlled conditions; contrast with *social/anthropological approach* (see Chapter 8).

Aims the desired outcomes of an exercise, programme, etc expressed in fairly general terms; cf *objectives* (see Chapter 3).

Algorithm a series of instructions or procedural steps that can be used to solve problems of a given type, reach decisions in a given area, etc.

Analog(ue) a term applied to something that is continuously proportional to some variable or to a device or system that handles or processes material in analog(ue) form (eg an analog computer); cf *digital.*

Analysis a *cognitive* process which involves breaking down an idea, system, process, etc into its constituent parts and examining the relationships between those parts; level 4 of Bloom's *cognitive domain* (see Chapter 3).

Analytic(al) method of marking a method of marking essays, projects, etc based on a separate assessment of specific aspects or features; cf *impression method of marking.*

Animation creation of an illusion of movement in a visual display by use of special effects.

Application a *cognitive* process in which a learner, given a new problem, will be able to make use of the appropriate theories, principles, facts, etc needed to tackle it; level 3 of Bloom's *cognitive domain* (see Chapter 3).

Applications software *computer programs* (or suites of programs) that are designed to carry out specific jobs for the user of the computer; cf *system software*

Artificial intelligence (AI) simulation of the characteristics and cognitive functions of the human brain using 'intelligent' computer systems such as the *fifth-generation computers* currently being developed.

Aspect ratio the numerical ratio of the horizontal length of a picture, screen, etc to its height.

Assessment grid a table or grid used in the *analytical method of marking* in order to help the marker assess specific aspects of an essay, project, etc independently.

Atomist a person whose preferred learning style is *atomistic learning*; cf *holist.*

Atomistic learning a *learning style* in which ideas are developed piece by piece, with the result that sequences of pieces can be repeated without the learner necessarily having a clear understanding of the whole.

Attention span the time during which a learner can give his full attention to a topic, programme, etc (see Chapter 4).

Attitude scale a linear instrument designed to assess a person's attitude to a specific issue, phenomenon, etc by determining his position on some form of *rating scale*.

Audible advance a term applied to a synchronized sound/vision presentation with an audible *synchronizing signal* which indicates when the next frame should be shown.

Audio relating to sound, or to the sound aspects of a system, signal, programme, etc.

Audio signal an electronic signal, either in *analogue* or *digital* form, representing a specific sound and capable of being used to reproduce that sound; cf *video signal.*

Audio tutorial (AT) an *individualized learning* system based on the use of audiotapes, generally in conjunction with other types of learning materials to which the learner is directed by the recorded commentary.

Audiovisual specifically, a term used to describe instructional materials or systems which use both sound and vision; more generally, a term used to describe all educational communications media.

Author(ing) language a *programming language* (such as MICROTEXT) designed to enable people with little or no conventional programming skills to write *computer-aided learning* materials. See also *authoring system.*

Authoring system the system with which an *author(ing) language* is designed to be used, consisting of a suitable *work station* together with all the necessary *software.*

Autonomous learner a learner who controls the selection and content of his learning material and also has control over the pace of the learning process (see Chapter 2).

Auto-threading a facility in a film projector, tape recorder or similar device whereby the film or tape is threaded into the machine automatically.

B

Backing store an extension to the *main store* of a computer, generally physically distinct from it.

Back projection projection of an image on to the back of a translucent screen for viewing from the opposite side.

Backward branching a type of *branching* in programmed instruction in which the learner is sent back to repeat items which he has not yet mastered; also known as *washback*.

Barrel distortion distortion of a projected image whereby straight lines parallel to the edges of the field curve inwards at their ends; cf *pincushion distortion*.

Batch mode, processing, system a method of using a computer in which all the data relating to a given task (or set of tasks) are fed into the computer at one time and processed to give a specific output (or set of outputs) based on this.

Battery any group of tests, scales, etc that are normally administered consecutively over a short period, the results being used to give an overall picture of performance, ability, attitude, etc in the area of interest.

Behavioural objective a precise statement indicating the performance expected of a learner (in terms of specific skills) as a result of exposure to given instructional material; see also *Magerian objective*.

Behavioural(-ist) psychology the school of psychology which holds that all behaviour of an organism can be explained in terms of the *stimulus-response mechanism*; also known as behaviourism.

Bit an abbreviation for binary digit. One bit represents the smallest amount of information that can be held in a computer store or carried by a communication channel. The two binary digits are 0 and 1.

Black box a term (originating from the name of Professor Black, an early worker in the field of systems theory) for an electronic device whose internal mechanism is hidden from (or is irrelevant to) the user, or, more generally, any system whose input and output are much more important than its internal mode of operation.

Bloom's taxonomies a set of taxonomies of learning objectives, compiled by the American psychologist B S Bloom and his co-workers, in which all such objectives are classified into three broad groups, or domains − the *cognitive, affective* and *psychomotor domains.* (See Chapter 3).

Booting (a) a computer term for transferring a *program* from a disk (usually a floppy disk) to the computer's *working memory* and running the program; (b) also used in computing to denote the use of an extremely simple process to initiate a more complex one.

Brainstorming a technique for generating ideas, solving problems, etc whereby members of a group are encouraged to originate ideas, no matter how wild or apparently unrelated to the topic under discussion, and then to consider their potential.

Branch see *branching program, branching programme.*

Branching program *a computer program* that incorporates *branches*, ie points at which alternative courses of action are possible.

Branching programme a *programmed learning* sequence that incorporates *branches*, ie points at which the learner is directed to alternative items depending on his response to the items just tackled (see Chapter 1).

Briefing an introductory session for the participants in a game, simulation or other exercise that is used to describe the background to the exercise, assign roles, etc.

Broadcast videotex(t) *videotex(t)* in which a limited number of pages of information are incorporated into ordinary television transmissions and can be 'called up' by owners of receivers that incorporate the necessary decoding facilities; the British CEEFAX and ORACLE systems are typical examples.

Bulletin board (a) a panel of cork, wood or other soft material to which pictures, notices and other display materials may be pinned; (b) a form of *electronic mail* system whereby computer users can pool and/or exchange information via a suitable *network*, or via the public telephone system.

Bulk eraser a device (incorporating a powerful electromagnet) that can erase the signals recorded on an entire reel or cassette of *magnetic tape* at one time, without the need to unwind the tape.

Bulletin typewriter a manual or electronic typewriter which produces very large print, suitable for *OHP transparencies*; also known as a *primary typewriter.*

Buzz session a short period in a lesson or exercise in which small groups of people (buzz groups) intensively discuss a given topic.

By-passing missing out part of an instructional programme because of successful performance of earlier parts, successful performance in a diagnostic test, etc. See also *forward branching, skip branching.*

Byte in computing and data processing, a group of adjacent *bits* (usually eight) that together form a larger unit, such as the code for a letter, number, etc.

C

Cablecasting dissemination of information via cables, as in *cable television.*

Cable television a television system in which the signal is distributed to subscribers via cable rather than by broadcasting; cable systems can carry a much larger number of channels than broadcast systems, and (in some cases) also enable users to communicate with the distribution centre; see also *switched-star system, tree-and-branch system.*

Cafeteria plan see *course unit plan*.

Capacitance, capacitive videodisc a *videodisc* which depends on the variation of the electrical capacitance between the disk and the sensor to read the information stored; cf *contact videodisc, optical videodisc*.

Caption generator an electronic device for creating alphanumerical captions using a keyboard and feeding them directly into a *video signal*.

Carrel a small enclosed space in a library, resources centre, language laboratory, etc designed for individual or private study. See also *dry carrel, wet carrel*.

Cartridge a type of *cassette* carrying a closed loop of audiotape, video-tape or film that does not require re-winding.

Case study an in-depth examination of a real-life or simulated situation carried out in order to illustrate special and/or general characteristics.

Cassette a closed container of film or magnetic tape designed for loading and unloading into a suitable projector, reader or recorder without prior threading.

Ceiling and floor effects reduction of the usefulness or effectiveness of a test or other form of assessment due to the upper and lower limits of performance (the ceiling and floor) being too close together.

Central processor, processing unit (CPU) the main part of a computer system, comprising the main store, arithmetic unit and control unit, or (in the case of some modern computers) simply the arithmetic and control units (see Chapter 10).

Chaining a mode of learning in which the learner connects two or more previously-learned *stimulus-response bonds* into a linked sequence.

Changeover cue another name for a *synchronizing signal*.

Characterization an *affective* process that involves the organization of values into a total and consistent philosophy; the highest level (level 5) of Bloom's *affective domain* (see Chapter 3).

Check list a predetermined list of items to be looked for or asked about, eg during observation of a process or in an interview.

Class analysis chart a chart on which the relative performances of the members of a class of pupils or students are displayed in graphical form.

Class interval the range of scores between the upper and lower bound-aries of a class of score in a test or other assessment.

Clip a term used to describe a short excerpt from a motion picture film or videotape, especially when it is used in a different context (eg in a lesson, or as part of a larger presentation).

Clip art ready-to-use illustrations that can be transferred on to artwork, overhead transparencies, etc from plastic sheets.

Closed access a practice whereby users are not normally given direct access to the stock of a library or resources centre or to parts thereof, such access being restricted to the staff of the library or centre (see Chapter 9).

Closed-circuit television (CCTV) a television system which limits distribution of the signal to those receivers or monitors which are directly connected to the origination point by coaxial cable, optical fibre or microwave link; see also *cable television.*

Closed question an examination or test question in which a unique answer is required and where there is no scope for divergent thinking, evaluation, explanation, etc.

Cloze procedure a language development technique that involves learners in trying to understand passages from which words have been deleted at regular intervals (typically every sixth or seventh word) or from which certain parts of speech have been deleted. See also *Cloze test.*

Cloze test a standard test for assessing the *readability* of textual material based on the use of the *Cloze procedure.*

Cognition a generic term for the rational processes of perception, discovery, recognition, imagining, judging, memorizing, learning and thinking through which an individual obtains knowledge and conceptual understanding.

Cognitive domain one of the three broad sets into which Bloom and his co-workers classify learning objectives, containing all those associated with the acquisition of knowledge or knowledge-related skills (see Chapter 3).

Cognitive psychology a school of psychology that holds that learning comes about as a result of the restructuring of perceptions and thoughts *within* the individual, thus enabling him to perceive new relationships and solve new problems.

Cognitive skill a skill associated with the acquisition, application or manipulation of knowledge, relating to *cognition* or the *cognitive domain.*

Cognitive style an alternative name for *learning style.*

Cohort a group (or set of groups) of individuals chosen for investigation, analysis, etc on the grounds of a particular criterion, eg the year in which they entered a course.

Collator a machine (or section of a machine) which uses a series of boxes or shelves to sort or order sheets, cards, etc automatically, eg in reprography or data processing.

Compact cassette the most commonly used type of audiotape *cassette* containing tape 4mm wide and having separate supply and take-up spools.

Compact disc a recently-developed ultra-high-fidelity sound disc on which the signal is recorded in *digital* form; such discs are only 5" in diameter (hence the name) and are played in a similar way to an *optical videodisc*, using a laser to read the signal.

Compact slide a 2" x 2" (35mm) *slide*, as opposed to a *lantern slide.*

Compatibility (of learning resources) the suitability of one learning resource as it relates to other learning resources in terms of content, format, target, population, etc.

Competency-based learning a form of individualized, self-instructional learning in which the learner is not allowed to progress to the next stage of the learning programme until he has demonstrated complete mastery of the present stage.

Compiler a special *computer program* that enables user programs written in a particular *high-level (programming) language* to be handled by a particular make or model of computer by translating the program into the appropriate *machine code.*

Completion item a test *item* in which an incomplete statement, calculation, figure, etc has to be finished by the person taking the test, usually by supplying a missing word, symbol, number, section, etc.

Comprehension a *cognitive* process whereby an individual understands a particular idea, set of knowledge, etc without necessarily being able to relate it to other material or appreciate its wider implications; level 2 of Bloom's *cognitive domain* (see Chapter 3).

Compressed speech recorded speech that is processed so as to increase the number of words per minute without any increase in pitch or distortion.

Computer any device, usually electronic, which is able to accept information, apply some processing procedure to it, and supply the resulting information in a form suitable to the user; see also *mainframe computer, minicomputer, microcomputer*, and also *first-, second-, third-, fourth-* and *fifth-generation computer.*

Computer-aided (assisted) assessment, examination, test an assessment, examination or test that is constructed and/or administered and/or marked with the aid of a computer.

Computer-aided (assisted) instruction (CAI) use of a computer as an integral part of an instructional system, the learner generally engaging in two-way interaction with the computer via a terminal (see Chapter 10).

Computer-aided (assisted) learning (CAL) learning with the aid of a computer through *computer-aided instruction, computer simulations*, etc.

Computer graphics the generation and/or display of graphic materials by computers, either on a *video display unit* or as *hard copy* produced by an electronic or mechanical plotter.

Computer-managed instruction (CMI) the use of a computer in a managerial or supervisory role, the computer prescribing work schedules, carrying out assessment, etc (see Chapter 10).

Computer-managed learning (CML) a term used virtually synonymously with *computer-managed instruction.*

Computer-marked assignment a technique (pioneered by the UK Open University) whereby a computer is used to mark assignments completed by students at home; the student fills in his responses on special sheets which can be read by the computer.

Computer program the coded instructions that are given to a computer in order to enable it to carry out a specific set of actions.

Computer store any computer sub-system or *peripheral* in which data can be stored in a form in which it can be read by the computer. See also *backing store, main store.*

Computer terminal an electronic device which permits communication between a user/learner and a computer; see also *data tablet, graphics terminal, intelligent terminal, keyboard terminal, remote terminal, smart terminal.*

Computerized item bank an *item bank* which is held in a computer store and can be accessed via a computer terminal.

Concept cards information-carrying cards included in *resource materials* to stimulate awareness of key concepts in a particular topic or subject.

Concept film, tape a short sequence, recorded on film or tape, which gives an illustration or demonstration of a single concept or idea.

Concrete materials physical objects (eg models) or *realia* used in teaching.

Conditioning manipulation or *reinforcement* of behaviour in an individual.

Confidence testing a method for discriminating between levels of partial knowledge relating to the content of a test item in which the testee indicates his degree of confidence in the answer chosen.

Conflation the fusing together of two sets of scores to give a single overall mark, eg combining a *continuous assessment* score with a *terminal assessment* score.

Console a generic name for a piece of equipment (often desk-like and non-moveable) carrying the control panels, monitoring equipment, etc needed to control a computer, television studio, etc.

Constant angular velocity (CAV) a *videodisc* or *digital optical disk* replay mode in which the disc(k) spins at a constant number of revolutions per second; cf *constant linear velocity (CLV)*.

Constant linear velocity (CLV) a *videodisc, compact disc* or *digital optical disk* replay mode in which the information is read at constant linear speed along a continuous spiral track similar to that on an ordinary gramophone record; cf *constant angular velocity (CAV)*.

Contact videodisc a type of *videodisc* on which the signal is read by electrical means using a stylus that is in actual contact with the surface of the disk; cf *optical videodisc, capacitance, capacitive videodisc*.

Content-centred a term applied to a *game, simulation* or other exercise whose educational objectives relate mainly to the subject matter on which the exercise is based; cf *process-centred*.

Continuous assessment on-going assessment of a learner throughout a course of instruction.

Contract-based learning, teaching, training *learning*, teaching or training in which an agreed contract of learning expectation or objectives is drawn up between the learner and the tutor, a contract which the learner is expected to fulfil for assessment purposes.

Control track (a) on an audiotape, a *track* carrying instructions on operations to be carried out during running; (b) on a videotape, a *track* used to carry synchronization and similar information.

Controlled discussion a discussion in which learners may raise questions or make relevant comments, but whose general direction is under the strict control of the teacher, tutor or instructor (see Chapter 6); cf *free group discussion*.

Convergent thinking a rational, systematic approach to problem-solving, normally leading to the single correct, best, most conventional, or most logical solution; cf *divergent thinking*.

Conversational language natural language used to communicate on-line with a computer; see also *conversational mode*.

Conversational mode on-line dialogue between a computer and a user.

Copyright the right to reproduce or to authorize reproduction or performance of a literary, dramatic, musical or artistic work.

Core course (a) a teaching course in which a skeleton framework of ideas and teaching activities is provided and in which the individual teacher is able to add his own methods, ideas, etc; (b) a course that has to be taken as part of the *core curriculum* of a school, college, etc.

Core curriculum (a) key elements or subjects in the curriculum operated by a school, college, etc that are taken by all pupils or students; (b) basic elements in a course that have to be taken by all students, regardless of their selection of optional modules, materials, etc.

Core module, subject a *module* or subject that forms part of the *core curriculum* of a course.

Correction for chance, guessing reduction of the total in a test score according to a standard correction formula that is designed to allow for correct answers made by the candidate purely as a result of guessing.

Correspondence course a form of *distance learning* course that relies mainly on the postal service to provide a link between the individual learner and the person or organization running the course.

Counselling (a) advice and support given to participants during a *game, simulation* or similar exercise; (b) guidance given to pupils or students regarding their courses, future careers, etc.

Course unit plan a type of modular course that enables a student to build up credits by taking a series of optional courses, which may have different credit values depending on their relative length, importance and difficulty; also known (in the USA) as the *cafeteria plan*, and (in the UK) as the *pathway scheme*.

Courseware (a) a term that is becoming increasingly widely used as a synonym for instructional *software*, in the broadest sense of the word; (b) the actual instructional material, including both the content and the instructional technique, that is incorporated in a computer-based instruction system, as opposed to the *software*, which is taken to refer to the *computer program* that controls the computer's operation.

Criterion a characteristic or measurement with which other characteristics or measurements are compared.

Criterion frame in *programmed learning*, another name for a *test frame*.

Criterion-referenced assessment assessment designed to determine an individual's achievement with reference to predetermined, clearly-defined performance standards (see Chapter 7); cf *norm-referenced assessment*.

Cross-fade to fade out the image from one slide projector at the same time as the image from a second projector (focused on the same screen) is faded in; a technique used to present slide or tape-slide programmes without any 'gaps' between successive slides.

Cross-media approach a methodology based on the principle that a variety of audiovisual media and experiences, correlated with other instructional materials, overlap and reinforce the value of one another.

Cue (a) a command or signal for a previously-specified event to take place; (b) in *programmed learning*, another name for a *prompt*.

Curriculum the subject areas or sections covered within a specified course of study.

Curriculum design, development the process of planning, validating, implementing and evaluating new curricula, etc.

Customized instruction instruction that is designed to meet the specific needs of individual learners, as in *programmed instruction.*

Cyclorama (cyc) a continuous curtain or back cloth suspended around the periphery of a film or television studio or stage.

D

Data base (database) a collection of data, bibliographic information, etc held on file and available for extraction or reference, usually via a computer terminal.

Data tablet a device whereby graphic material can be inputted into a computer by 'writing' on its (electromagnetically-sensitive) surface using a *light pen* or other forms of electronic stylus; also known as a *graphics tablet.*

Daylight projection a projection system that produces an image bright enough to be seen without darkening the room.

Daylight screen a projection screen so constructed that clear images from a slide or other projector are visible in an undarkened room.

Debriefing review and discussion of the processes and outcomes of a *game, simulation* or similar exercise.

Decoy another term for a *distractor* in multiple-choice testing.

Dedicated a term applied to a computer, machine, system, etc that is set apart for special use.

Deductive method a method of teaching, study or argument which proceeds from general or universally-applicable principles to particular applications of these principles and shows the validity of the conclusions.

Deep processing a type of study method in which a learner reads material in order to gain deep understanding of the material being studied; cf *surface processing.*

Delivery system (a) in teaching, training, individualized learning, etc, a combination of medium and method of usage that is employed to present instructional information to a learner; (b) in *distance learning,* the method by which distribution of instructional materials to learners is organized.

Desktop publishing producing multiple copies of paper-based materials in one's own office or work situation using the methods of *electronic publishing.*

Developmental testing testing of a course, programme, exercise, system, etc carried out while it is actually being developed in order to identify and eliminate weaknesses.

Diagnosis the process of determining the existing capabilities of a learner by analysing his performance of a hierarchy of essential tasks in a specific subject, with the object of facilitating his learning by assigning appropriate remedial or advanced learning tasks.

Didactic method a method of instruction that emphasizes rules, principles, standards of conduct and authoritarian guidelines, usually conveyed directly to the learner by someone else.

Differential weighting assigning different weights (marks) to different options in a multiple-choice question in order to give some reward for partly correct answers.

Difficulty index another name for *facility value.*

Difficulty score a score that indicates the highest level of difficulty achieved by an individual in the assessment of a particular skill, quality, etc.

Digital a term applied to an information processing, storage or transfer system in which the signal is translated into binary code before processing, storage or transmission, or to the signal handled by such a system; cf *analog(ue).*

Digital optical disk (DOD) a disk designed for the recording, storage and retrieval of *digital* information, using laser optics; see also *EDOD, OROM, WOOD.*

Digitizer a device for converting a graphical image into a *digital* signal capable of being handled by a digital computer.

Diorama a three-dimensional representation of a scene, usually created by placing objects, figures, etc in front of a two-dimensional painted background.

Direct access (a) a situation where users of a library, resources centre, computer, etc have unrestricted access to all (or part) of the stock, or to the system; (b) in computing, another term for random access, as in *random access memory.*

Directed observation guided observation provided for the purpose of improving the study, understanding and evaluation of that which is observed.

Directed private study individualized instruction, normally carried out at home, that is built into a course which also uses other methods such as face-to-face instruction.

Directed reading a type of *directed private study* that involves reading specific books or sections thereof.

Discovery area a portion of an *open classroom* which is provided with reading, audiovisual and manipulative materials relating to one particular interest, activity or subject.

Discovery learning a method of instruction that attempts to teach principles or general concepts by providing the learner with a set of relevant experiences from which it is hoped he will arrive at the principles or concepts by the process of induction; see also *inductive method*.

Discrimination index a measure of the ability of a *multiple-choice item* to discriminate between students of high and low ability; it is equal to the difference between the *facility values* for the top and bottom thirds of the candidates (see Chapter 7).

Disk drive a computer *peripheral* using data which can be read into or out of a *hard disk* or *floppy disk*.

Dissolve a gradual transition between two visual images in which one fades out as the other fades in.

Distance learning learning carried out by a student who is geographically remote from the body or person organizing the instruction (see Chapter 5).

Distractor a wrong answer in a *multiple-choice item* (see Chapter 7).

Divergent thinking a creative approach to solving problems and tackling tasks which produces a range of original solutions, procedures, etc.

Dot matrix printer a low-quality *printer* in which each character is made up of a series of dots; cf *letter-quality printer*.

Double-frame a term used to describe a *filmstrip* where the horizontal axis of the pictures is parallel to the length of the film; also known as *full frame*.

Down a term used to describe a computer or other system which is out of action due to malfunction, etc.

Down-time the period (absolute or fractional) for which a learning resource (usually a device or system) is out of action due to breakdown, routine servicing, etc; cf *up-time*.

Drill an ordered, repetitive learning activity intended to help develop or fix a specific skill or aspect of knowledge.

Dry carrel a 'bare' carrel which has no electrical connections and is fitted with no special equipment, being intended for study of paper-based materials only; cf *wet carrel*.

Dubbing (a) combining two or more *audio signals* into a composite recording; (b) transferring an *audio signal* from one medium or machine to another; (c) making a copy of a tape; (d) in film production, recording new dialogue to be substituted for the original.

Dumb terminal a *computer terminal* with no independent data processing capability; cf *intelligent terminal, smart terminal*.

E

Earphones another name for *headphones*.

Easement a legal process whereby a copyright holder grants limited performance, reproduction, publication or other rights to another person, body, etc while retaining ownership of the actual copyright.

Editing (a) selecting and re-arranging recorded audio and/or video signals or film into a new continuity by manual or electronic means; see also *electronic editing, mechanical editing*; (b) removing unwanted material from and/or inserting new material into a document, file, computer file, etc prior to storage, publication or use.

EDOD *e*rasable *d*igital *o*ptical *d*isk; a type of *digital optical disk* that is being developed as a possible replacement for magnetic disks.

Educational age (EA) another name for *mental age*.

Educational technology (a) the development, application and evaluation of systems, techniques and aids to improve the process of human learning; (b) the application of scientific knowledge about learning, and the conditions of learning, to improve the effectiveness and efficiency of teaching and training. In the absence of scientifically established principles, educational technology implements techniques of empirical testing to improve learning situations; (c) a systematic way of designing, implementing and evaluating the total process of learning and teaching in terms of specific objectives, based on research in human learning and communication and employing a combination of human and non-human resources to bring about more effective instruction (see Chapter 1).

Egrul(e) an *inductive method* of instruction in which the learner is led through a series of examples (the "eg's) before having to formulate the 'rule' that explains them or ties them together; cf *ruleg*.

Eidophor a type of television projector which first produces an intense primary image by electronic means and then projects this by means of a system of lenses similar to those in a film projector.

Eight millimetre (8mm) film a standard size of motion picture film 8mm wide and with sprocket holes along only one edge; see also *standard 8, super 8*.

Eight-track a term applied to an audiotape (usually in a cartridge) with eight separate tracks of sound recorded on it; the term may also apply to the players and recorders used with such audiotapes.

Electronic classroom a classroom (such as a language laboratory) in which instruction can be given to and feedback received from individual learners by electronic means, usually via individual *carrels* connected to a master *console* operated by the teacher or instructor.

Electronic editing a form of audiotape or videotape *editing* in which the signal from one recorder is re-recorded on another machine.

Electronic mail a general term for systems that enable letters, messages, etc to be sent from one individual, department, institution, etc to another solely by electronic means, without the use of a conventional postage or internal mail system.

Electronic publishing the reproduction and distribution of documents using the electronic media of *new information technology* rather than by conventional printing and publishing methods; see also *desktop publishing*.

Electrostatic copying a reprographic process that first produces an electrostatically-charged image of the original material on a plate or drum and then uses this to transfer pigment particles to the copy paper; also known as *xerography*.

Elliptic questioning a method of question writing (widely used in *programmed learning*) whereby a learner is not asked questions directly but is left to complete statements by adding missing words.

Enactive learning a term (first used by Olson and Bruner) to denote learning through direct experience as opposed to learning via *media* of some sort (*mediated learning*).

End spurt in learning, a final increase in effort made at the end of a period or sequence of work; see also *beginning spurt*.

Enhancement materials instructional materials which are used to extend understanding of basic course material in specific areas.

Entry behaviour the set of skills which a learner possesses at the time he enters or begins a course or sequence of instruction.

Entry level performance a set of statements specifying the prior skills and concepts necessary for undertaking a particular learning task, sequence of instruction, course, etc.

Entry skills another term for *entry behaviour*.

Episcope a name for an *opaque projector* that is commonly used in the UK.

EPROM *e*rasable *p*rogrammable *r*ead-*o*nly *m*emory; a *PROM* (programmable read-only memory) from which the encoded *program* can be erased, thus allowing the device to be re-programmed; cf *read-only memory (ROM)*.

Erase head the *head* in a tape recorder which removes any previous recording from the tape prior to new material being recorded.

Error score the difference between an individual's *raw score* in a test or assessment and his *true score*.

Essay test, examination a test or examination that involves writing essays of a given length on one or more topics (see Chapter 7).

Evaluation (a) a *cognitive* process which involves making judgements about the value of ideas, works, solutions, methods, materials, etc for some specific purpose; the highest level (level 6) of Bloom's *cognitive domain* (see Chapter 3); (b) a series of activities designed to measure the effectiveness or value of a course, instructional programme, exercise, etc (see Chapter 8).

Evaluation instrument any of the means by which one obtains information for the purpose of *evaluation*, eg questionnaires, rating scales.

Experiential learning learning which is based on participants' reactions to the activities experienced during an exercise.

Expert system (a) a computer system which is programmed with all the knowledge that is currently available in a particular specialized field and is capable of making 'intelligent' evaluations in the field; (b) sometimes used as a synonym for an *artificial intelligence* system or intelligent learning system. Also known as a *knowledge-based system.*

Expert witness method a group instruction technique in which students question or cross-examine one or more experts in a particular field.

Expository display a display which presents information only; cf *inquisitory display.*

Expository organizer a preliminary lesson in which learners are introduced to material that is completely new and unfamiliar to them by using principles and concepts with which they are already familiar to form a 'cognitive bridge' to the new material; see also *advance(d) organizer.*

Expository teaching methods teaching methods that are based on exposition, ie presentation of material to a class in a lesson, lecture, etc.

F

Facilitator a group discussion leader whose primary function is to act as a catalyst in stimulating discussion rather than providing information.

Facility index, value the fraction (expressed as a decimal) of candidates choosing the correct answer or *key* in a multiple-choice question (see Chapter 7).

Facsimile transmission (fax) an electronic system whereby an exact copy of a document can be produced at a distance, in *hard copy* form.

Feedback (a) the information received by a learner immediately after each of his responses during a sequence of programmed instruction which indicates the correctness (or otherwise) of the response;

(b) communication of responses to a teacher by learners, as in a *feedback classroom.*

Feedback classroom a special classroom where student positions are electronically or electrically connected to the teacher's desk so that responses to multiple-choice questions or similar items can be monitored by the teacher.

Feltboard a flat display surface covered with felt, flannel or similar material on to which pictures, symbols or shapes backed with the same or similar material will adhere; also called a *flannel board* or *flannelgraph.*

Fibrevision a cable television distribution system that employs optical fibres to carry the signals; such systems can carry many more channels than conventional systems; see also *switched-star system.*

Field test, trial the assessment of a near-final system (eg an instructional exercise or programme) in an appropriate realistic setting prior to full-scale production and/or use.

Fifth-generation computer a term applied to the new type of *computers* currently being developed to act as *expert systems*; cf *first-, second-, third-, fourth-generation computer.*

Film clip a short sequence of motion picture film used as an insert in a presentation to illustrate a specific point.

Film gauge the width of a motion picture or photographic film; the most commonly used gauges are 8mm, 16mm, 35mm and 70mm.

Filmstrip a strip of 35mm film carrying a sequence of positive photographic images intended for projection (or viewing) as still pictures (see Chapter 4).

Firmware a term applied to a *computer program* that is recorded in a storage medium from which it cannot be accidentally erased, or to an electronic device containing such a program, eg a *ROM, PROM* or *EPROM*; cf *software.*

First-generation computer a term applied to any *computer* based on the technology of electronic valves (vacuum tubes); all the early computers built during the late 1940s and 1950s were of this type; cf *second-, third,-, fourth-, fifth-generation computer.*

Fishbowl session a group discussion technique whereby a number of the class sit in an inner circle and hold a discussion while the remaining members sit around the outside and observe the interaction.

Fixed-response item a type of objective test *item* which provides all the options from which a testee must select correct responses; cf *free-response item.*

Flannelboard, flannelgraph alternative names for a *feltboard.*

Flashcard a card or other opaque material carrying words, pictures or other information designed to be displayed briefly, usually by hand, during a programme of instruction.

Flesch formula a standard formula that is used to give a quantitative measure of the *readability* of textual material based on the number of syllables in a typical sample of 100 words and the number of sentences (including any incomplete sentence) in the sample.

Flexistudy an individualized learning system in which students are provided with learning materials for home-based study, counselling, tutorial support and access to college facilities (see Chapter 5).

Flip chart a set of large sheets of paper attached to an easel unit so that they can be flipped over the top of the unit into or out of view as a presentation progresses (see Chapter 4).

Floppy disk a small flexible magnetically-coated disk (usually 8", 5¼", 3½" or 3" in diameter) used as a medium for storing data in *digital* form; cf *hard disk*.

Fog index a numerical indicator of the *readability* of a text.

Follow-up activities additional and/or enrichment activities that are used to build upon the work of a lesson, the content of a programme, etc.

Font originally a set of printer's type of uniform style and size; now extended to denote a particular alphanumeric character set available within a system such as a *video display unit* or *word processor*.

Forced-choice item another term for a *fixed-response item*.

Formal prompt (cue) in *behavioural psychology* or instructional design, a *prompt (cue)* which provides information about the form of the expected response; cf *thematic prompt (cue)*.

Formative evaluation evaluation of instructional programmes or materials while they are still in some stage of development (see Chapter 8).

Forward branching in programmed learning, *branching* in which the learner is sent forward by several frames if he makes a correct response; also known as *washahead*.

Foundation course (studies) a course designed to provide a basis for more advanced or more extended studies.

Fourth-generation computer a term applied to a *computer* based on the technology of integrated circuits; such computers, which started to be built in the late 1970s, are much more compact than earlier computers and also have much greater calculating powers than earlier machines of comparable price; cf *first-, second-, third-, fifth-generation computer*.

Four-track a term applied to an audiotape with four separate sound recording tracks.

Frame (a) each separate presentation of a small basic unit of material, eg an individual picture in a series of pictures such as a motion picture film or filmstrip; (b) one of the discrete stages into which a *programmed learning* sequence is broken down, ie a *step*.

Frame game a type of *game* or *simulation* which is structured in such a way that a variety of roles, ideas and relationships may be inserted as and when required or appropriate.

Free group discussion a group discussion in which the specific topics covered and the direction that the discussion takes are largely controlled by the learners (see Chapter 6); cf *controlled discussion*.

Free-response item a test *item* in which responses can be made freely, provided that they satisfy set criteria, eg as in a *completion item*; cf *fixed-response item*.

Frieze a long wallchart on which scenes are built up by pupils.

Front-end processor a separate processing system (such as an analog-to-digital converter or microcomputer) that is used to pre-process signals or data before they are fed into a computer.

Front projection projection of an image on to the front of an opaque screen, for viewing from the same side as the projector; cf *back projection*.

Full-frame another term for *double-frame*, as applied to a *filmstrip*.

Full-track a term applied to an audiotape with a single recording track covering almost the whole width of the tape.

G

Gain score the measured amount of favourable change in an individual of some trait or variable due to treatment or instruction.

Game in an instructional context, any exercise that involves competition (either between participants or against the game system) and rules (arbitrary constraints within which the participants have to operate).

Gate frame in *programmed instruction*, a *frame* in a *branching programme* that poses a key question, the answer to which determines the next frame to which the user is routed.

Gate-keeper function the 'qualifying' function of an examination or assessment that has to be passed in order to progress to further instruction.

Gateway course a course that is taken with the specific object of attaining the qualifying standard for another course such as a first or higher degree.

General purpose language a computer *programming language* whose use is not restricted to a single type of computer or to a small range of computers; examples are BASIC, COBOL, FORTRAN and PASCAL.

Ghost (a) an 'after image' that remains on a chalkboard, whiteboard, etc after material has been rubbed or wiped off; (b) a secondary image on a television screen, due to faulty transmission or reception.

Goal-free evaluation *evaluation* in which the evaluator examines the actual effects of a programme without prior consideration of the programme goals.

Goal specification the detailed description of the desired results of an action or programme prior to the action or programme.

Graded difficulty a term applied to a series of tasks that are made progressively more difficult in order to extend a learner's capabilities gradually; a technique commonly used in *programmed learning.*

Grading on the curve a grading system in which grades or marks are allocated to the students in a class or large group so that they conform to the *normal distribution*; a form of *norm-referenced assessment* (see Chapter 7).

Graphical plotter an electro-mechanical device that can draw graphs, diagrams, etc on the basis of signals supplied by a computer.

Graphics tablet another name for a *data tablet.*

Graphics terminal a *computer terminal* on which graphical materials may be created, altered, displayed, etc.

Group dynamics the methods by which a group of people function as a collective whole.

Group learning *learning* that takes place through some form of interactive small-group activity, eg in a game or simulation (see Chapter 6).

Group pacing a type of programmed group instruction in which all the members of the group progress in lockstep (that is, all doing the same tasks at the same time).

Guided discovery learning a form of *discovery learning* in which the activities of the learner are partly structured or pre-determined by the teacher.

H

Half-frame another term for *single-frame*, as applied to a *filmstrip.*

Half-track a term applied to an audiotape with two separate recording tracks on it, each approximately half the width of the tape.

Halo effect in assessment, bias resulting from the assessor being influenced by favourable traits or behaviour on the part of the person being assessed.

Haptic (learner) a term applied to a learner who, in a visual sense, analyses the visual presentation of material into discrete elements; the visual version of an *atomist* or *serialist*; cf *visual learner*.

Hard copy information printed, typed or otherwise reproduced on paper, as opposed to information temporarily displayed on a screen, held in a store, coded on tape, etc (known as *soft copy*).

Hard disk a large, rigid disk (or stacked system of disks) on which digital data can be stored in magnetic form; such disks can carry much more data than *floppy disks*.

Hardware a generic term for the equipment used in instruction, computing, etc; cf *software*.

Hawthorne effect in learning, where improvement apparently brought about by the use of a new technique is wholly or partly due to the increased interest and motivation produced by the use of the technique rather than to the intrinsic properties of the technique itself.

Head (a) a component of a tape recorder, compact disc player, videodisc player, computer peripheral, etc whereby a signal can be read into or out of the system or existing signals erased; (b) the system that carries the characters in a daisy wheel printer, golf ball printer or similar device.

Headphones two small audio transducers connected to a headband for individual listening to audio sources; also known as *earphones*.

Hectograph (gelatin) duplication a type of *spirit duplicating* process in which copies of writing, drawing, etc are made from a pre-prepared gelatin surface to which the original image has been transferred.

Helical scanning a video recording technique in which the tape is wrapped helically round a fixed drum while the recording head rotates within a slot in the side of the tube, thus producing a diagonal scan across the tape as it moves through the machine.

Heuristic a term used to describe the method of instruction or problem-solving that involves using successive evaluations of trial and error in an attempt to arrive at a final result; see also *discovery learning*.

Hidden curriculum the informal and subtle ways in which a school, college or similar establishment mirrors and supports the accepted values of the social system or organization that runs it; see also *informal curriculum*.

Higher cognitive a term applied to educational objectives, learning skills, etc that fall in the upper part of the *cognitive domain (application,* *analysis, synthesis* and *evaluation)*; cf *lower cognitive* (see Chapter 3).

High-level (programming) language a computer programming language (such as ALGOL, BASIC or FORTRAN) which provides a range of facilities and standard constructions designed to simplify the writing of computer programs.

Histogram a graphical representation of a frequency distribution in the form of a vertical bar chart.

Holist a term applied by Pask to a person who learns, remembers and recapitulates material as a whole; cf *serialist*.

Hologram a visual recording, produced using a laser, which presents the illusion of three dimensions, including parallax.

Home experiment kit a package supplied or sold to students so that they can perform practical experiments at home, eg as part of a *distance learning* course.

Home study (a) course-related work carried out by pupils or students at home in their own time; (b) study carried out at home, eg as part of a *distance learning* course, *correspondence course*, etc.

Hook-and-loop board a display board covered with a nylon (or nylon-type) surface containing a large number of tiny loops on to which materials backed with tape strips carrying tiny hooks will adhere firmly.

Horizontal transfer (of learning) a form of *transfer of learning* in which no new higher-order skills are learned, but in which existing skills are applied to a new task (or set of tasks) of similar level of difficulty; also known as *lateral transfer*.

Humanist psychology a school of psychology that emphasizes the concepts of 'self' and 'person' and the study of man's 'humanness' in an integrated or holistic manner as opposed to an analytical or psychometric style (see Chapter 1).

Hypnopaedia literally 'education in sleep' (from the Greek); learning carried out while the learner is asleep, eg by playing audiotapes; also known as *sleep teaching*.

I

Ice breaker (a) an activity designed to establish rapport and generate a receptive atmosphere in a group of people who are about to take part in an exercise, course, etc; (b) a preliminary question or short paper taken by students before starting an examination in order to accustom them to the examination room environment and help overcome nervousness; it is not usually marked as part of the examination proper.

Icon in computing, a pictorial representation of a *menu* function, eg use of a picture of a pencil to indicate a drawing facility.

Illuminative evaluation another name for the *social/anthropological approach (to evaluation)*.

Impression method of marking a technique of marking a composition, essay, etc purely on the basis of the overall impression it creates; cf *analytic(al) method of marking*.

Inaudible advance a term applied to a synchronized sound/vision presentation with an inaudible *synchronizing signal*.

In-basket (in-tray) technique a method of training or instruction in which an individual is called upon to play a specific role and must, in isolation, respond to a number of hypothetical situations as they arise.

Independent learning, study an instructional system in which learners, carrying on their studies without attending formal classes, consult periodically with instructors or tutors for direction and assistance (see Chapter 5).

Individualized instruction, teaching, learning the tailoring of instruction, teaching or learning to meet the needs of the individual learner rather than the learning group as a whole (see Chapter 5).

Inductive method a method of instruction that involves presenting the learner with a sufficient number of specific examples to enable him to arrive at a definite rule, principle or fact embracing the examples; see also *egrul(e)* and cf *didactic method, deductive method.*

Informal curriculum material learned informally by association with fellow pupils, students or trainees; see also *hidden curriculum.*

Information technology the technology associated with the creation, storage, selection, transformation and distribution of information of all kinds; see also *new information technology.*

Inlay an image inserted or incorporated in another image, as, for example, in television production.

Inquisitory display a display which asks a question; cf *expository display.*

Instant lettering rub-down adhesive letters which can be transferred from plastic or paper carrier sheets on to artwork.

Intelligence quotient (IQ) the ratio (multiplied by 100) of an individual's *mental age*, as measured by intelligence tests, to his or her chronological age.

Intelligent terminal a *computer terminal* which can be used to perform some local data processing without the assistance of a central processor.

Interactive a term used to describe an exercise which involves participants in communicating with one another in some way; see also *interactive mode*.

Interactive courseware development a technique whereby a teacher plans, writes and evaluates a computer-based course or instructional programme using a computer terminal.

Interactive mode a method of using a *computer* whereby the user carries out an *on-line* dialogue with the computer via a suitable terminal.

Interactive video a hybrid individualized learning system in which a *videocassette* or *videodisc* recorder is linked to a *computer* (see Chapter 4).

Interactive videotex(t) *videotex(t)* in which the user is connected to a a computer *data base* by cable (usually a telephone line) and can therefore interact directly with the data base; the British PRESTEL system is a typical example.

Interdisciplinary a term used to describe an exercise, programme, course, etc that draws its material from a number of different subject areas and illustrates the links and relationships that exist between them.

Inventory test (a) a general term for personality tests and questionnaires designed to assess or identify attitudes, traits or personality characteristics; (b) a stock-taking test used to determine the level of prior knowledge or later achievement in short components of a course of instruction; see also *pre-test* and *post-test*.

Item (a) in assessment, a single component or question in a test; (b) in programmed learning, another name for a *frame* or *step*.

Item bank a bank of multiple-choice *items* from which multiple-choice tests can be made up by selecting suitable items.

Item difficulty gradient the extent to which items in a test or examination are arranged in order of increasing difficulty (a common practice in objective tests).

Item editing, trial testing, validation see *shredding*.

J

Job aid any form of 'aide memoire' designed to facilitate either the learning or the performance of a task.

Joystick a lever with two degrees of freedom that is used to control a cursor, 'write' on a *video display unit*, etc.

K

k (a) in conventional scientific usage, an abbreviation for kilo; used as a prefix to denote multiplication by 1000, as in kW; (b) in computing, an abbreviation for 2^{10} (ie 1024, not 1000 as is sometimes mistakenly supposed); used as the standard unit in which capacity of computer *memory* is measured, 1k of memory corresponding to a storage capacity of 1024 *bytes*.

Keller Plan a type of individualized learning strategy based on the self-paced study of (mainly) written material backed up by tutoring and monitored by means of mastery tests at the end of each unit (see Chapters 2 and 5).

Key the correct answer to a *multiple-choice item* (see Chapter 7).

Keyboard terminal a computer terminal that incorporates a keyboard similar to that on a typewriter.

Keypad a small hand-held keyboard of the type used to call up pages of a videotex(t) system.

Keystoning the production of a trapezoid (out-of-square) image on a projection screen due to the fact that the screen is not perpendicular to the axis of projection.

Knowledge a cognitive process which involves the remembering of facts, ideas, etc without necessarily understanding them or being able to make use of or manipulate them; the lowest level (level 1) of Bloom's *cognitive domain* (see Chapter 3).

Knowledge-based system another name for an *expert system*.

L

Laboratory mode CAL *computer-assisted learning* in which the computer acts as a 'substitute laboratory' using which the learner can carry out simulated experiments (see Chapter 10); cf *tutor-mode CAL*.

Landscape (format) a term used to describe the format of a page, book, document, drawing, photograph, etc with an *aspect ratio* greater than 1:1; cf *portrait (format)*.

Language laboratory a room equipped for language instruction in which taperecorders, projectors, record players and other devices are used singly or in combination in order to present material, provide feedback, etc (see Chapter 5).

Lantern slide a *slide* with an image area roughly 3¼″ square.

Laser printer an ultra-high-speed, high-quality *printer* system that uses a laser to produce the characters on the copy paper.

Lateral thinking a term (first used by de Bono) that describes the process of solving a problem by indirect or interactive methods rather than by adopting a logical, direct approach.

Lateral transfer another name for *horizontal transfer.*

Leaderless group a group of learners who are required to carry out some activity on their own without any member of the teaching staff being present to act as leader; such a group may, however, choose a leader from within itself.

Lead-lecture a lecture designed to present material and information for later discussion or given in preparation for participative work.

Learner-based (-controlled, -managed) education education in which the individual learner has considerable influence over what is taught, how it is taught, the pace of instruction, etc (see Chapter 2).

Learning (a) in *behavioural psychology*, a change in the stable relationship between (i) a *stimulus* that an individual organism perceives and (ii) a *response* that the organism makes, either covertly or overtly; (b) a relatively permanent change in *behaviour* that results from past experience, produced either inadvertently or deliberately.

Learning (aids) laboratory an alternative name for a *resources centre.*

Learning block a flaw or weakness in an individual's cognitive function that causes him to have difficulty in mastering a particular item, subject, group of subjects, etc.

Learning-by-appointment system a system in which learners can obtain access to teachers, instructors, self-instructional materials, hardware, etc as and when they need them by making appropriate appointments or booking arrangements.

Learning contract see *contract-based learning, teaching, training.*

Learning curve a graphic representation of the rate of progress of a learner (or group of learners) produced by plotting some appropriate measurable variable against time.

Learning resources all the *resources* which may be used by a learner (in isolation or in combination with other learners) to facilitate learning.

Learning resources centre an alternative name for a *resources centre.*

Learning style the preferred mode of problem-solving, thinking or learning that is employed by an individual; sometimes called *cognitive style.*

Lesson plan an outline of the important points of a lesson arranged in the order in which they are to be presented to the learners by the teacher.

Lesson unit a discrete individual lesson designed to form part of a larger course or sequence of lessons.

Lettering device, system any system designed for use in adding lettering to graphic or other materials.

Letter-quality printer a *printer* that produces output of similar quality to a standard typewriter; such printers generally employ golf ball or daisy wheel printing heads, and generally print on to single sheets of paper.

Light box a back-illuminated translucent surface used for viewing and working with transparent graphic and photographic materials.

Light-emitting diode (LED) a solid-state electronic component which emits light when an electric current is passed through it; used to display data, as on/off indicators, etc.

Light pen a pen-like implement that may be moved across the face of a computer *data tablet* in order to enter new data or alter existing data.

Likert scale an *attitude scale* involving the use of a list of statements to which an individual has to respond, normally from a range of degrees of agreement/disagreement (see Chapter 8).

Linear programme a type of instructional programme in which no *branching* occurs (see Chapter 1).

Line printer a printer mechanism that produces a *hard copy* printout from a computer, word processor, etc one line at a time.

Liquid crystal display (LCD) a data display technique that produces visible characters as opaque liquid crystals by application of suitable electric fields.

Listening centre an audio distribution device to which several sets of headphones can be connected in order to enable more than one learner to hear an audio programme at the same time.

Listening group an organized group that meets to hear an audio presentation of some sort (eg a radio broadcast or audiotape) as part of an instructional programme.

Listing a computing term for a line-by-line *readout* or *printout* of a *computer program* (or section thereof), a set of data, etc.

Long-term memory that part of the human *memory* in which material is stored on a long-term or permanent basis as opposed to a short-term, temporary basis; cf *short-term memory.*

Loop film a length of motion picture film joined as an endless band to facilitate continuously-repeated projection; usually contained in a *cartridge.*

Lower cognitive a term applied to educational objectives, learning skills, etc that fall in the lower part of the *cognitive domain* (*knowledge* and *comprehension*); cf *higher cognitive* (see Chapter 3).

Low-level (programming) language a computer *programming language* (such as *machine code*) which requires the programmer to specify his program in minute detail, but also gives access to the more intimate facilities of the hardware.

M

Machine code a *low-level (programming) language* in which the instructions that cause a particular computer to operate are written.

Magazine (a) a container for slides, a filmstrip, a film, etc for use in conjunction with a projector; (b) a light-proof film container for use with a camera, processor, etc.

Magerian objective a *behavioural objective* which indicates what the learner should be able to do, under what conditions, and at what level of competence (see Chapter 3).

Magnetic board a flat sheet of ferromagnetic material (or steel) to which objects may be stuck with magnets for display purposes (see Chapter 4).

Magnetic chalkboard, markerboard a chalkboard (markerboard) made of ferromagnetic material so that it can also serve as a magnetic board, thus combining the advantages of the two types of board (see Chapter 4).

Magnetic film a type of motion picture film that uses a *magnetic soundtrack*.

Magnetic soundtrack a strip of magnetic oxide along one edge of a motion picture film used to carry the sound signal.

Magnetic tape (a) magnetic oxide-coated tape on which audio or video signals or data can be recorded; (b) heavy magnetized tape used for attaching light materials to a magnetic board or preparing displays for use on such boards.

Mainframe computer a large, 'fixed' computer facility (see Chapter 10); see also *minicomputer* and *microcomputer*.

Main store the rapid-access memory system incorporated in the *central processing unit* of a *computer*.

Manipulative materials learning resources such as model-making kits, educational toys and tools that are actually handled and manipulated by the person using them.

Manual (a) (noun) a detailed and comprehensive guide to practice, use, manufacture or service, usually in book or booklet form; (b) (adjective) a term applied to an exercise such as an educational game that does not involve the use of an internal or external computer or data processor.

Markerboard a smooth light-coloured surface on which display material may be written or drawn using crayons, felt pens or other easily erased materials (see Chapter 4).

Marking scales scales that are established by examining bodies, schools, etc in order to guide examiners in marking examination papers (see Chapter 7).

Marking scheme any system that is used for evaluating and reporting achievement in a learner's work.

Master a copy or, in some cases, the original of a document, tape, film, etc from which further copies (or extracts) can be made.

Mastery learning the theory that mastery of a topic, subject, field, etc is (in principle) possible for *all* individuals provided that the appropriate amount of teaching time and the optimum quality of instruction are given to each student.

Mastery model the model for correct, error-free or minimally-acceptable performance of a task or set of tasks.

Matching item a type of objective test *item* which requires the testee to pair one word, object, symbol, etc with an associated response.

Mathmagenic information additional or augmenting information that is provided in order to facilitate learning, eg use of devices such as *prompts*, questions in text, *feedback* and *algorithms*.

Matt(e) screen a projection screen with a flat, even surface and dull finish which provides an even brilliance at all viewing angles.

Mechanical editing a general term for the various editing methods used with audiotapes or motion picture films that involve cutting them up and physically joining the pieces into the required continuity; cf *electronic editing*.

Mediated learning a term (first used by Olson and Bruner) to denote learning via media of some sort as opposed to learning through direct experience *(enactive learning)*.

Mediated observation observation of a situation carried out using some type of audiovisual medium (eg film or television) rather than direct observation.

Memory (a) the part of the mind/brain system in which impressions, facts, etc are stored; see also *long-term memory, short-term memory*; (b) in computing and data processing, a generic term for any system in which data can be stored in *digital* form.

Mental age an estimate of the intellectual development of an individual given in terms of the chronological age of the average population to which he is equivalent in intellectual terms.

Menu a list of options presented by a computer to a user, usually via a *video display unit.*

Microcomputer a small desk-top computer based on microcircuit technology; see also *mainframe computer* and *minicomputer.*

Microcopy a copy of printed or other material so reduced in size in comparison with the original that it cannot be read without the aid of a suitable magnifying device.

Microfiche a transparent sheet of photographic film bearing a matrix of *micro-images* (usually pages of text) together with an eye-legible title strip.

Microfiche reader a projector by means of which an eye-readable image of one or more pages of a *microfiche* can be produced for individual or group study.

Microfilm a roll or strip of photographic film carrying a series of *micro-images.*

Microfilm reader a projector by means of which an eye-readable image of one or more frames of a *microfilm* can be produced for individual or group study.

Microform a general term for any medium used to record *micro-images.*

Micro-image an image, obtained by means of an optical device, so reduced in size in comparison with the original that it cannot be read or studied with the naked eye; see also *microfiche, microfilm, micro-opaque.*

Micro-opaque a matrix of *micro-images* recorded on an opaque medium such as a card or sheet of photographic paper.

Microphone a device which converts sounds into electrical signals, usually for feeding into an amplifying, mixing or sound recording system of some sort.

Microphone characteristic the directional properties of a microphone, usually given in terms of a polar response diagram that indicates its relative sensitivities in different directions.

Microprocessor a self-contained solid-state microcircuit unit that can be used to build more complicated devices such as computers and control systems.

Microprojector a device designed to enlarge and project microscopic transparencies such as microscope slides for viewing by large groups.

Microsleep a term for the type of attention break that a learner undergoes periodically during a lecture, talk, etc that lasts longer than his *attention span* (see Chapter 4).

Microteaching training of teachers, lecturers, etc in specific skills or sets of skills in a scaled-down teaching situation, often using video playback to let them see and criticize their own performance.

Mimeograph, mimeographing see *rotary stencil duplication.*

Mimeoscope another name for a *light box.*

Minicomputer a term that is used to denote a computer intermediate in size between a *mainframe computer* and a *microcomputer.*

Minidisk an extra-small *floppy disk* 3½" or 3" in diameter.

Mix in sound recording or television work, to combine two or more signals from different sources into a single signal.

Mobile a three-dimensional non-projected display composed of elements hung from a system of threads so that they can rotate and move about (see Chapter 4).

Modem in computing, a contraction of *modulator-demodulator* − a device that can be used to convert a *digital* signal into an *analogue* signal capable of being transmitted along an ordinary telephone line or to re-convert such an analogue signal back into digital form after transmission.

Moderator an internal or external examiner who checks the standard of marking and/or examining in a course or section thereof.

Module (a) an organized collection of learning experiences assembled in order to achieve a specified group of related objectives; (b) a self-contained section of a course or programme of instruction.

Modular course a flexible course that allows individual learners to select the course programme that best suits them from a structural hierarchy of *modules*, some of which are compulsory and some optional.

Modulator-demodulator see *modem.*

Modular examination an examination in which candidates can elect to take a number of optional elements of equal difficulty in related subjects, topics or areas.

Moirée pattern, fringes patterns produced when two separate sets of parallel lines are superimposed at a small angle to one another.

Monaural a term used to describe a sound recording or sound repro-duction system with only a single sound channel.

Monitor (noun) (a) see *(television) monitor*; (b) a person who acts as a tutor, supervisor, or assessor in an individualized instruction system such as *Keller Plan*; (c) (verb) to listen to a sound signal as it is being recorded or played back or check a system for correct operation.

Monitoring carrying out an on-going assessment or appraisal of a system while it is in operation.

Monophonic a term used synonymously with *monaural.*

Mouse a hand-held device by which the user of a *digitizer* or *data tablet* can enter graphical information into the system, alter existing material, etc.

Multi-access a term used to describe a computer system whereby several users or operators may, through multiple or remote terminals, each use the same computer facilities at the same time; see also *time-sharing.*

Multi-channel learning *learning* that involves the use of more than one perception channel, eg the simultaneous use of hearing and sight.

Multi-choice item, question see *multiple-choice item, question.*

Multi-image of a presentation, the simultaneous use of two or more separate images, usually projected.

Multi-media a term used to describe (a) collections or groups of documents in several media; (b) a work designed to be presented through the integrated use of more than one medium (eg a tape-slide programme).

Multi-media kit, package a package of materials in several media dealing with a specific topic or subject area and forming an integrated whole.

Multiple-choice item, question a type of objective test or questionnaire question in which the testee has to choose the correct answer from a number of alternatives supplied (see Chapter 7).

Multiple-choice test a form of *objective test* composed of several *multiple-choice items* (see Chapter 7).

Multiple-completion item another name for a *multiple-response item.*

Multiple marking examination, essay, project or other marking carried out independently by more than one person in order to arrive at a collective mark that is (it is to be hoped) free from subjective influence and thus has a greater *reliability* (see Chapter 7).

Multiple-response item an *item* in an objective test of the multiple-choice type in which two or more responses are correct.

Multiple-track a term used to describe (a) a recording tape that carries more than one recording track; (b) a set of programmed materials with more than one track through them, ie a *branching programme.*

Multi-screen a term used to describe a presentation that employs two or more screens for showing projected images simultaneously.

Multi-sensory learning (teaching) aids learning or teaching aids which utilize or bring into play more than one of the physical senses (eg video materials or tape-slide programmes).

N

Negative transfer (of learning) a reduction in the efficiency of learning because of earlier learning carried out in a different situation.

Negotiated learning a form of *contract-based learning* in which the details of the contract are negotiated between the learner and the tutor.

Network a general term for any *system* consisting of a number of physically separated but interconnected sub-systems, eg computers, word processors, radio or television stations, agencies, institutions, organizations, etc.

New information technology the application of new electronic and other technology (computers, communication satellites, fibre optics, videorecording, etc) to the creation, storage, selection, transformation and distribution of information of all kinds.

No-failure programme a course or programme designed to avoid outright failure by a system of adjustment of tuition and learning materials and/or transfer to other courses.

Non-book (non-print) media *media* that carry or transmit information or instructions by non-typographic means, eg by sound, pictorial representations, projected images, etc.

Non-directive tutorial (group) a tutorial (group) in which students are encouraged to contribute views and questions spontaneously, with the tutor acting as a leader and guide, but not to the extent of dominating the group or firmly structuring the course of the discussion (see Chapter 6).

Non-functioning distractor a *distractor* which attracts less than 5 per cent of the responses to a *multiple-choice item*.

Non-projected visual aids, materials visual materials which do not require the use of a projector for their display; also called *self-display materials*.

Non-verbal communication the meaningful transfer of thought or emotion through methods other than words or speaking, eg using body language.

Norm the average performance or measure in a specified function of a specified homogeneous population.

Normal distribution (curve) a symmetrical bell-shaped distribution that has, or approximates to, the shape of a Gaussian distribution; many statistical measures (eg intelligence) are found to follow such a distribution.

Norm-referenced assessment assessment designed to determine an individual's achievement in comparison with the group or population to which he belongs (see Chapter 7); cf *criterion-referenced assessment.*

O

Objective a desired outcome of an instructional process or programme expressed in highly-specific (generally behavioural) terms; cf *aims* (see Chapter 3).

Objective assessment, examination, test an assessment, examination or test that can be marked with total *reliability* by anyone, including non-subject specialists, or (in some cases) by computer (see Chapter 7).

Objective item (question) an *item* (question) in an *objective assessment, examination* or *test.*

Observational learning learning that takes place through the observation of a model system; see also *discovery learning.*

Obsolescence time the length of time before a learning resource becomes so outdated that it is no longer of any use.

Off-campus study education carried out outside the formal school/college/university system, eg via *distance learning.*

Off-line a computing term applied to a terminal or peripheral that is not at the time in question under the control of the central processing unit, ie is switched off or operating quite separately from the main computer.

OHP transparency see *overhead transparency.*

Omnibus test a test which covers a range of different skills or mental operations in an extended sequence of *items*, but which produces a single overall score.

One-two-four snowball technique a *snowball group* technique in which the members are first asked to reflect individually on a question or stimulus, then to form pairs in order to compare thoughts, then finally to form groups of four in order to arrive at a consensus response.

On-line a computing term applied to a terminal or peripheral that is under the control of the central processing unit at the time in question; cf *off-line.*

Opaque projector the US name for a device designed to project images of opaque, flat objects on to a screen by using light scattered from the object; in the UK, such a device is generally referred to as an *episcope.*

Open access (a) a practice whereby users are given direct access to all or part of the stock of a library or resources centre (see Chapter 9); (b) a system whereby admission to a course is open to anyone who wishes to participate, regardless of his qualifications or experience;

(c) an informal *individualized learning* system in which a student can have access to the facilities of the host institution more or less at any time (see Chapter 5).

Open-book examination, test an examination or test in which students are allowed to bring into the examination room, or consult any reference material they wish.

Open classroom a classroom environment based on the concepts of *open education*, generally incorporating a system of *discovery areas*.

Open education an approach to education that includes an emphasis on learning (rather than teaching), personal and affective growth, exploring and questioning, decision-making, and the role of the teacher as a partner and guide rather than as an authoritarian figure (see Chapter 2).

Open-ended a term applied to a question, test, examination, exercise, project, etc in which many acceptable answers or outcomes are possible rather than one single correct solution or result.

Open learning an instructional system in which many aspects of the learning process are under the control of the individual learner, who decides what, how and when to study, usually under some form of guidance (see Chapter 5).

Open plan a learning environment that is designed in an open, flexible manner rather than divided into traditional 'closed-door' classrooms, thus allowing a wide range of teaching and learning methods to be employed (traditional expository teaching, team teaching, group learning, individualized learning, etc).

Open reel a term applied to an unenclosed audiotape, videotape or film reel (as opposed to the enclosed reels contained in *cassettes* or *cartridges*) and to audio or video systems which employ such reels.

Operating, operation(al) costs the total recurring expenditure of funds associated with operating a learning resource after any initial purchase and installation costs have been met.

Operational objective another term for a *behavioural objective.*

Optical character recognition (OCR) a technique (device) whereby characters that are illegible to the (unaided) human eye may be read by optico-electronic means.

Optical soundtrack a *soundtrack* which has been recorded and/or printed on a motion picture film in the form of an optical band of varying density or width along one edge of the film.

Optical videodisc a type of *videodisc* in which the signal is read optically, usually using a laser; cf *capacitance videodisc, contact videodisc.*

Oral examination examination by spoken word and answer, as opposed to a written examination; also known as a viva voce examination, or viva.

Organization an *affective* process that involves the conceptualization of values and ordered relationships between values; level 4 of Bloom's *affective domain* (see Chapter 3).

Orientation course a short course designed to introduce pupils or students to a subject, course, institution, etc.

OROM optical read-only memory — a type of *digital optical disk* that is used in the *constant angular velocity* mode; such disks have extremely large capacities.

Overhead projector (OHP) a device designed to project easily visible images from transparent materials (usually roughly 10" x 10" in size) on to an external screen in a completely lighted room (see Chapter 4).

Overhead (OHP) transparency a transparent sheet of material (usually roughly 10" x 10" in size) intended for use with an *overhead projector* or *light box* as a means of showing graphic, textual or other information.

Overlay a transparent sheet which registers over another sheet or transparency, giving additional or alternative information.

P

Pacing the act of indicating the speed to be achieved by an individual learner, group or class in carrying out a given programme of work; see also *self-pacing.*

Package (a) a collection of all the materials needed to organize, run or participate in an exercise, course or programme of some sort; (b) a computing term for a generalized *program* or set of programs designed to meet the needs of several users.

Paddle a manual control device used in conjunction with a computer, eg in video games and *interactive video.*

Page a *viewdata* term for a collection of information that can be called up by means of its page number.

Paper-and-pencil test, examination any test or examination which involves only question papers, answer papers and writing instruments.

Parent page a term used in *viewdata (interactive videotex)* for the *routing page* immediately prior to the page containing the information that the user requires.

Participative simulation a *simulation* whose main purpose is to enable people to participate in some activity (or group of activities); cf *predictive simulation.*

Passive learning learning in which the learner has a purely passive role, receiving information from the instructor or from the materials being studied without taking any active part in the proceedings.

Pathway scheme see *course unit plan.*

Peer group a group of individuals having similar age, background, qualifications, etc.

Peer (group) assessment a method of assessment that is based on the consensus opinion of a *peer group* on the respective contributions to the work of the group made by each individual.

Peer teaching, tutoring a technique in which the teaching (tutoring) of learners is not done by a teacher but by other learners, usually either older or of the same age, who have already met the learning objectives involved.

Peripheral (equipment, unit) in computer parlance, a terminal or backing store device that is (or can be) connected to the central processing unit of a computer system.

Personalized instruction another name for *individualized instruction.*

Personalized system of instruction (PSI) a generic name given to *individualized instruction* systems of the *Keller Plan* type.

Pictogram a diagram in which items or objects are drawn in different sizes or quantities in order to represent actual sizes or quantities more forcefully.

Pilot testing carrying out early trials of an exercise, programme, etc during its development; a type of *formative evaluation.*

Pincushion distortion distortion of a projected image whereby straight lines parallel to the edges of the field move outwards at their ends; cf *barrel distortion.*

Pixel the smallest picture element on a television or video display unit screen.

Platen the flat surface or platform in an *opaque projector* on which the material to be projected is placed.

Playback head a *head* in a tape recorder that is used to play back a signal recorded on the tape; in audiotape recorders, such heads are generally used only for playback purposes, but in videotape recorders, they also generally double as *record heads.*

Plenary session a session involving all the participants in an exercise, programme, course, etc.

Plotter a visual display or computer output device where the values of one variable quantity are automatically plotted against those of another; see also *x-y plotter.*

Point system a system used in English-speaking countries to measure type size, one *point* being equivalent to 1/72 of an inch (0.351mm); thus, type 1″ high would be described as 72 point type.

Polarized animation simulation of movement in *overhead transparencies, slides* and other display materials by the use of variably-oriented polarized light transmitted through special materials.

Port a point at which access can be gained to the *central processing unit* of a *computer*.

Portability a term used to give an indication of the ease with which an educational or other device can be moved and its resistance to damage when being transported.

Portapack a portable television camera and videorecorder system operated by rechargeable batteries.

Portrait (format) a term used to describe the format of a page, book, document, drawing, photograph, etc with an *aspect ratio* less than 1:1; cf *landscape (format)*.

Positive transfer (of learning) facilitation of learning brought about as a result of learning a previous task which contained similar elements.

Posterization reproducing a photographic or video image using only a few specific tones or flat colours, with most of the tonal gradation and detail suppressed.

Post-test a test carried out after the completion of a course or programme of instruction in order to determine the extent to which the learner has achieved the specified objectives; cf *pre-test*.

Pounce paper transfer a system of transferring an outline of an illustration from one surface to another (eg from paper to a chalkboard) by making small holes along the lines of the original; the pattern can then be transferred to another surface by dusting along the lines with chalk dust, powder, etc.

Power test a test in which the score or level of performance attained is more important than the time taken to achieve the score or level; cf *speed test*.

Practice frame in *programmed instruction*, a *frame* that provides practice in the material just presented; cf *teaching frame, test frame*.

Practice items trial items that are included in a test, examination or questionnaire in order to familiarize the subject with its form.

Pre-coded question a question in which the answer has to be chosen from a number of alternatives supplied, usually by ticking or otherwise marking one of them.

Predictive simulation a *simulation* whose main purpose is to predict future behaviour, performance, trends, etc; cf *participative simulation*.

Pre-knowledge relevant knowledge which a learner or participant should have before embarking on a programme, course, etc or taking part in an exercise.

Pre-recorded materials recorded materials (such as audiotapes or video-tapes) where the recorded signal was present at the time of purchase or acquisition.

Presentation programmer an electronic system which controls the synchronization of sound reproduction and/or projection devices in multi-media or multi-device presentations (eg cross-fade tape-slide programmes).

Pre-test a test carried out prior to a course or programme of instruction in order to determine the *entry behaviour* of the learner(s); cf *post-test*.

Primary typewriter another name for a *bulletin typewriter*.

Printer (a) a generic name for a *peripheral* to a *computer, word processor*, etc that gives *hard copy* output; (b) a system for producing photographic prints (usually positive) from original film (usually negative).

Printout the *hard copy* output that a *computer* or *word processor* provides via a *line printer* or similar device.

Problem method a method of instruction in which learning is stimulated by the creation of challenging situations that demand solution.

Process-centred a term applied to a *game, simulation* or other exercise in which the subject matter is far less important than the activities that the exercise involves; cf *content-centred*.

Prognostic test a type of diagnostic test that is used to predict the future performance of an individual in a specific task, course of study, etc.

Program a coded sequence of instructions whereby a programmer communicates with a computer; cf *programme*.

Programme an ordered sequence of learning or other activities; cf *program*.

Programmed instruction, learning a general term for instruction or learning that takes place in a systematic, highly-structured manner, generally in a step-by-step fashion with feedback taking place between steps (see Chapter 1).

Programmed text a set of programmed learning materials produced in the form of a printed text.

Programming language the code that a computer programmer uses to communicate with a computer; see also *high-level programming language, low-level programming language*.

Projected (projection) television a television display system that produces a large projected picture on an external screen by optical or electronic means; see also *idophor*.

Projected visual aids visual materials that require the use of a projector for their display.

Project method a method of instruction in which learners (individually or in groups) carry out projects, working largely free of supervision or control.

PROM *programmable read-only memory*; a *read-only memory (ROM)* which can be programmed by the user provided that he has access to the necessary specialized equipment; see also *EPROM*.

Prompt in *behavioural psychology, programmed instruction*, etc, a *stimulus* (eg a verbal or pictorial hint of some sort) that is added to another stimulus (eg a question) in order to make it more likely that a learner will give a correct *response*; see also *formal prompt, thematic prompt*.

Psychodrama the dramatic presentation of a personal conflict or crisis for diagnostic or therapeutic purposes, eg via *role play*; see also *sociodrama*.

Psychomotor associated with the co-ordination of mind and body in carrying out physical (motor) actions; see also *psychomotor domain*.

Psychomotor domain one of the three broad sets into which Bloom and his co-workers classify learning objectives, containing all those associated with the co-ordination of mind and body in carrying out physical (motor) actions.

Pygmalion effect the theory that a teacher's expectations of a pupil's achievement can sometimes become a self-fulfilling prophecy in that the pupil will perform to meet the teacher's preconceptions of him.

Q

Quadraphonic a term applied to a sound recording or sound reproduction system that makes use of four discrete but related sound tracks, channels or sources.

Quarter-track a synonym for *four-track*.

Qwerty keyboard a keyboard in which the alphanumerical and standard control keys are laid out in the same way as on a standard typewriter; the name is derived from the top left row of letters.

Quiz mode a *programmed learning* technique that involves providing the learner with the correct response immediately after he has made a response to each item.

R

Radio listening group a group of people who meet in order to listen to and discuss educational radio broadcasts, usually with the help of related *study guides.*

Radio microphone a *microphone* connected to a small radio transmitter that can relay its signal back to the audio system with which it is being used without the need for connecting wires.

Radiovision an audiovisual instructional system which uses special filmstrips, booklets, or other visual material linked with radio broadcasts.

Random Access Memory (RAM) a computing term for a fast, random-access *store* of the type found in the *central processing units* of computers.

Random access slide projector a slide projector which can show slides in the magazine in any order rather than merely in the sequence in which they were loaded into the magazine.

Rank order a list of learners' scores, etc given in order of merit, attainment or some other attribute(s).

Rating scale a numerical scale (generally with no more than five or six points) upon which aspects of an exercise, programme, course, etc can be scored as part of a diagnostic or evaluation process.

Raw score a score which has not (so far) been modified by mathematical operations.

Read to scan the information held in a particular location or set of locations in a *store* (read out or *readout*) or feed information into a particular location or set of locations from another source (read in).

Readability a measure of the appropriateness of reading material to the age or ability of the reader.

Reader a projection device used to produce an eye-readable image of a *microcopy* on a small screen, which may be either opaque or translucent.

Reader-printer a microcopy *reader* with additional built-in facilities for producing an eye-legible *hard copy* of any page or section required.

Readiness test a test designed to determine whether a would-be learner has the characteristics needed to cope satisfactorily with a particular course, programme of instruction, etc.

Reading age a measure of the reading ability of an individual in terms of the chronological age of the average population to which he is equivalent in reading ability.

Read-only memory (ROM) a computing term for a *store* from which information can be read as often as required, but, once entered, cannot normally be changed; cf *read/write memory*. See also *PROM, EPROM*.

Readout (a) the display of output from a *computer* or *word processor* in *soft copy* form, normally on the screen of a *video display unit*; cf *printout*; (b) see *read*.

Read/write head a *head* in a *computer terminal* or similar device that can be used both to *read* data out of, and *write* data into, the system.

Read/write memory a computing term for a *store* from which information can be read as often as required and can also be altered as and when necessary; cf *read-only memory*.

Realia real objects, as opposed to models, representations, etc.

Real time the actual time over which a game, simulation or other exercise operates, as opposed to any simulated time scale built into its structure; see also *real-time processing*.

Real-time processing computer processing of data as it arises, so that the information obtained can be of immediate use in analysing or controlling external events happening concurrently.

Rear projection see *back projection*.

Rearrangement test a test that involves arranging items in the correct order or pattern.

Recall test a type of *objective test* in which the subject is required to supply missing items of information (usually words, numbers or phrases) to complete statements.

Receiving an *affective* process that involves showing awareness of, and willingness to receive, certain stimuli such as the aesthetic properties of an object, system, etc; the lowest level (level 1) of Bloom's *affective domain*.

Recognition test a type of recall test in which a learner has to recognize objects, symbols, patterns, words, etc previously encountered or learned.

Record(ing) head a *head* in a tape recorder, data storage device, etc which is used to transfer an incoming signal on to the storage medium.

Recurrent education education that continues throughout an individual's life rather than terminating at the end of the formal education that precedes entry into employment.

Reel-to-reel a term describing a process or machine in which tape or film moves from one open reel or spool to a separate take-up reel or spool during processing, play-back or projection.

Refresher course a course that is designed to reinforce previously-learned skills, knowledge, etc which may have deteriorated through disuse or lapse of time.

Register (a) (verb) to place in exact position or alignment, eg when placing an *overlay* on an overhead transparency or drawing; (b) (noun) a computer *store* which holds information, addresses or instructions on a temporary basis, eg during a multi-stage calculation.

Reinforcement (a) in behavioural psychology, a process in which a *stimulus* presented immediately following a *response* increases the likelihood of the response being repeated when the same situation recurs; (b) the process of helping a learner to master new facts, principles, etc by repetition, rehearsal, demonstrating applications, etc.

Reliability (a) a measure of the consistency with which an item, test, examination, etc produces the same results under different but comparable conditions; (b) the capability of a device to function properly over a period of time.

Reliability co-efficient a statistical measure used to quantify the *reliability* of a test or between two forms of a test.

Remedial frame(s) a frame (or sequence of frames) in a *programmed learning* sequence that covers material previously covered in the programme, usually in order to help the learner master material that he did not succeed in mastering the first time (see Chapter 1).

Remedial instruction a specific unit (or system of units) of instruction based on comprehensive diagnostic findings and intended to overcome a particular learning deficiency (or set of learning deficiencies) in a student.

Remedial loop a loop in an instructional programme that employs *backward branching* whereby a learner is made to repeat a section he has failed to master or is exposed to other remedial material (see Chapter 1).

Remote control a mechanical or electronic facility that enables an operator to control a device such as a camera, projector, videoplayer or television set from a distance, or from another room or building.

Remote terminal a computer terminal sited in a place convenient to a user rather than in the vicinity of a central processing unit; it may be anywhere from the next room to the other side of the world.

Resource a system, set of materials or situation that is deliberately created or set up in order to enable an individual student to learn (see Chapter 9).

Resource-based learning a highly-structured, individualized, student-centred learning system that makes full use of appropriate *resources*, both material and human, in creating an effective learning situation (see Chapter 9).

Resource materials (a) the basic components of a package used in an exercise, programme, course, etc; (b) a general term for *resources* and instructional materials used by learners or teachers.

Resource(s) centre a place — which can be anything from part of a room to a complex of buildings — that is set up specially for the purpose of housing and using a collection of *resources*, both in printed and in non-printed form (see Chapter 9).

Responding an *affective* process that involves showing an interest in an object, system, etc as opposed to merely being aware of it; level 2 of Bloom's *affective domain* (see Chapter 3).

Response (a) in *behavioural psychology*, any implicit or overt change in an organism's behaviour brought about by the application of a *stimulus*; (b) the behaviour a learner emits following an instructional *stimulus* (usually a question or request to perform some activity).

Response card, sheet a printed card or sheet used in an *objective test* as a vehicle for the person being tested to record his answers.

Response frame (a) a *frame* in an *interactive videotex(t)* system that requires a response from the user; (b) in *programmed instruction*, a *frame* which follows on from a *test frame* in a *branching programme*, providing either *reinforcement* or appropriate remedial material depending on whether the response was correct or incorrect.

Restricted response in instructional design, assessment, etc, a *response* which is constrained in some way (as, for example, in a *multiple-choice question*).

Retention test a test administered some time after the completion of a course or programme of instruction in order to determine the extent to which knowledge, skills, etc have been retained by the learner.

Review items items or frames in a *programmed learning* sequence that cause the learner to repeat or review material, usually for *reinforcement* purposes.

Role play a technique (used in *games* and *simulations*) in which participants act out the parts of other persons or categories of persons.

ROM see *read-only memory.*

Rosenthal effect another name for the *Pygmalion effect.*

Rotary stencil duplication a duplicating process in which a special perforated *master* (known as a mimeograph master or stencil) is first prepared and then attached to a rotary drum; the printing takes place by forcing ink through the holes in the master on to the copy paper; also known as *mimeographing*, or *stencil duplication.*

Rote learning a type of learning *drill* in which material is learned by simple repetition.

Routine in computing, a sequence of instructions designed to make a computer carry out a single process or set of related processes.

Routing page a *viewdata* term for a *page* whose function is to indicate a choice of other pages.

Rubric (a) instructions on an examination or test paper; (b) an introduction to a printed syllabus, course description or similar document.

Ruleg a didactic technique that involves first giving a general principle, formula, classification, etc (the 'rule') and then giving illustrative examples, instances, etc (the 'egs'); cf *egrul(e)*.

S

Sandwich course a course in which a learner or trainee alternates between periods of full-time study at a college, university, etc and periods of training and/or work experience in industry, commerce, teaching, etc.

Scale an ordered series of symbols or numbers by means of which a measure of some aspect(s) of a person's behaviour or some aspect(s) or attribute(s) of a system can be given; see also *rating scale*.

Scaling adjustment of examination or other marks so that they conform to an agreed standard or yardstick, thus allowing meaningful comparisons or inferences to be made; see also *grading on the curve*.

Scenario background information relating to the setting of a *game, simulation* or other exercise.

Scene the basic unit of continuity sequence in a film or television production, planned for shooting as continuous, uninterrupted action.

Scrambled text, book a text (book) in which the sequence of pages does not follow logically and whose order of use is determined by the response of the reader to questions; a type of *branching programme*.

Script (a) the detailed scene-by-scene or frame-by-frame instructions for the production of a film, television programme, tape-slide programme, etc; (b) the written answers produced by a person sitting an examination or test.

Scroll a continuous roll of transparent film designed for use with an *overhead projector*.

Scrolling adding a new line of information to an overhead projector display, video display unit screen, etc and accommodating it by moving the existing display upwards or downwards so that part of it disappears from the field of view.

Second-chance institution an institution that provides educational opportunity (particularly at post-school level) for people who did not receive such education at the normal age.

Second-generation computer a *computer* (of the type built during the 1960s) based on the technology of the discrete transistor; see also *first-, third-, fourth-, fifth-generation computer.*

Self-assessment assessment of progress, attainment of objectives, etc by the actual learner, generally by using some sort of questionnaire or criterion-referenced test.

Self-completion questionnaire a questionnaire that is completed by the recipient or interviewee rather than by the interviewer.

Self-display materials another name for *non-projected visual aids.*

Self-help group a group of students on a *distance learning* or other course who get together in order to share ideas, problems and experience and generally help one another with the work of the course (see Chapter 6).

Self-help materials instructional materials or *resources* designed for use by an individual in order to help him carry out some specific task.

Self-instruction an instructional technique which involves the use by learners of individualized instructional materials or *resources* that require minimal (or no) intervention on the part of the teacher (see Chapter 5).

Self-pacing a method where the individual learner controls the speed at which he carries out a given programme or course of work, eg the *Keller Plan* (see Chapter 5).

Self-study centre another name for a *resources centre.*

Self-study material(s) another name for *self-instructional material(s).*

Semantic differential technique a diagnostic technique involving the use of pairs of antonyms joined by a *rating scale* (see Chapter 8).

Semantic prompt (cue) in *behavioural psychology* and instructional design, a *thematic prompt (cue)* that is based on the meaning of language; cf *syntactic prompt (cue).*

Semester system division of the academic year into two equal *semesters*, each of roughly 15-18 weeks' duration, rather than into three terms.

Seminar (a) a small class organized in order to discuss a particular topic; (b) a conference of specialists in a particular field; (c) a short, intensive course on a particular subject or topic.

Sentence completion a type of *completion item* in which the learner has to complete a sentence by adding a missing word (or words).

Sequential access a term applied to any system in which a specific item or section can only be reached by running through the entire system up to the item or section required; cf *random access.*

Serial access another name for *sequential access.*

Serial learning learning to make a series of responses in the correct order, as in the manner of a *serialist.*

Serialist according to Pask, a person who learns, remembers and recapitulates a body of information in terms of string-like cognitive structures where items are related by simple data links; cf *holist.*

Setting *streaming* of pupils in different subjects according to their ability in each subject.

Short-answer question, item an examination or test question requiring only a short answer rather than an extended essay, discussion, proof, etc.

Short-term memory that part of the human *memory* in which material is stored on a short-term, temporary basis before either being forgotten or transferred to the *long-term memory.*

Shot (a) in film or television production, a *scene* or sequence that is photographed or recorded as one continuous piece of action; (b) a particular photograph taken with a still camera.

Shredding submitting possible *multiple-choice items* to a battery of diagnostic procedures in order to determine whether they are suitable for inclusion in a multiple-choice test or examination, ie a combination of item editing and item trial testing; see *validation.*

Simulation (a) in general, any operating representation of a real system or process (or part thereof); (b) an educational, training or research exercise that incorporates such features; see also *participative simulation, predictive simulation, simulation game* (see Chapter 6).

Simulation game an exercise that includes all the essential characteristics of both a *game* and a *simulation.*

Single concept film loop (loop film) a *loop film* that illustrates a particular concept, idea, process, etc and can be shown or viewed at an appropriate point in an instructional programme.

Single-frame a term used to describe a *filmstrip* where the horizontal axis of the pictures is at right angles to the length of the film.

Single-track a term used to describe (a) a recording tape that carries only one recording track; (b) a set of *programmed learning* materials with only a single track through them, ie a *linear programme.*

Situational assessment assessment of a learner's ability to handle particular situations (often simulated) involving decision-making and other skills (see Chapter 7).

Skill(s) analysis a detailed analysis of a task, job or activity in terms of the basic skills involved; also known as task analysis.

Skip branching a type of *branching programme* in which not all the frames are necessarily worked on, depending on the progress of the learner.

Sleep teaching another name for *hypnopaedia.*

Slide a single positive image on transparent material (a slide transparency) held in a mount and designed for projection; see also *compact slide, lantern slide* (see Chapter 4).

Slow motion the technique of slowing down a motion picture film by running the camera faster than normal and then showing the resulting film at normal speed; cf *slow play.*

Slow play the technique of slowing down a motion picture film or videorecording by operating the projector or playback machine slower than normal; cf *slow motion.*

Smart terminal a *computer terminal* which has a certain amount of inbuilt data processing ability, but not so much as an *intelligent terminal.*

Snap change a very rapid slide change between two projectors of a dual- or multi-projector system.

Snowball group a discussion group which moves or is guided through successive phases of idea sharing, with one idea leading on to another; see also *one-two-four snowball technique.*

Social/anthropological approach (to evaluation) a subjective approach to evaluation that is more concerned with studying the on-going process of education than with trying to measure specific outputs (see Chapter 8); also known as *illuminative evaluation.*

Sociodrama the use of *role play* as a means of providing experience of or seeking a solution to a social problem of some sort; see also *psychodrama.*

Soft copy computer output displayed on a *video display unit* or fed into a storage medium, as opposed to *hard copy.*

Soft keyboard a representation of a keyboard on the screen of a *video display unit* that can be used to input data into a computer by pointing a *light pen* at each required character in turn.

Software a general term for material which is used in conjunction with *hardware* (see Chapter 1), although its use is sometimes restricted to describe the programs that control computers; see also *courseware.*

Sound film a motion picture film with a self-contained optical or magnetic *soundtrack.*

Sound filmstrip a *filmstrip* accompanied by an audiorecording, usually a tape cassette.

Sound synchronizer a device linking an audiotape recorder to an automatic slide or filmstrip projector which causes the projector to advance by means of signals recorded on the audiotape.

Soundtrack the optical or magnetic strip on a *sound film* that carries the sound signal; see also *magnetic soundtrack, optical soundtrack.*

Speech compressor an electronic device capable of compressing or expanding an *audio signal* (usually human speech) without changing the pitch.

Speech synthesis the production of speech by artificial means, eg by using a computer to generate the component sounds.

Speed test a test in which the total number of items or questions answered is an important factor; cf *power test.*

Spirit duplicating a method of producing multiple copies of a document from a specially-prepared *master* carrying a reversed image by pressing the copy material, moistened with spirit, against the master.

Splice (a) to make a physical join between the ends of two sections of tape or film using cement or adhesive tape; (b) the resulting cemented or taped join.

Split screen (projection) projection or showing of two or more different images on different parts of the same screen.

Spot questions test or examination questions requiring short, usually factual answers rather than more discussive, essay-style answers (see Chapter 7).

Spreadsheet in computing, a facility whereby a complete table (or set of tables) of data, information, etc can be presented, and where alteration of any one item causes any resulting changes in other items to be made automatically by the computer.

Sprite a small *computer graphics* element (such as a face) which can be controlled and moved as a unit.

Squeezezoom a device that enables the geometry of a video image to be manipulated for artistic or other effects.

S-R bond, connection, mechanism see *stimulus-response bond, mechanism.*

Stand-alone (capability) the capability of an item of equipment to function independently of any other equipment.

Standard 8 standard 8mm motion picture film, as opposed to *super 8* (see Chapter 4).

Start-up costs the total costs involved in launching a project, programme, etc, over and above any operating costs subsequently incurred.

Stem the introductory part of a *multiple-choice item* containing the information on the basis of which the candidate makes his choice of answer from the various options that follow (see Chapter 7).

Stencil duplication another name for *rotary stencil duplication.*

Step in *programmed learning,* one of the discrete stages into which the programme is broken down (see Chapter 1); also known as a *frame.*

Step size in *programmed learning,* the size of a *step* measured in terms of (a) the length of time needed to complete it, (b) the number of words; (c) the amount of information contained (see Chapter 1).

Stereograph a pair of slides or transparencies designed to produce a three-dimensional effect when viewed using a suitable projector or viewer.

Stereophonic a term used to describe a sound recording or sound reproduction system that employs two discrete but related sound-tracks, channels or sources.

Stereoscope an optical device for viewing *stereographs.*

Still motion slide a stationary *slide* or transparency in which an illusion of motion is produced by use of polarized light, *moirée fringes* or some other technique.

Stimulus (a) in *behavioural psychology,* an external or internal force, burst of energy, or other signal that is supplied to an organism in an attempt to activate sensory receptors and internal data processing systems and hence elicit a *response;* (b) in learning theory, a signal, message, question, etc that is given to a learner in an attempt to elicit a desired *response.*

Stimulus-response (S-R) bond, connection, mechanism the link between a *stimulus* and the *response* that it elicits.

Stop motion the technique of exposing one frame of a motion picture film at a time in *time-lapse photography* or *animation* work.

Store a computer memory unit; see also *backing store, main store.*

Storyboard a series of sketches or pictures and any accompanying text used in the planning of an audiovisual programme.

Streaming dividing children of the same chronological age into separate classes on the basis of overall ability or ability in a particular subject; see also *setting.*

String in computing, data processing etc, a linear sequence of *bits,* characters or words recording a particular set of connected data.

Structural communication test a test in which the subject is presented with a grid containing a number of (correct) statements pertaining to a particular topic and has to select and arrange relevant pieces of information in response to questions on the topic (see Chapter 7).

Structured programming a systematic way of designing, building, validating and documenting *computer programs* which, if carried out correctly, leads to the production of error-free, efficient and reliable *software*.

Student-centred approach, learning, teaching an approach to instruction that concentrates on the needs of the individual student, and in which the teacher and the host institution play supportive rather than central roles (see Chapter 2).

Student-paced learning aids, materials learning aids (materials) that are designed in such a way as to allow each individual student to work at his own natural pace (see Chapter 9).

Study guide a document that provides learners with instructions and/or guidance designed to help them cope with the work of a particular course, learning programme, etc, particularly if it is of the self-instructional type.

Study skills the set of skills that a learner needs to develop in order to study effectively.

Stylus (a) a 'needle' used to read the *audio signal* from the groove of a conventional gramophone record; (b) a pen-like device used to input data into a *data tablet*, select material from a computer *menu*, etc; (c) a pointed scriber used in stencil preparation, graphics work, etc.

Subroutine in computing, a minor sequence of instructions that is often repeated, and which is held in a *store* so that it can be called up as and when required rather than entered in full every time it is used in a *program*.

Suite (a) a set of inter-related *computer programs* which can be run consecutively as a single job; (b) a related set of learning packages, instructional exercises, etc; (c) a set of rooms or equipment set aside for a particular purpose (eg an editing suite in a film or television studio).

Summative evaluation evaluation carried out at the conclusion of a project, activity, etc in order to provide data for product validation or to determine the overall effectiveness of a course or other activity.

Super 8 a type of 8mm motion picture film with a larger image than *standard 8* (see Chapter 4).

Surface processing a type of study method in which a learner scans material in order to acquire straightforward factual knowledge or an overview of the content, rather than an in-depth understanding of the latter; cf *deep processing*.

Switched-star system a high-capacity *cable television* distribution system currently being developed in the UK; subscribers are connected via optical fibre cables to local distribution centres, which are, in turn, linked to the main distribution centre.

Synchronizing signal, pulse an audible or inaudible signal or pulse (stored on an audiotape or sound disc) used as a component of a synchronized sound/vision presentation in order to cause the frame to be advanced manually or automatically.

Synchronizing unit an electronic device that enables a pulsed *tape-slide programme* to be played using an ordinary taperecorder and automatic slide projector.

Syndicate a small group of course students or participants in an exercise who are separated from the rest of the students or participants in order to undertake a specified task or investigation.

Syntactic prompt (cue) in instructional design, a *formal prompt (cue)* that is based on the nature of grammar or the structure of language; cf *semantic prompt (cue)*.

Synthesis a *cognitive* process which involves the rearranging of elements, parts, items, etc into a new and integrated whole; level 5 of Bloom's *cognitive domain*.

System the structure or organization of an orderly whole, clearly showing the interrelationship between the different parts (sub-systems) and between the parts and the whole (see Chapter 1).

System software *computer programs* (usually prepared and supplied by the manufacturer of a computer) that provide the link between user programs and the computer *hardware*, eg the programs that control the operation of the computer itself and *compilers* for the high-level programming languages that can be used with it.

Systems approach a term used to describe the systematic application of educational technology to an educational or training problem. starting with the input (*entry behaviour*) and output (*terminal behaviour*) and determining how best to progress from the former to the latter (see Chapter 1).

T

T-group a group in which the members study their own social interactions and try to improve their interpersonal and social skills.

Tablet arm a writing surface attached to, or built into, the arm of a chair in order to facilitate note-taking and similar activities.

Talking book a spoken text recorded either on audiotape or on a sound disc, eg for use with the visually handicapped.

Tape-slide programme, presentation an instructional programme or presentation in the form of a slide sequence accompanied by an audiotape, the two being synchronized by means of audible or inaudible cues recorded on the tape.

Target population that proportion of the total learner population selected for exposure to a specific unit of instruction, instructional product, etc.

Task an activity which forms an observable and/or measurable unit of work, has a direct and immediate outcome, and contributes directly to the accomplishment of a goal or purpose.

Teacher's guide an explanatory handbook for teacher use produced to accompany a textbook or instructional package.

Teacher/institution centred approach the 'traditional' educational system in which instruction is almost entirely under the control of the host institution and teaching staff (see Chapter 2).

Teaching frame in *programmed instruction*, a *frame* that provides the user with new knowledge or helps him/her to re-structure knowledge already possessed; cf *practice frame, test frame.*

Teaching machine a term applied to the various mechanical and electro-mechanical devices that were developed during the 1960s and early 1970s as *delivery systems* for the *programmed learning* materials that were being developed at the time (see Chapter 1).

Team project a project carried out by a co-operative group, often as part of the work of a course (see Chapter 6).

Team teaching a teaching technique in which two or more teachers share responsibilities for a given instructional programme with the same group of learners.

Teazle board, teazlegraph alternative names for a *hook-and-loop board.*

Telebeam projector another name for a *television projector.*

Teleconference a conference arranged by connecting geographically-separated individuals or groups through the public telephone system, using either audio links only (an audioconference) or audio links plus slow-scan television pictures (a television conference).

Telecourse another name for a *distance learning* course.

Telelecture an arrangement which enables a speaker or lecturer to communicate with several classes in different locations simultaneously, using public telephone links.

Telephone instruction education or teaching in which practically all direct communication between the teacher and the student is carried out via the public telephone system; also known as telephone tutoring.

Tele-type terminal another name for a *keyboard terminal.*

(Television) monitor an electronic device which translates television signals into pictures on a cathode ray tube screen and sound; a *monitor* differs from a television receiver in that the input signal is unmodulated and the picture quality is higher; monitors are used mainly in television production and broadcasting, and as *video display units*.

Television projector an electronic device which projects television images on to a large screen, usually for viewing in large rooms or spaces and/or by large groups of people.

Telewriter a device which transmits hand-written or hand-drawn material over a telephone line for display or viewing elsewhere; see also *facsimile transmission (fax)*.

Terminal (a) a device for sending and/or receiving information over a communications channel; (b) see *computer terminal*; (c) relating to the end of a course or programme.

Terminal assessment assessment that is carried out at the end of a course (or section thereof).

Terminal behaviour the set of knowledge, skills, behaviours, etc that a learner is expected to have acquired by the end of a course　or programme of instruction.

Terminal course a course in a subject which is not likely to be taught again during a student's subsequent studies.

Terminal frames *frames* that end or terminate a *programmed learning* sequence; such frames are often used to revise or summarize earlier material.

Test frame in *programmed instruction*, a *frame* (usually at the end of a sequence of *teaching frames* and *practice frames*) that tests the user's mastery of the material covered therein; also known as a *criterion frame*.

Thematic prompt (cue) in *behavioural psychology* or instructional design, a *prompt (cue)* which takes the form of the presentation or implying of meaningful associations that are likely to help the subject or learner to give the desired *response*; cf *formal prompt*.

Thermal copier a reprographic device that makes use of some type of thermographic process, ie makes use of heat for the formation of the image.

Third-generation computer a *computer* that uses microcircuits (complete electronic circuits, including networks of transistors and switches, contained in thin silicon chips) as its main components; such computers started to be built during the early 1970s; see also *first-, second-, fourth-, fifth-generation computer*.

Throw the distance from a projector to the projection screen with which it is used.

Time base corrector an electronic device for synchronizing the *frame* speed of a *video signal* (eg from a videotape) with that of the system into which it is being fed.

Time chart a type of chronological wallchart used in the teaching of history, geology, etc, divisions of time being represented by spaces of corresponding width and events being depicted in those spaces.

Time lapse photography a technique for visualizing normally invisibly slow processes by shooting one frame of a motion picture film at a time at prescribed intervals, and then showing the resulting sequence at normal speed.

Time-sharing a system whereby several users may, through *remote terminals*, each use the facilities of the same large computer at the same time so that each appears to have exclusive use of his own computer.

Toner the black powder that is used to produce the dark image in electrostatic copying.

Tool subject a subject (such as mathematics) through which key skills needed for use in studying other subjects are acquired.

Touch screen terminal a *terminal* with a screen via which information can be fed into a *computer* or similar device by touch, eg using a *soft keyboard.*

Track (a) that discrete area of a film, videotape or (usually) audiotape on which a particular signal is recorded; (b) a term used in *programmed learning* — see *multiple-track, single-track.*

Trackerball a ball-operated control that enables a cursor to be moved around a video screen.

Tractor-feed printer a *printer* that uses continuous stationery, the paper being pulled through the system by sprocket wheels.

Transceiver a *terminal* (such as a teleprinter) which can be used both to transmit and to receive information.

Transcribe to copy a recording or set of data from one storage system or medium to another.

Transducer (a) a device for converting electrical signals into mechanical vibrations or vice versa; (b) an *information technology* term for any device designed to convert signals from one medium to another.

Transfer (a) a term used in *behavioural psychology* to denote the effects of previous experience on later learning — see *horizontal, negative, vertical transfer (of learning)*; (b) a term applied to film, lettering, images, etc that can be transferred from one sheet to another by pressure or other means — see *transfer film, lettering, type.*

Transfer film transparent or translucent film with a pressure-sensitive adhesive back that can be used to add colour, shading, etc to overhead transparencies.

Transfer lettering, type a generic name for sheets of letters which can be transferred to other material by application of pressure (or some other process) during the preparation of graphic material, etc.

Transfer of learning see *transfer*.

Translucent screen a type of screen with a translucent surface used in *back projection*.

Transverse scanning a video scanning system in which the head moves across the recording tape rather than along it as in *helical scanning*.

Tree-and-branch system a *cable television* distribution system in which subscribers are connected to the distribution centre by a branching system of coaxial cables.

True-false test an *objective test* in which the testee has to mark items as either 'true' or 'false'.

True score a score that has been corrected for errors, subjected to standardization, etc; cf *raw score*.

Tuning carrying out fine adjustments to a system in order to optimize its operation.

Turtle a small robot, shaped like a turtle, that is controlled via a *microcomputer*, eg in systems that use the LOGO *high-level programming language*.

Tutor-mode CAL a type of *computer-assisted learning* in which the computer interacts with the learner in a similar way to a live tutor, engaging in a dialogue whose course depends on the responses made by the learner; cf *laboratory mode CAL*.

Twinning stand a stand for mounting two automatic slide projectors one above the other for use in dual projection displays.

U

Underware a term sometimes applied to those aspects of educational technology which underlie the use of *hardware* and *software*; but which cannot be placed in either category (see Chapter 1).

Unique answer question an examination or test question that has a single correct answer or solution, as opposed to an *open-ended* question.

Unobtrusive assessment assessment based on observation that is carried out without the knowledge of the individual or group of people being assessed (see Chapter 7).

Unobtrusive measure an evaluation tool where the actual measurement process is not immediately apparent to, or is remote from, the individual or group being observed (see Chapter 8).

Up-time the time (absolute or fractional) during which a learning resource (usually a device or system) is fully available for use; cf *down-time*.

Use life the maximum amount of time (or number of times) for which a system can be used under normal conditions before deteriorating past the point of usefulness.

User friendly a term applied to a machine or system which is specifically designed so as to be as simple as possible to operate or use.

User-oriented language a computer *programming language* that is designed for use by ordinary computer users rather than by specialist computer staff; see also *high-level programming language*.

V

Validation determination of the effectiveness of instructional materials or systems by the use of appropriate *summative evaluation* techniques. techniques.

Validity the extent to which a test or other measuring instrument fulfils the purpose for which it is designed (see Chapter 7).

Valuing an *affective* process that involves accepting that an object, system, etc, has value; level 3 of Bloom's *affective domain*.

Variable speech a technique used in audio instruction whereby the listener can vary the rate at which spoken information is presented without altering the pitch or introducing distortion.

Velcro board a type of *hook-and-loop board*.

Vertical file materials items such as pamphlets, newspaper or magazine clippings, pictures, etc which, because of their form, can be stored in vertical files in drawers or filing cabinets for ready retrieval and reference.

Vertical transfer (of learning) a form of *transfer of learning* in which a low-order learned skill, concept or fact is put to use in a higher-order or more complex situation of which it is a component.

Vestibule course a course whose purpose is to prepare learners for another course or to introduce them to a particular subject, area or field.

Video (a) (adjective) a term applied to all visual aspects of television signals, equipment, etc; (b) (noun) a loose term for a *videorecording* or for any machine that can be used to record and/or play back such recordings (videocassette recorders, videotape recorders, etc).

Video cartridge a *cartridge* containing *videotape.*

Videocassette a *cassette* containing *videotape.*

Videodisc a disc on which visual images, with or without sound, are electronically or optically recorded; see also *capacitance videodisc, contact videodisc, optical videodisc.*

Video display unit (VDU) a television-like computer terminal on which verbal, numerical or graphical information generated by the computer and user can be displayed.

Video signal an electronic signal, either in *analogue* or *digital* form, representing a visual scene and capable of being used to reproduce that scene; cf *audio signal.*

Videotape special magnetic tape on which encoded television signals are (or may be) recorded.

Videotex(t) a generic term for electronic systems that make computer-stored information available via video display units or television sets; see also *broadcast videotex, interactive videotex.*

Video typewriter another name for a *caption generator.*

Viewdata an alternative name for *interactive videotex(t).*

Vision mixer an electronic control panel for combining separate *video signals* to form a synchronized composite signal; used in television production.

Visual display unit (VDU) another name for a *video display unit.*

Visual learner a learner who, in a visual sense, views a system as a whole rather than analysing it in terms of discrete elements; the visual version of a *holist*; cf *haptic (learner).*

Visual noun a term used to describe a basic element of visual material (eg a chart, *slide* or *loop film*) which can be used in a variety of instructional contexts.

Vocoder a device used in *speech synthesis*; it produces speech that is semantically clear, but does not resemble 'natural' speech in tone quality, etc.

Voice over a narrative accompaniment to a film or television pro-gramme, heard without the speaker being seen.

Vu-foil, vu-graph US names for an *OHP transparency.*

W

Wallchart a relatively large opaque sheet exhibiting information in graphic or tabular form designed to be attached to a wall for display purposes.

Washahead another name for *forward branching*.

Washback another name for *backward branching*.

Weighting the assignment of differential values to test items, scores, etc in order to give them the required degree of relative importance.

Wet carrel a *carrel* that is fitted with one or more mains outlets, so that electrically-operated equipment can be used in it; cf *dry carrel*.

Whiteboard a marker board with a white surface.

Winchester disk a widely-used type of *hard disk*.

Window (a) in *computer graphics*, a specified area that is selected for enlargement, thus effectively defining a 'window' through which that particular part of the display can be viewed in more detail; (b) see *windowing*.

Windowing a facility available with some *microcomputer* systems whereby multiple *inlays (windows)* can be incorporated in existing screen displays, the user then being able to work on any chosen section of the display.

WOOD *w*rite *o*nce *o*ptical *d*isk; a type of *digital optical disk* on which a user can record data, but, once recorded, it cannot be erased or re-recorded.

Word processor a keyboard/microcomputer system that enables text to be composed, edited and filed; the text is held in the computer store and any part can be called up, visually displayed, printed in *hard copy* form, or fed into a different system at any time.

Workbook a text produced as a study or learning guide, usually containing exercises, problems, practice materials, etc.

Work card a re-usable card carrying instructions relating to a particular piece of work, and (usually) giving background information relating to same.

Working memory that part of the *memory* in the *central processing unit* of a digital computer that is actually available to the user at any given time, ie the part not taken up by the operating programs that are in use at the time.

Worksheet a sheet carrying instructions, information, etc relating to part of (or some aspect of) the work of an exercise; such sheets often incorporate spaces where information, answers, results, etc have to be filled in.

Workshop a practical session designed to illustrate the underlying principle, logistics or mechanics of an exercise, programme, etc without necessarily working all the way through it.

Work station (a) in general, a place in a workshop, factory, office, teaching laboratory, language laboratory, etc where an individual works; (b) a *terminal* whereby an individual can gain access to the facilities of a *computer, word processor, data base, interactive video* system, etc, or to a combination of systems of this type.

Write to feed data into a computer *store.*

X

Xerography a widely-used name for *electrostatic copying.*

x-y plotter a *plotter* in which the two variables are respectively plotted along a horizontal x-axis and a vertical y-axis.

Z

Zap to erase material from a computer store.

Zig-zag book a *scrambled text* in which pages are divided into cut sections which can be turned forward or backward independent of one another.

Zoom (a) a visual effect in which it appears that a camera is moving rapidly towards or away from a subject; it is often achieved using a *zoom lens*; (b) a similar effect in *computer graphics.*

Zoom lens a projector or camera lens system with a continuously-variable focal length.

Bibliography

Readers wishing to study any of the topics covered in the various chapters in greater depth may find the following books and articles of interest.

Chapter 1: The Nature of Educational Technology

Beard, R (1972) *Teaching and Learning in Higher Education* (Second Edition). Penguin, Harmondsworth.

Bjerstedt, A (1972) *Educational Technology.* Wiley-Interscience, New York.

Bolam, R (1975) The management of educational change. In Houghton, Y, McHugh, R and Morgan, C (eds) *Management in Education.* Ward Lock International, London.

Bruner, J S (1960) *The Process of Education.* Harvard University Press, Cambridge, Massachusetts.

Bugelski, B R (1971) *The Psychology of Learning Applied to Teaching.* Bobbs-Merrill, New York.

Buzan, T (1979) *How to Study.* Encyclopaedia Britannica, London.

CET (1979) *The Contribution of Educational Technology to Higher Education in the 1990s.* Council for Educational Technology, London.

Champness, B and Young, I (1980) Social limits in educational technology. *European Journal of Education,* 14, 3, pp 229-39.

Clarke, J L (1981) *Educational Development: A Select Bibliography.* Kogan Page, London.

Cleary, A, Mayes, T and Packham, D (1976) *Educational Technology: Implications for Early and Special Education.* Wiley, London.

Cowan, J (1980) Is systematic curriculum design always feasible? *Programmed Learning and Educational Technology,* 17, 2, pp 115-17.

Davies, I K and Hartley, J (eds) (1972) *Contributions to an Educational Technology.* Butterworths, London.

De Cecco, J P (1968) *The Psychology of Learning and Instruction.* Prentice-Hall, Englewood Cliffs, New Jersey.

Elton, L R B (1977) Educational technology —today and tomorrow. In Hills, P and Gilbert, J (eds) *Aspects of Educational Technology* **XI**. Kogan Page, London.

Eraut, M and Squires G (1973) *An Annotated Select Bibliography of Educational Technology* (Second Edition). Council for Educational Technology, London.

Gagné, R M (1970) *The Conditions of Learning* (Second Edition). Holt, Rinehart and Winston, New York.

Gagné, R M and Briggs, L J (1979) *Principles of Instructional Design* (Second Edition). Holt, Rinehart and Winston, New York.

Gagné, R M (ed) (1987) *Instructional Technology: Foundations* Lawrence Erlbaum Associates, Inc., Hillsdale, New Jersey.

Galloway, C (1976) *Psychology for Teaching and Learning.* McGraw-Hill, New York.

Gibbs, G (1981) *Teaching Students to Learn: A Student-Centred Approach.* Open University Press, Milton Keynes.

Glock, M D (ed) (1971) *Guided Learning. Readings in Educational Psychology.* Wiley, New York.

Habeshaw, T, Gibbs, G and Habeshaw, S (1987) *53 Interesting Ways of Helping Your Students to Study.* Technical and Educational Services, Bristol.

Hartley, J and Davies, I K (1978) *Contributions to an Educational Technology, 2.* Kogan Page, London.

Hawkridge, D G (1981) The telesis of educational technology. *British Journal of Educational Technology,* **12**, 1, pp 4-18.

Houghton, V, McHugh, R and Morgan, C (eds) (1975) *Management in Education.* Ward Lock Educational, London.

Huczynski, A (1983) *Encyclopaedia of Management Development Methods.* Gower Press, Farnborough.

Lewis, B N (1980) The professional standing of educational technology. In Howe, A (ed) *International Yearbook of Educational and Training Technology 1980/81.* Kogan Page, London.

Lewis, R (ed) (1984) *Open Learning in Action.* Council for Educational Technology, London.

Morgan, R N (1978) Educational technology: adolescence to adulthood. *Educational Communication and Technology,* **26**, 2.

Nickson, M (1971) *Educational Technology. A Systematic Approach for Teachers.* Ward Lock Educational, London.

Osborne, C W (ed) (1986) *International Yearbook of Educational and Instructional Technology 1986/87.* Kogan Page, London.

Popham, W J and Baker, E L (1970) *Systematic Instruction.* Prentice-Hall, Englewood Cliffs, New Jersey.

Race, W P (1981) Help yourself to success — improving polytechnic students' study skills. In Percival, F and Ellington. H I (eds) *Aspects of Educational Technology,* **XV**. *Distance Learning and Evaluation.* Kogan Page, London.

Ramsden, P (1987) *Improving Learning: A New Perspective.* Kogan Page, London.

Reif, F (1978) Towards an applied science of education. *Instructional Science*, 7, pp 1-14.

Richey, R (1986) *The Theoretical and Conceptual Bases of Instructional Design*. Kogan Page, London.

Richmond, W K (1969) A systems approach to educational reform: the Swedish example. In *The Education Industry*. Methuen, London.

Richmond, W K (1970) *The Concept of Educational Technology*. Weidenfeld and Nicolson, London.

Rogers, C (1969) *Freedom to Learn*. Merrill, Columbus, Ohio.

Romiszowski, A J (1974) *The Selection and Use of Instructional Media: A Systems Approach*. Kogan Page, London.

Romiszowski, A J (1983) *Designing Instructional Systems*. Kogan Page, London.

Romiszowski, A J (1985) *Producing Instructional Systems*. Kogan Page, London.

Rowlands, S and Rowlands, N (1986) *Into Open Learning*. Open Learning Systems, London.

Rowntree, D (1976) *Learn How to Study*. McDonald and Jane's, London.

Rowntree, D (1982) *Educational Technology in Curriculum Development* (Second Edition). Harper and Row, London.

Saettler, P (1978) The roots of educational technology. *Programmed Learning and Educational Technology*, 15, 1.

Skinner, B F (1968) *The Technology of Teaching*. Appleton-Century-Crofts, New York.

Stenhouse, L (1971) *An Introduction to Curriculum Development and Research*. Heinemann, London.

Tickton, S G (ed) (1970) *To Improve Learning*. Bowker, New York.

Trott, A J, Strongman, H and Giddins, L (1983) *Aspects of Educational Technology*, **XVI**. *Improving Efficiency in Education and Training*. Kogan Page, London.

Unwin, D and McAleese, R (1978) *Encyclopaedia of Educational Media, Communications and Technology*. Macmillan, London.

UTMU (1976) *Improving Teaching in Higher Education*. University of London Teaching Methods Unit, London.

Chapter 2: Basic Educational Strategies

Allen, P S (1978) Developing a remedial Keller Plan course. *Studies in Higher Education*, 3, 2.

Ausubel, D P and Robinson, F G (1969) *School Learning*. Holt, Rinehart and Winston, New York.

Bennett, S N (1976) *Teaching Styles and Pupil Progress*. Open Books, London.

Berstein, B (1971) Open Schools, Open Society. In Cosin, B R *et al* (eds) *School and Society: A Sociological Reader*. Routledge and Kegan Paul, London.

Boud, D (ed) (1987) *Developing Student Autonomy in Learning.* Kogan Page, London.

Bremer, J and Von Moschzisker, M (1971) *The School Without Walls.* Holt, Rinehart and Winston, New York.

Brewer, I M (1985) *Learning More and Teaching Less. A Decade of Innovation in Self-Instruction and Small Group Learning.* SRHE and NFER-Nelson, Guildford.

Coffey, J (1978) *Development of an Open Learning System in Further Education* (Working Paper 15). Council for Educational Technology, London.

Daly, D W and Robertson, S M (1978) *Keller Plan in the Classroom.* Scottish Council for Educational Technology, Glasgow.

Davies, T C (1977) *Open Learning Systems for Mature Students* (Working Paper 14). Council for Educational Technology, London.

Earl, T (1987) *The Art and Craft of Course Design.* Kogan Page, London.

Galton, M, Simon, B and Croll, P (1980) *Inside the Primary Classroom.* Routledge and Kegan Paul, London.

Gross, N. Giacquinta, J B and Bernstein, M (1971) *Implementing Organizational Innovations.* Harper and Row, New York.

Haddon, F A and Lytton, H (1968) Teaching approach and the development of divergent thinking abilities in primary schools. *British Journal of Educational Psychology,* **38**, 2, pp 171-9.

Hooper, R S (ed) (1971) *The Curriculum: Context Design and Development.* Oliver and Boyd, Edinburgh.

Keller, F S (1968) Goodbye teacher . . . *Journal of Applied Behaviour Analysis,* 1, pp 79-89.

Keller, F S and Sherman, J (1974) *The Keller Plan Handbook* Benjamin, Menlo Park, California.

Mackenzie, N, Postgate, R and Scupham, J (1975) *Open Learning Systems and Problems in Post Secondary Education.* UNESCO Press, London.

Miller, A H (1987) *Course Design for University Lecturers.* Kogan Page, London.

Percival, F, Craig, D and Buglass, D (1987) *Aspects of Educational Technology,* **XX**. *Flexible Learning Systems.* Kogan Page, London.

Romiszowski, A J (1981) *Designing Instructional Systems.* Kogan Page, London.

Rowntree, D (1974) *Educational Technology in Curriculum Development.* Harper and Row, London.

Rowntree, D (1981) *Developing Courses for Students.* McGraw-Hill, London.

Spencer, D C (1980) *Thinking About Open Learning Systems* (Working Paper 19). Council for Educational Technology, London.

Tucker, R (ed) (1986) *The Integration of Media into the Curriculum.* Kogan Page, London.

Weston, P B (1980) *Negotiating the Curriculum: A Study in Secondary Schooling.* NFER Publishing, Slough.

Chapter 3: Educational Objectives

Beard, R (1972) *Teaching and Learning in Higher Education.* Penguin, Harmondsworth.

Bloom, B S (ed) (1972) *Taxonomy of Educational Objectives. Book 1: Cognitive Domain.* Longman, London.

Bloom, B S, Hastings, J T and Madaus, J F (1971) *Handbook on Formative and Summative Evaluation of Student Learning.* McGraw-Hill, New York.

Bloom, B S, Krathwohl, D R and Masia, B (1964) *Taxonomy of Educational Objectives. Book 2: Affective Domain.* Longman, London.

Bosten, R E (1972) *How to Write and Use Performance Objectives to Individualize Instruction. Volumes 1-4.* Educational Technology Publications, Englewood Cliffs, New Jersey.

Byrne, M S and Johnstone, A H (1987) Can critical-mindedness be taught? *Education in Chemistry,* 20, 3, pp 75-7.

Calder, J R (1980) In defense of the systematic approach to instruction and behavioural objectives. *Educational Technology,* 20, pp 21-5.

Eisner, E W (1967) Educational objectives: help or hindrance? *School Review,* 75, pp 250-60.

Harrow, A J (1972) *A Taxonomy of the Motor Domain.* McKay, New York.

Henrysson, S and Franke-Wikberg, S (1979) Long term effects of higher education. *International Newsletter,* 12, pp 7-9. Society for Research into Higher Education.

Kapfer, M B (ed) (1971) *Behavioural Objectives in Curriculum Development.* Educational Technology Publications, Englewood Cliffs, New Jersey.

Macdonald-Ross, M (1973) Behavioural objectives — a critical review. *Instructional Science,* 2, 1, pp 1-52.

Mager, R F (1962) *Preparing Instructional Objectives.* Fearon, Palo Alto, California.

Ormell, C P (1974) Bloom's taxonomy and the objectives of education. *Educational Research,* 17, 1.

Ormell, C P (1974) Objections to Bloom's taxonomy. *Journal of Curriculum Studies,* 6, pp 3-18.

Peters, R S (ed) (1969) *Proceedings of UTMU Conference on Objectives in Higher Education.* University of London Institute of Education, London.

Plowman, P D (1971) *Behavioural Objectives.* Science Research Associates, Chicago.

Pope, D (1983) *The Objectives Model of Curriculum Planning and Evaluation.* Council for Educational Technology, London.

Pring, R (1971) Bloom's taxonomy: a philosophical critique. *Cambridge Journal of Education,* 2, pp 83-91.

Rowntree, D (1973) Which objectives are most worthwhile? In Leedham, J F and Budgett, R E B (eds) *Aspects of Educational Technology,* **VII.** Pitman, London.

Rowntree, D (1982) *Educational Technology in Curriculum Development* (Second Edition). Harper and Row, London.

Simpson, E (1971) Educational objectives in the psychomotor domain. In Kapfer, M B (ed) *Behavioural Objectives in Curriculum Development.* Educational Technology Publications, Englewood Cliffs, New Jersey.

Stenhouse, L (1975) Some limitations of the use of objectives in curriculum research and planning. *Paedagogica Europaea,* 6, pp 73-83.

Stones, E (1972) *Educational Objectives and the Teaching of Educational Psychology.* Methuen, London.

UTMU (1976) *Improving Teaching in Higher Education.* University of London Teaching Methods Unit, London.

Warren Piper, D J (1969) An approach to designing courses based on the recognition of objectives. In Peters, R S (ed) *Proceedings of UTMU Conference on Objectives in Higher Education.* University of London Institute of Education, London.

Chapter 4: Mass Instruction Techniques

Beard, R (1972) *Teaching and Learning in Higher Education.* Penguin, Harmondsworth.

Bligh, D A (1972) *What's the Use of Lectures?* Penguin, Harmondsworth.

Bligh, D A *et al* (1975) *Teaching Students.* Exeter University Teaching Services, Exeter.

Brown, G A (1978) *Lecturing and Explaining.* Methuen, London.

Ellington, H I (1985) *Producing Teaching Materials: A Handbook for Teachers and Trainers.* Kogan Page, London.

Ellington, H I (1987) *Some Hints on How to be an Effective Lecturer.* CICED Publications, Dundee College of Technology, Dundee.

Erickson, C W H (1972) *Fundamentals of Teaching with Audio-Visual Technology.* Collier-Macmillan, New York.

Gibbs, G, Habeshaw, S and Habeshaw, T (1986) *53 Interesting Things to Do in Your Lectures.* Technical and Educational Services, Bristol.

Hawkridge, D (1981) *Organizing Educational Broadcasting.* Croom Helm, London.

Henderson, J and Humphreys, F (1981) *The Audio Visual Handbook.* Kogan Page, London.

Johnstone, A H and Percival, F (1981) Attention breaks in lectures. *Education in Chemistry,* 13, 3, pp 49-50.

McInnes, J (1980) *Video in Education and Training.* Focal Press, London on Teaching Methods 1). Cambridge Institute of Education, Cambridge, UK.

McRae, R K (1975) *The Overhead Projector.* Association for the Study of Medical Education, Dundee.

Ogborn, J (ed) (1977) *Practical Work in Undergraduate Science.* Heinemann, London.

Powell, L S (1978) *A Guide to the Use of Visual Aids.* (Fourth Edition). British Association for Commercial and Industrial Education, London.

Powell, L S (1980) *A Guide to the Overhead Projector.* British Association for Commercial and Industrial Education, London.

Romiszowski, A J (1987) *Developing Auto-Instructional Materials.* Kogan Page, London.

Romiszowski, A J (1987) *The Selection and Use of Instructional Media.* Kogan Page, London.

Rowatt, R W (1980) *OHP − A Guide to the Use of the Overhead Projector.* Scottish Council for Educational Technology, Glasgow.

UTMU (1976) *Improving Teaching in Higher Education.* University of London Teaching Methods Unit, London.

Waters, C D J and Lawrie, N L (1981) The use of television equipment in Scottish secondary schools. In Percival, F and Ellington, H I (eds) *Aspects of Educational Technology,* **XV.** Kogan Page, London.

Chapter 5: Individualized Learning Techniques

Barnet College of Further Education (1978) *Flexi-Study: A Manual for Local Colleges.* National Extension College, Cambridge, UK.

Bates, A W (1982) Learning from audio-visual media: the Open University experience. In *Teaching at a Distance: Research Supplement 1.* Open University, Milton Keynes.

Birch, D W and Cuthbert, R E (1981) *Costing Open Learning in Further Education.* Council for Educational Technology, London.

Block, J H (1971) *Mastery Learning: Theory and Practice.* Holt, Rinehart and Winston, New York.

Boud, D J (ed) (1987) *Developing Student Autonomy in Learning.* Kogan Page, London.

Boud, D J and Bridge, W (1974) Keller Plan: a case study in individualized learning. In *Towards Independence in Learning.* The Nufffield Foundation, London.

Brewer, I M (1985) *Learning More and Teaching Less. A Decade of Innovation in Self-Instruction and Small Group Learning.* SRHE and NFER-Nelson, Guildford.

Bridge, W and Elton, L R B (eds) (1977) *Individual Study in Undergraduate Science.* Heinemann, London.

Butts, D (1981) Distance learning and broadcasting. In Percival, F and Ellington, H I (eds) *Aspects of Educational Technology,* **XV.** Kogan Page, London.

Clarke, J and Leedham, J (eds) (1976) *Aspects of Educational Technology,* **X**. *Individualized Learning.* Kogan Page, London.

Coffey, J (1978) *Development of an Open Learning System in Further Education: A Report.* (Working Paper 15). Council for Educational Technology, London.

Daly, D W and Robertson, S M (eds) (1978) *Keller Plan in the Classroom.* Scottish Council for Educational Technology, Glasgow.

Davies, T C (1977) *Open Learning Systems for Mature Students.* (Working Paper 14). Council for Educational Technology, London.

Davies, W J K (1978) *Implementing Individualised Learning in Schools and Colleges.* (Guidelines 4). Council for Educational Technology, London.

Davies, W J K (1980) *Alternatives to Class Teaching in Colleges and Schools* (Guidelines 9). Council for Educational Technology, London.

Ellington, H I (1985) *Producing Teaching Materials: A Handbook for Teachers and Trainers.* Kogan Page, London.

Gagné, R M (ed) (1967) *Learning and Individual Differences.* Macmillan, New York.

Goldschmid, B and Goldschmid, M L (1976) Peer teaching in higher education: a review. *Higher Education,* **5**, 1, pp 9-33.

Graves, J and Graves, V (1979) *Designing a Tape-Slide Programme.* Association for the Study of Medical Education, Dundee.

Harding, A G (1973) The project: its place as a learning situation. *British Journal of Educational Technology,* 4, pp 216-32.

Harris, W J A and Williams, J D S (1977) *A Handbook on Distance Education* (Manchester Monograph 7). Manchester University, Manchester.

Hartley, J (1985) *Designing Instructional Text.* Kogan Page, London.

Heidt, E U (1976) *Instructional Media and the Individual Learner.* Kogan Page, London.

Heidt, E U (1980) Differences between media and differences between learners: can we relate them? *Instructional Science,* **9**, pp 365-91.

Hills, P J (1976) *The Self-Teaching Process in Higher Education.* Croom Helm, London.

Holmberg, B (1977) *Distance Education — A Survey and Bibliography.* Kogan Page, London.

Holmberg, B (1981) *Status and Trends of Distance Education.* Kogan Page, London.

Keller, F S (1968) Goodbye teacher . . . *Journal of Applied Behavioural Analysis,* 1, pp 79-89.

Keller, F S and Sherman, J (1974) *The Keller Plan Handbook.* Benjamin, Menlo Park, California.

Lewis, R (1981) *How to Tutor in an Open Learning Scheme.* Council for Educational Technology, London.

Lewis, R (1981) *How to Write Self-Study Materials* (Guidelines 10). Council for Educational Technology, London.

Lewis, R (ed) (1984) *Open Learning in Action*. Council for Educational Technology, London.

Lewis, R and Jones, G (eds) (1980) *How to Write a Distance Learning Package: A Self-Study Pack for Authors*. Council for Educational Technology, London.

Lickley, A (1977) *Towards Individualized Learning in Teacher Education*. Council for Educational Technology, London.

Long, D G (1987) *Self Directed Learning: The Key to Lifelong Learning and Development*. Kogan Page, London.

Mackenzie, M L (1978) *Deciding to Individualize Learning: A Study of the Process*. Council for Educational Technology, London.

Mackenzie, N, Postgate, R and Scupham, J (1975) *Open Learning Systems for Post-Secondary Education*. UNESCO Press, London.

Manpower Services Commission (1981) *An 'Open Tech' Programme: A Consultative Document*. Manpower Services Commission, London.

Manwaring, G (1977) *Individualized Learning*. Dundee College of Education, Dundee (Audio-visual package).

Neil, M W (ed) (1981) *Education of Adults at a Distance: A Report of the Open University's Tenth Anniversary Conference*. Kogan Page, London.

Nuffield Foundation (1974) *Towards Independence in Learning*. The Nuffield Foundation, London.

O'Neill, G (1987) Interactive video as an aid to learning. *Programmed Learning and Educational Technology*, 24, 2, pp 137-44.

Percival, F, Craig, D and Buglass, D (1987) *Aspects of Educational Technology, XX. Flexible Learning Systems*. Kogan Page, London.

Percival, F and Ellington, H I (eds) (1981) *Aspects of Educational Technology, XV. Distance Learning and Evaluation*. Kogan Page, London.

Romiszowski, A J (ed) (1976) *Programmed Learning and Educational Technology*, 13, 1 (Special issue on 'Individualization in Higher Education').

Romiszowski, A J (1987) *Developing Auto-Instructional Materials*. Kogan Page, London.

Rowatt, R W (1980) *Slide-Tape — A Guide to the Production of Slide-Tape Programmes*. Scottish Council for Educational Technology, Glasgow.

Rowlands, S and Rowlands, N (1986) *Into Open Learning*. Open Learning Systems, London.

Rowntree, D (ed) (1976) *Programmed Learning and Educational Technology*, 13, 4 (Special issue on 'The Open University').

Rowntree, D and Conners, B (eds) (1980) *How to Develop Self-Instructional Teaching. A Self-Instructional Guide to the Writing of Self-Instructional Materials*. The Open University, Milton Keynes.

Rowntree, D (1986) *Teaching Through Self-Instruction*. Kogan Page, London.

Ruskin, R S (ed) (1977) *Educational Technology*, **17**, 9 (Special issue on 'The Personalized System of Instruction (PSI)').

Spencer, D C (1977) *Independence in Learning* (Coombe Lodge Information Paper 1193). Coombe Lodge, Bristol.

Spencer, D C (1980) *Thinking About Open Learning Systems* (Working Paper 19). Council for Educational Technology, London.

SRHE (1976) *The Use of Project Methods in Higher Education.* Society for Research in Higher Education, London.

Twining, J (ed) (1982) *Open Learning for Technicians.* Stanley Thorne, Cheltenham.

Young, M et al (1980) *Distance Teaching for the Third World.* Routledge and Kegan Paul, London.

Chapter 6: Group Learning Techniques

Abercrombie, M L J (1979) *Aims and Techniques of Group Teaching* (Fourth Edition). Society for Research into Higher Education, Guildford.

Abercrombie, M L J and Terry, P M (1978) *Talking to Learn: Improving Teaching and Learning in Small Groups.* Society for Research into Higher Education, Guildford.

Boocock, S S and Schild, E O (eds) (1968) *Simulation Games in Learning.* Sage Publications, Beverly Hills, California.

Bramley, W (1979) *Group Tutoring: Concepts and Case Studies.* Kogan Page, London.

Brewer, I M (1985) *Learning More and Teaching Less. A Decade of Innovation in Self-Instruction and Small Group Learning.* SRHE and NFER-Nelson, Guildford.

Brown, G A (1975) *Microteaching, a Programme of Teaching Skills.* Methuen, London.

Christopher, E M and Smith, L E (1987) *Management Training through Gaming: Power, People and Problem Solving.* Kogan Page, London.

Ellington, H I (1985) *Producing Teaching Materials: A Handbook for Teachers and Trainers.* Kogan Page, London.

Ellington, H I, Addinall, E and Percival, F (1981) *Games and Simulations in Science Education.* Kogan Page, London.

Ellington, H I, Addinall, E and Percival, F (1982) *A Handbook of Game Design.* Kogan Page, London.

Ellington, H I, Addinall, E and Percival, F (1984) *Case Studies in Game Design.* Kogan Page, London.

Ellington, H I and Percival, F (1977) Educating 'through' science using multi-disciplinary simulation games. *Programmed Learning and Educational Technology*, **14**, 2, pp 117-26.

Greenblat, C S and Duke, R D (1981) *Principles and Practice of Gaming-Simulation.* Sage Publications, Beverly Hills, California.

Habeshaw, S, Habeshaw, T and Gibbs, G (1986) *53 Interesting Things to Do in Your Seminars and Tutorials.* Technical and Educational Services, Bristol.

Hargie, O and Maidment, P (1978) *Microteaching in Perspective.* Blackstaff Press, Dundonald, Co Down.

Hill, W F (1977) *Learning Thru' Discussion.* Sage Publications, Beverly Hills, California.

Jaques, D (1984) *Learning in Groups.* Croom Helm, London.

Jones, K (1980) *Simulations: A Handbook for Teachers.* Kogan Page, London.

Jordan, W J J (1961) *Synectics.* Harper and Row, London.

Marshall, S and Williams, N (1986) *Exercises in Teaching Communication.* Kogan Page, London.

Megarry, J (ed) (1977) *Aspects of Simulation and Gaming.* Kogan Page, London.

Megarry, J (1979) Developments in simulation and gaming. In Howe, A and Romiszowski, A J (eds) *International Yearbook of Educational and Instructional Technology 1978/79.* Kogan Page, London.

Ogborn, J (ed) (1977) *Small Group Teaching in Undergraduate Science.* Heinemann, London.

Pfeiffer, J W and Jones, J E (1969-1983) *Annual Handbooks for Group Facilitators.* University Associates, La Jolla, California.

Rowntree, D (1982) *Educational Technology in Curriculum Development* (Second Edition). Harper and Row, London.

Ruddock, J (1978) *Learning Through Small Group Discussion.* Society for Research into Higher Education, Guildford.

Simons, H, Squires, G and Ruddock, J (1976) *Small Group Teaching: Selected Papers.* The Nuffield Foundation, London.

Steeds, D, Habeshaw, S, Gibbs, G and Habeshaw, T (1987) *53 Interesting Communication Exercises for Science Students.* Technical and Educational Services, Bristol.

Tansey, P J (ed) (1971) *Educational Aspects of Simulation.* McGraw-Hill, London.

Tansey, P J and Unwin, D (1969) *Simulation and Gaming in Education.* Methuen, London.

Taylor, J L and Walford, R (1978) *Learning and the Simulation Game.* Open University Press, Milton Keynes.

Teather, D L B (1978) Simulation and games. In Unwin, D and McAleese, R (eds) *Encyclopaedia of Educational Media, Communications and Technology.* Macmillan, London.

Twelker, P A (1971) Simulation and media. In Tansey, P J (ed) *Educational Aspects of Simulation.* McGraw-Hill, London.

Vincent, B and Vincent, T (1985) *Information Technology and Further Education.* Kogan Page, London.

Van Ments, M (1983) *The Effective Use of Role Play.* Kogan Page, London.

Wentworth, D R and Lewis, D R (1973) A review of research on instructional games and simulations in social science education. *Social Education* May. pp 432-48.

Chapter 7: Student Assessment

Clift, J C and Imrie, B W (1981) *Assessing Students, Appraising Teachers.* Croom Helm, London.

Davies, D (1986) *Maximizing Examination Performance.* Kogan Page, London.

Ebel, R L (1972) *Essentials of Educational Measurement.* Prentice-Hall, Englewood Cliffs, New Jersey.

Edwards, D (1979) A study of reliability of tutor-marked assignments in the Open University. *Assessment in Higher Education,* 5, 1, pp 16-44.

Fairbrother, R (1975) The reliability of teachers' judgements of the abilities tested by multiple-choice items. *Educational Research,* 17, 3, pp 202-10.

Frith, D and Macintosh, H G (1984) *A Teacher's Guide to Assessment.* Stanley Thornes, Cheltenham.

Gibbs, G, Habeshaw, S and Habeshaw, T (1986) *53 Interesting Ways to Assess Your Students.* Technical and Educational Services, Bristol.

Harris, D and Bell, C (1986) *Evaluating and Assessing for Learning.* Kogan Page, London.

Hudson, B (1973) *Assessment Techniques.* Methuen, London.

Illiffe, A H (1966) Objective tests. In Heywood, J and Illiffe, A H (eds) *Some Problems of Testing Academic Performance.* Department of Higher Education, University of Lancaster.

Ingenkamp, K (1977) *Educational Assessment* NFER Publishing, Slough.

Klug, B (ed) (1975) *A Question of Degree: Assorted Papers on Assessment.* The Nuffield Foundation, London.

Knox, J D (1975) *The Modified Essay Question.* Association for the Study of Medical Education, Dundee.

Lennox, B (1974) *Hints on the Setting and Evaluation of Multiple Choice Questions of the One from Five Type.* Association for the Study of Medical Education, Dundee.

Miller, C and Parlett, M (1974) *Up to the Mark: A Study of the Examination Game.* Society for Research into Higher Education, Guildford.

Popham, W J (ed) (1971) *Criterion-Referenced Measurement.* Educational Technology Publications, Englewood Cliffs, New Jersey.

Rowntree, D (1987) *Assessing Students: How Shall We Know Them?* (Revised Edition). Kogan Page, London.

Rowntree, D (1982) *Educational Technology in Curriculum Development* (Second Edition). Harper and Row, London.

Satterly, D (1981) *Assessment in Schools.* Blackwell, Oxford.

SED (1979) *Issues in Educational Assessment.* HMSO, Edinburgh.

Sumner, R (1982) *Assessment in Schools.* Croom Helm, London.

Sumner, R and Bradley, K (1977) *Assessment in Transition.* NFER Publishing, Slough.

Sumner, R and Robertson, T S (1976) *Criterion-Referenced Measurement and Criterion-Referenced Tests: Some Published Work Reviewed.* NFER Publishing, Slough.

Tittle, C K and Miller, K M (1976) *Assessing Attainment.* Independent Assessment and Research Centre, London.

Tuckman, B W (1975) *Measuring Educational Outcomes: Fundamentals of Testing.* Harcourt Brace Jovanovich, New York.

Tyler, R W and Wolf, R M (eds) (1976) *Critical Issues in Testing.* McCutchan, Berkeley, California.

Wardrop, J L (1976) *Standardized Testing in the Schools: Uses and Roles.* Brooks/Cole, Monterey, California.

Webb, E J, Campbell, D T, Schwartz, R D and Sechrest, L (1969) *Unobtrusive Measures: Non-Reactive Research in the Social Sciences.* Rand McNally, Chicago.

Chapter 8: Evaluation

Beard, R (1972) *Teaching and Learning in Higher Education.* Penguin, Harmondsworth.

Becher, T (1981) Evaluation and educational technology. In Percival, F and Ellington, H I (eds) *Aspects of Educational Technology, XV.* Kogan Page, London.

Birch, D W and Cuthbert, R E (1981) *Costing Open Learning in Further Education.* Council for Educational Technology, London.

Bligh, D (1972) Evaluation of teaching in groups by interaction analysis. In *Varieties of Group Discussion in University Teaching.* University of London Institute of Education, London.

Bloomer, J (1975) Paradigms of evaluation. *SAGSET Journal, 5,* 1, pp 36-7.

Clift, J C and Imrie, B W (1981) *Assessing Students, Appraising Teachers.* Croom Helm, London.

Ellington, H I (1981) Course development by error elimination — a Popperian approach. *Coombe Lodge Report: Course Monitoring and Evaluation.* Coombe Lodge, Bristol.

Elton, L (1987) *Teaching in Higher Education: Appraisal and Training.* Kogan Page, London.

Eraut, M R (1970) The role of evaluation. In Taylor, G (ed) *The Teacher as a Manager.* Council for Educational Technology, London.

Falk, B and Lee Dow, K (1971) *The Assessment of University Teaching.* Society for Research into Higher Education, London.

Fielden, J and Pearson, P K (1978) *Costing Educational Practice.* Council for Educational Technology, London.

Fielden, J and Pearson, P K (1978) *The Cost of Learning with Computers: Report of the Financial Evaluation of the National Development Programme in Computer Assisted Learning.* Council for Educational Technology, London.

Flood-Page, C (1974) *Student Evaluation of Teaching: The American Experience*. Society for Research into Higher Education, London.

Habeshaw, T, Habeshaw, S and Gibbs, G (1987) *53 Interesting Ways to Evaluate Courses and Teaching*. Technical and Educational Services, Bristol.

Hamilton, D *et al* (1977) *Beyond the Numbers Game: A Reader in Educational Evaluation*. Macmillan, London.

Harlen, W (1975) *Evaluation in Curriculum Development: Twelve Case Studies*. Macmillan, London.

Harris, N D C and Bell, C D (1981) An evaluation resource pack: issues and implications. In Percival, F and Ellington, H I (eds) *Aspects of Educational Technology*, **XV**. Kogan Page, London.

Harris, D and Bell, C (1986) *Evaluating and Assessing for Learning*. Kogan Page, London.

Harris, N D C, Bell, C D and Carter, J E H (1981) *Signposts for Evaluating: A Resource Pack*. Council for Educational Technology, London.

Henderson, E S and Nathenson, M B (1976) Developmental testing: an empirical approach to course improvement. *Programmed Learning and Educational Technology*, **13**, 4, pp 31-42.

Knapper, C K (1980) *Evaluating Instructional Technology*. Croom Helm, London.

Lawless, C J (1981) Evaluating the process of learning. In Percival, F and Ellington, H I (eds) *Aspects of Educational Technology*, **XV**. Kogan Page, London.

McIntyre, D I (1980) Systematic observation of classroom activities. *Educational Analysis*, **2**, 2, pp 3-30.

Nathenson, M B and Henderson, E S (1980) *Using Student Feedback to Improve Learning Materials*. Croom Helm, London.

Oppenheim, A N (1966) *Questionnaire Design and Attitude Measurement*. Heinemann, London.

Pace, C R (1972) *Thoughts on Evaluation in Higher Education*. American College Testing Programme, Iowa.

Parlett, M and Hamilton, D (1972) *Evaluation as Illumination: A New Approach to the Study of Innovatory Programmes*. (Occasional Paper 9). Centre for Research in the Educational Sciences, University of Edinburgh.

Percival, F (1978) Evaluation procedures for simulation/gaming exercises. In McAleese, R (ed) *Perspectives on Academic Gaming and Simulation 3*. Kogan Page, London.

Percival, F (1981) The student questionnaire — a vehicle for on-going course development. *Coombe Lodge Report: Course Monitoring and Evaluation*. Coombe Lodge, Bristol.

Percival, F and Ellington, H I (eds) (1981) *Aspects of Educational Technology*, **XV**. *Distance Learning and Evaluation*. Kogan Page, London.

Popper, K R (1972) *The Logic of Scientific Discovery* (Third Edition). Hutchinson, London.

Rowntree, D (1982) *Educational Technology in Curriculum Development* (Second Edition). Harper and Row, London.

Stake, R E (1978) *Evaluating the Arts in Education — A Responsive Approach.* Merrill, Columbus, Ohio.

UTMU (1975) *Evaluating Teaching in Higher Education.* University of London Teaching Methods Unit, London.

UTMU (1976) *Improving Teaching in Higher Education.* University of London Teaching Methods Unit, London.

Chapter 9: Resources Centres

Atherton, B (1980) *Adapting Spaces for Resource-Based Learning* (Guidelines 8). Council for Educational Technology, London.

Barker, A L and Cowan, J (1978) Cataloguing and retrieval of interrelated resource material. *British Journal of Educational Technology,* **9**, 1, pp 59-70.

Beswick, N J (1975) *Organising Resources: Six Case Studies.* Heinemann, London.

Beswick, N J (1977) *Resource-Based Learning.* Heinemann, London.

Boyce, L (1987) Student-centred learning: some implications for learning resources provision. *Coombe Lodge Report,* **19**, 9, pp 547-58.

CET (1974) *Non-Book Materials: Cataloguing Rules* (Working Paper 11). Library Association/Council for Educational Technology, London.

Clarke, J (ed) (1975) *Programmed Learning and Educational Technology,* **12**, 3 (Special issue on 'Resource Centres in Education').

Clarke, J (1978) *Learning Resources for an Institution of Higher Education: A Feasibility Study.* Dundee College of Education, Dundee.

Clarke, J (1982) *Resource-Based Learning for Higher and Continuing Education.* Croom Helm, London.

Crabb, G (1975) Copyright and the resource centre. *Programmed Learning and Educational Technology,* **12**, 3, pp 191-8.

Davies, W J K (1977) *Learning Resources? An Argument for Schools* (Guidelines 1). Council for Educational Technology, London.

Davies, W J K (1978) *Implementing Individualized Learning in Schools and Colleges* (Guidelines 4). Council for Educational Technology, London.

Donovan, K G (1981) *Learning Resources in Colleges: Their Organization and Management.* Council for Educational Technology, London.

Dove, J (1975) *The Audio Visual. The Availability and Exploitation of Non-Print Material with Special Reference to Libraries.* Andre Deutsch, London.

Evans, C (1987) The organisation and management of library and learning services. *Coombe Lodge Report*, **19**, 9, pp 567-75.

Fairfax, O, Durham, J and Wilson, W (1976) *Audio-visual Materials: Development of a National Cataloguing and Information Service* (Working Paper 12). Council for Educational Technology, London.

Gordon, C (1978) *Resource Organization in Primary Schools* (Guidelines 5). Council for Educational Technology, London.

Hannabus, C S (1981) The impact of independent and open learning systems on UK libraries since 1970. In Percival, F and Ellington, H I (eds) *Aspects of Educational Technology*, **XV**. Kogan Page, London.

Manwaring, G (1976) Self-instructional biology — a resource centre for individualized learning. In Clarke, J and Leedham, J (eds) *Aspects of Educational Technology*, **X**. Kogan Page, London.

Matthews, J and Buckingham, D (1976) Resource-based learning: a pragmatic approach. *Studies in Higher Education*, **1**, 2, pp 156-68.

Noble, P (1980) *Resource-Based Learning in Post-Compulsory Education*. Kogan Page, London.

Raddon, R (1980) *An Annotated Bibliography on Educational Resource Organization and Related Topics*. Council for Educational Technology, London.

Routh, J C (1975) Independent learning systems and their implications for libraries. *Coombe Lodge Report*, **8**, 2, pp 52-7.

SCET (1973) *A Resources Centre is a State of Mind*. Scottish Council for Educational Technology, Glasgow.

SCET (1976) *The Setting Up of a Resources Centre: Book 1: Basic Ideas*, Malcolm, A.H; *Book 2: Planning and Staffing*, Tucker, R.N; *Book 3: Retrieval Systems*, Malcolm, A H (ed). Scottish Council for Educational Technology, Glasgow.

SCET (1978) *Sources and Resources*. Scottish Council for Educational Technology, London.

Tucker, R N (ed) (1987) *The Development of Resource Centres: a UNESCO study*. Kogan Page, London.

Wilson, G V (1980) *Audio-Visual Resources in Secondary Schools: Their Organization and Management*. Council for Educational Technology, London.

Chapter 10: Computers in Education

Ahmed, K, Ingram, D and Dickinson, C J (1980) *Software for Educational Computing*. MTP Press, Lancaster.

Baker, F B (1978) *Computer Managed Instruction*. Educational Technology Publications, Englewood Cliffs, New Jersey.

Beech, G (ed) (1978) *Computer Assisted Methods in Science Education*. Pergamon, Oxford.

Beveridge, W T (1982) *Educational Computer Package Evaluation and Design*. Scottish Microelectronics Development Programme, Glasgow.

Bork, A (1981) *Learning with Computers*. Digital Press, Bedford.

CET (1978) *Microelectronics: Their Implications for Education and Training*. Council for Educational Technology, London.

CET (1980) *Microcomputers: Their Uses in Primary Schools*. Council for Educational Technology, London.

CET (1981) *Thinking about Microcomputers: First Steps* (Information Sheet 1). Council for Educational Technology, London.

Crabb, G (1980) *Copyright and Computers*. Council for Educational Technology, London.

Dean, C and Whitlock, Q (1983) *A Handbook of Computer-Based Training*. Kogan Page, London.

Ellingham, D (1982) *Managing the Microcomputer in the Classroom*. Council for Educational Technology, London.

Ellis, A B (1974) *The Use and Misuse of Computers in Education*. McGraw-Hill, New York.

Evans, C (1981) *The Micro Millenium*. Washington Square Press/ Pocket Books, New York.

Fielden, J and Pearson, P K (1978) *The Cost of Learning with Computers. Report of the Financial Evaluation of the National Development Programme in Computer Assisted Learning*. Council for Educational Technology, London.

Gosling, W (1978) *Microcircuits, Society and Education* (Occasional Paper 8). Council for Educational Technology, London.

Gray, L (1983) Teachers' unions and the impact of computer-based technologies. In Megarry, J, Walker, D R F, Nisbet, S and Hoyle, E (eds) *Computers and Education (World Yearbook of Education 1982/83)*. Kogan Page, London.

Hawkridge, D (1982) *New Information Technology in Education*. Croom Helm, London.

Henderson, J and Humphreys, F (eds) (1982) *The Audio Visual and Micro-computer Handbook*. Kogan Page, London.

Hooper, R (1977) *The National Development Programme in Computer Assisted Learning. Final Report of the Director*. Council for Educational Technology, London.

Hooper, R and Toye, I (1975) *Computer Assisted Learning in the United Kingdom. Some Case Studies*. Council for Educational Technology, London.

Howe, J A M and Ross, P M (1981) *Microcomputers in Secondary Education*. Kogan Page, London.

Jones, R (1982) *Five of the Best: Computer Programs in Primary Schools*. Council for Educational Technology, London.

Jones, R (1982) *Microcomputers in the Primary School. A Before-You-Buy Guide*. Council for Educational Technology, London.

Kemmis, S, Atkin, R and Wright, E (1977) *How Do Students Learn? Working Papers on Computer Assisted Learning*. Centre for Applied Resource in Education, University of East Anglia, Norwich.

McKenzie, J, Elton, L and Lewis, R (eds) (1978) *Interactive Computer Graphics in Science Teaching*. Ellis Horwood, Chichester.

McMahon (1978) Progress and prospects in computer-managed learning in the United Kingdom. *Programmed Learning and Educational Technology*, **15**, 2, pp 104-13.

Maddison, J (1982) *Information Technology and Education. An Annotated Guide to Printed, Audiovisual and Multimedia Resources.* The Open University Press, Milton Keynes.

Meadows, A J, Gordon, M and Singleton, A (1982) *Dictionary of New Information Technology.* Kogan Page, London.

Megarry, J (1983) Thinking, learning and educating: the role of the computer. In Megarry, J, Walker, D R F, Nisbet, S and Hoyle, E (eds) *Computers and Education (World Yearbook of Education 1982/83).* Kogan Page, London.

Megarry, J, Smart, N and Tomasso, C (1981) Microcomputers and Scottish education. In Percival, F and Ellington, H I (eds) *Aspects of Educational Technology*, **XV**. Kogan Page, London.

Megarry, J, Walker, D R F, Nisbet, S and Hoyle, E (eds) (1983) *Computers and Education (World Yearbook of Education 1982/83).* Kogan Page, London.

O'Neill, G (1987) Interactive video as an aid to learning. *Programmed Learning and Educational Technology*, **24**, 2, pp 137-44.

O'Shea, T and Self, J (1982) *Learning and Teaching with Computers.* Harvester Press, Brighton.

Rushby, N J (ed) (1979) *An Introduction to Educational Computing* Croom Helm, London.

Rushby, N J (ed) (1981) *Selected Readings in Computer-Based Learning.* Kogan Page, London.

Rushby, N J (ed) (1987) *Technology-Based Learning: Selected Readings.* Kogan Page, London.

Shepherd, I D H, Cooper, Z A and Walker, D R F (1980) *Computer Assisted Learning in Geography.* Council for Educational Technology/Geographical Association, London.

Sledge, D (1980) *Microcomputers in Education: A Selection of Introductory Titles.* Council for Educational Technology, London.

Smith, C (ed) (1982) *Microcomputers in Education.* Ellis Horwood, Chichester.

Chapter 11: A Glimpse into the Future

Brook, D and Race, P (1978) *Aspects of Educational Technology*, **XII**, *Educational Technology in a Changing World.* Kogan Page, London.

CET (1978) *Microelectronics: Their Implications for Education and Training.* Council for Educational Technology, London.

CET (1980) *Microcomputers: Their Uses in Primary Schools.* Council for Educational Technology, London.

Hawkridge, D (1982) *New Information Technology in Education.*
Croom Helm, London,

Howe, J A M and Ross, P M (1981) *Microcomputers in Secondary Education.* Kogan Page, London.

Megarry, J (1978) Retrospect and prospect. In McAleese, W (ed) *Perspectives on Academic Gaming and Simulation 3.* Kogan Page, London.

Megarry, J, Walker, D R F, Nisbet, S and Hoyle, E (eds) (1982) *Computers and Education (World Yearbook of Education 1982/83).* Kogan Page, London.

O'Neill, G (1987) Interactive video as an aid to learning. *Programmed Learning and Educational Technology,* **24**, 2, pp 137-44.

Rushby, N J (ed) (1977) *Computer Managed Learning in the 1980s. A Future Study Report* (Technical Report 16). National Development Programme in Computer Assisted Learning, London.

Smith, C (ed) (1982) *Microcomputers in Education.* Ellis Horwood, Chichester.

Winterburn, R and Evans, L (1980) *Aspects of Educational Technology,* **XIV**. *Educational Technology to the Year 2000.* Kogan Page, London.

Zuber-Skerritt, O (ed) (1984) *Video in Higher Education.* Kogan Page, London.

List of Organizations involved in the Educational Technology Field

The following list contains some of the main bodies which are involved in the educational technology field, together with the addresses at which they may be contacted. For convenience, the list is organized on a national basis, dealing in turn with the United Kingdom, the USA, Canada, Australia and New Zealand.

United Kingdom

Association for Educational and Training Technology (AETT). A UK-based international organization that is concerned with all aspects of educational and training technology; address: BLAT Centre, BMA House, Tavistock Square, London WC1.

British Universities Film Council (BUFC). A national organization that was formed to promote the use of film and other audiovisual materials in British universities and other institutions of higher education; address: 72 Dean Street, London W1V 5HB.

Council for Educational Technology for the United Kingdom (CET). The central organization in the UK for promoting the application of educational technology in all sectors of education and training; address: 3 Devonshire Street, London W1N 2BA.

Educational Foundation for Visual Aids (EFVA). An organization set up to produce educational films and filmstrips and provide advice on the use of visual media; address: 33 Queen Anne Street, London W1.

Educational Television Association (ETA). An organization set up to promote the use of television and allied media in education and training address: 86 Micklegate, York YO1 1JZ.

Network of Practitioners of Educational and Training Technology (NPETT). An association of individuals and organizations that are involved in the use of educational technology; address: 2 Haigh House Hill, Lindley Moor, Huddersfield, W Yorks HD3 3SZ.

Scottish Council for Educational Technology (SCET). The main official organization responsible for promoting educational technology in Scotland; address: Dowanhill, 74 Victoria Crescent Road, Glasgow G12 9JN.

Society for the Advancement of Gaming and Simulation in Education and Training (SAGSET). A UK-based international organization that promotes the use of gaming and simulation techniques in all branches of education and training; address: c/o Centre for Extension Studies, University of Technology, Loughborough LE11 3TU.

USA

Agency for Instructional Television (AIT). An organization whose aim is to promote education through television throughout the USA and Canada; address: Box A, Bloomington, IN 47402.

Association for Computer-Based Instructional Systems. An American organization set up to facilitate exchange of information on the use of computers in education; address: Box 70189, Los Angeles, CA 90070.

Association for Educational Communications and Technology (AECT). A major American professional organization concerned with learning and educational technology; address: 1126 16th Street, NW, Washington, DC 20202.

Educational Film Library Association. An organization that acts as a national clearinghouse for information about educational 16mm films, videorecording and other non-print media; address: 17 W 60th Street, New York, NY 10023.

International Congress for Individualized Instruction. A US-based international body concerned with research and evaluation in the field of individualized instruction; address: c/o Biology Dept, Fordham University, Bronx, NY 10458.

International Council for Computers in Education. A US-based international body primarily concerned with the use of computers at pre-tertiary level; address: Dept of Computer and Information Science, University of Oregon, Eugene, OR 97403.

International Tape Exchange. A body that acts as a clearinghouse for the exchange of educational audiotapes; address: 834 Ruddiman Avenue, North Miskegon, MI 49445.

National Audiovisual Center (NAC). A federal body that acts as a national clearinghouse and distribution centre for all audiovisual materials produced by the US Government and its agencies; address: General Services Administration, Reference Section, Washington, DC 20409.

National Center for Audio Tapes (NCAT). A national bank and distribution centre for audiotapes produced by American schools, colleges, official organizations, etc; address: c/o Educational Media Center, Stadium, University of Colorado, Boulder, CO 80309.

National Information Center for Educational Media (NICEM). A national centre that publishes lists of currently-available non-print instructional materials; address: University of Southern California, University Park, Los Angeles, CA 90007.

National Society for Performance and Instruction (NSPI). An interdisciplinary professional organization for teachers, trainers, educational and training technologists, researchers and producers of hardware and software; address: Box 266, Charles Town, WV 25414.

National Video Clearinghouse Inc. A national reference centre for all available video software; address: PO Box 3, Syosset, NY 11791.

North American Simulation and Gaming Association (NASAGA). A body set up to promote the use of gaming and simulation techniques in the USA and Canada; address: c/o Dr W T Nichols, Box 100, Westminster College, New Wilmington, PA 16142.

Society for Computer Simulation. An organization set up to promote the use of computer simulation in education, training, research, etc; address: PO Box 2228, La Jolla, CA 92038.

University Film Association. A professional association of people interested in the use of film for instructional and communication purposes; address: 217 Flint Hall, University of Kansas, Lawrence, KS 66045.

Canada

Association for Media and Technology in Education in Canada (AMTEC). A national organization set up to promote the dissemination of educational technology research findings; address: PO Box 174, Station W, Toronto, Ontario, M6M 4Z2.

Teaching and Instructional Support Division. A government body set up to help schools select and use audiovisual media and equipment; address: Dept of Education, PO Box 2000, Charlottetown, PE1.

Australia

Australian and South Pacific External Studies Association (ASPESA). An international organization set up to promote external studies in the South Pacific area; address: Dept of External Studies, University of New England, Armidale, NSW 2351, Australia.

Australian Society of Educational Technology (ASET). A national body, with state chapters, promoting all aspects of educational technology in Australia; address: PO Box 143, Kensington, NSW 2033.

Modern Teaching Methods Association. An organization which runs an audiocassette library and promotes the use of 'modern' teaching methods; address: 101 Wallan, Victoria 3654.

New Zealand

Department of Education, Resources Development Division. A government organization responsible for promoting the use of learning resources in schools; address: Department of Education, Wellington.

National Film Library of New Zealand. An organization that maintains a bank of films for lending to schools and other bodies; address: PO Box 9583, 6th Floor, Cubewell House, Kent Terrace, Wellington.

Keyword Index

Note: This Keyword Index refers only to the main text of the book, *not* to the Glossary or Bibliography. Where more than one page reference is given under a particular heading, any particularly important reference is given in italics.

12392

DATE DUE

HIGHSMITH 45-220